# Language Learning, Digital Communications and Study Abroad

# NEW PERSPECTIVES ON LANGUAGE AND EDUCATION

*Founding Editor*: Viv Edwards, *University of Reading, UK*
*Series Editors*: Phan Le Ha, *University of Hawaii at Manoa, USA,* Joel Windle, *Monash University, Australia* and Kyle R. McIntosh, *University of Tampa, USA.*

Two decades of research and development in language and literacy education have yielded a broad, multidisciplinary focus. Yet education systems face constant economic and technological change, with attendant issues of identity and power, community and culture. What are the implications for language education of new 'semiotic economies' and communications technologies? Of complex blendings of cultural and linguistic diversity in communities and institutions? Of new cultural, regional and national identities and practices? The New Perspectives on Language and Education series will feature critical and interpretive, disciplinary and multidisciplinary perspectives on teaching and learning, language and literacy in new times. New proposals, particularly for edited volumes, are expected to acknowledge and include perspectives from the Global South. Contributions from scholars from the Global South will be particularly sought out and welcomed, as well as those from marginalized communities within the Global North.

All books in this series are externally peer-reviewed.

Full details of all the books in this series and of all our other publications can be found on http://www.multilingual-matters.com, or by writing to Multilingual Matters, St Nicholas House, 31-34 High Street, Bristol, BS1 2AW, UK.

NEW PERSPECTIVES ON LANGUAGE AND EDUCATION: 120

# Language Learning, Digital Communications and Study Abroad

Identity and Belonging in Translocal Contexts

**Levi Durbidge**

**MULTILINGUAL MATTERS**
Bristol • Jackson

DOI https://doi.org/10.21832/DURBRI5058
Library of Congress Cataloging in Publication Data
A catalog record for this book is available from the Library of Congress.
Names: Durbidge, Levi, author.
Title: Language Learning, Digital Communications and Study Abroad: Identity and Belonging in Translocal Contexts/Levi Durbidge.
Description: Bristol; Jackson: Multilingual Matters, 2024. | Series: New Perspectives on Language and Education: 120 | Includes bibliographical references and index. | Summary: "This book argues for a view of study abroad as emergent of tensions between localised and globalised imaginaries of language, identity, and place. It offers the first in-depth exploration of mobile technology's role in language learning and identity formation during study abroad"—Provided by publisher.
Identifiers: LCCN 2024003146 (print) | LCCN 2024003147 (ebook) | ISBN 9781800415041 (paperback) | ISBN 9781800415058 (hardback) | ISBN 9781800415065 (pdf) | ISBN 9781800415072 (epub)
Subjects: LCSH: Language and languages—Study and teaching. | Foreign study. | Digital communications.
Classification: LCC P53.41155 .D83 2024 (print) | LCC P53.41155 (ebook) | DDC 407.1—dc23/eng/20240229
LC record available at https://lccn.loc.gov/2024003146
LC ebook record available at https://lccn.loc.gov/2024003147

British Library Cataloguing in Publication Data
A catalogue entry for this book is available from the British Library.

ISBN-13: 978-1-80041-505-8 (hbk)
ISBN-13: 978-1-80041-504-1 (pbk)

**Multilingual Matters**
UK: St Nicholas House, 31-34 High Street, Bristol, BS1 2AW, UK.
USA: Ingram, Jackson, TN, USA.

Website: https://www.multilingual-matters.com
X: Multi_Ling_Mat
Facebook: https://www.facebook.com/multilingualmatters
Blog: https://www.channelviewpublications.wordpress.com

Copyright © 2024 Levi Durbidge.

All rights reserved. No part of this work may be reproduced in any form or by any means without permission in writing from the publisher.

The policy of Multilingual Matters/Channel View Publications is to use papers that are natural, renewable and recyclable products, made from wood grown in sustainable forests. In the manufacturing process of our books, and to further support our policy, preference is given to printers that have FSC and PEFC Chain of Custody certification. The FSC and/or PEFC logos will appear on those books where full certification has been granted to the printer concerned.

Typeset by Deanta Global Publishing Services, Chennai, India.

*For Steve*
*(1980–2022)*

# Contents

| | | |
|---|---|---|
| | Tables and Figures | ix |
| | Acknowledgements | xi |
| | Transcription Conventions | xiii |
| | Introduction | 1 |
| 1 | Digital Sociality, Immersion and Translocality | 16 |
| 2 | Approach and Participants | 36 |
| 3 | Nikko: Translingual Participation In and Beyond Hungary | 60 |
| 4 | Nagisa: Translocal Ties and Online Identity in Brazil | 82 |
| 5 | Megumi: Racialisation and Marginalisation in Germany | 104 |
| 6 | Manabu: Negotiating Multilingual Identity in Francophone Canada | 119 |
| 7 | Misa: Social Support and Language Learning in the US Midwest | 138 |
| 8 | Translocal Language Learning and Belonging during and beyond Study Abroad | 151 |
| | References | 171 |
| | Index | 185 |

# Tables and Figures

**Tables**

| | | |
|---|---|---|
| Table 2.1 | Interview informants | 50 |
| Table 2.2 | Motivation clusters | 58 |
| Table 2.3 | Outcomes clusters | 58 |

**Figures**

| | | |
|---|---|---|
| Figure 2.1 | Self-actualisation score across interview informants | 56 |
| Figure 2.2 | Transformation score across interview informants | 57 |

# Acknowledgements

While this book bears my name, it has only come together through the effort, time, sacrifice and support of so many others. First I would like to thank Robyn Spence-Brown who enthusiastically supported the project this book is based on. She has been generous and tireless in her advocacy and guidance and I am deeply thankful for her mentorship. My sincere thanks also go to Naomi Kurata who provided invaluable feedback, criticism and advice during the project.

Over the years, I have been privileged to have received support, mentorship and critical feedback from many colleagues directly and indirectly associated with the project. I am particularly indebted to Liz Ellis, Nadine Normand-Marconnet, Satoshi Nambu, Jeremy Breaden, Brook Bolander, Anne McLaren, Celeste Kinginger, Gary Barkhuizen, John Plews, Takaji Aoki, Takeshi Kawazoe and Mariko Fujita.

I also wish to acknowledge my graduate research 先輩 and fellow travellers at Monash University whose camaraderie and willingness to listen and share have been an invaluable source of insight and joy. Special thanks go to Gwyn McClelland, Olivier Elzingre, Rikki Corry, Luluh Alfurayh, Kathryn MacFarlane, Cathy Sell, Xinxin Li, Margherita Angelucci, Wes Robertson, Nicola Helps, Janice Keynton and Enung Rostika.

I would also like to acknowledge the invaluable contribution of the anonymous participants who gave up their time to share their experiences studying abroad, especially the interview informants who agreed to share the details of their life abroad and return to Japan, as well as the generous cooperation of Chiba 様, Fujisawa 様 and the rest of the team at AFS Intercultural Programs Japan.

I would also like to express my sincere thanks to Anna Roderick and the rest of the team at Multilingual Matters for their support in guiding the book to publication, Joel Windle for his guidance and insight and the two anonymous reviewers whose insightful comments and suggestions contributed to a much stronger final manuscript.

Finally, I cannot begin to express my thanks to my family. To Mum and Dad for your belief, encouragement and gifting me with the critical and independent mindset that got me here. To Yuka, whose unconditional support and encouragement cannot be fully expressed in any of the words I know. 様々なことをぎせいにして、ずっと応援してくれてありがとう。And to Sophia and Seigen, whose love, kindness and insistence on living in the moment were the brightest part of the many years spent on this project. You constantly remind me to stop and appreciate the beauty of the everyday, even if I would have preferred those days to begin after 6am.

*This research was supported by an Australian Government Research Training Program (RTP) scholarship.*

# Transcription Conventions

English

| | |
|---|---|
| . | end of clause |
| , | pause |
| ? | question intonation |
| "language" | reported speech (indicated by change in voice) |
| [ ] | insertion |
| […] | omitted section |
| [??] | unclear section |
| (( )) | backchannelling by interviewer |
| @ | laughter |

Japanese

| | |
|---|---|
| 。 | end of clause |
| 、 | pause |
| ? | question intonation |
| 「言語」 | reported speech (indicated by change in voice) |
| [ ] | insertion |
| […] | omitted section |
| [??] | unclear section |
| ( ) | backchannelling by interviewer |
| @ | laughter |

Transcription Conventions

# Introduction

Community, place, time. So much of what goes on during a sojourn abroad is tied up in these notions. On the surface, it is relatively straightforward; an individual travels to a new place and through interactions and experiences available to them in the host community, they return home transformed. Study abroad has been widely conceived of as a localised immersive experience of unfamiliar linguistic and cultural practices that leave sojourners indelibly changed. Yet, as so much of the research has shown, beyond the glossy promotional posters that promise life-affirming experiences in exotic locations, a sojourn abroad can raise difficult questions of identity, belonging and relationship to language. The experiences of those studying abroad are inevitably tangled with those they encounter, each with their own histories, desires and understandings. What happens during and beyond a sojourn abroad is complex and highly particular precisely because nothing is certain to happen; interactions are dynamic and unpredictable, shaped by the agency of individuals as they move through and engage with changing social, material and symbolic environments.

Simultaneously exhilarating and perplexing, the contexts of study abroad have become an important site to investigate the dynamics of language learning. This has been made more so as interconnected networks of digital communication have led to an 'intensification of worldwide social relations which link distant localities in such a way that local happenings are shaped by events occurring many miles away' (Giddens, 1990: 64). Supercharged by the advent of social media, online social interaction is increasingly mediated through privately owned communications platforms that seek to capture the interactional and attentional behaviour of users even as they contribute to rapid and far-reaching processes of social upheaval. Following these developments, the interactions of sojourners with host and home communities are no longer limited to chronological time or geographical space, and the previously well-defined nature of a sojourn abroad is decidedly less clear-cut. Several decades ago, Appadurai (1990) coined the notion of *flows* to conceptualise how the dissemination of images, information and interaction at speeds and scales never seen before was altering experiences of global migration and understandings of culture and identity. With flows of information and people continuing to traverse geographical boundaries at increasing rates, study abroad research must look to concepts that grapple with the complex ways in which individuals, ideas, practices and resources move across geographical spaces and interact within and between different localities.

In an article that examined the increasing use of digital communications technology by UK participants in a study abroad programme to Senegal, Coleman and Chafer (2010: 165) argued in their closing remarks that, 'thanks to telecommunications technologies, abroad is less abroad than it once was'. Perhaps this was intended more rhetorically than dialectically, yet it expresses an attitude that has been present in the reflections and analysis of many who have coordinated and researched programmes of study abroad over the past several decades – that the development and expansion of digital communications has been accompanied by a diminishment in the 'immersive' nature of study abroad contexts. This view remains bound up in ideological conceptions of study abroad as a clearly demarcated stay in environs where the sojourner can, and should, continuously engage with 'authentic' local cultural and linguistic practices. Under this view, maintaining communication with home contravenes the imperative to involve oneself directly with the host community. Yet, this picture is, as I demonstrate in this book, misguided in its assumptions.

Reflecting on her 1993 memoir *French Lessons* 25 years after the fact, Alice Kaplan (2018) notes how the communicative landscape of studying abroad has shifted for her students in the intervening years:

> …as long as it lasts, the miraculous process of stepping into another person's language persists. And for that purpose, technology is a friend, not a foe, of learning. The same apps that keep students constantly in touch with home, that map Starbucks and Bagelstein for them, also allow them to 'friend' their French friends on Facebook, to write in French on informal blogs, without the pressure of an academic assignment—and to send text messages in French. […] Once students return home from studying abroad, there are a hundred new ways to stay in touch, day by day, with foreign friends. My students are messaging friends in Senegal, Korea and Peru everyday. (Kaplan, 2018: 218)

As Kaplan points out, sojourners are using digital communications technology not only to remain connected to people from home, but also to connect with, and stay connected to, people they meet abroad. While there are certainly differences in the ways and degrees that different communities are able to access resources online (van Dijk, 2017), communications technology and its attendant new media are now a fundamental part of the social landscape of the communities to which sojourners travel. Linguistic practices, as they emerge online, are situated in the lived contexts of users and are therefore integral to language learning (Barton & Potts, 2013). With global flows of people, ideas and capital reshaping notions of community, language learning abroad must be understood within wider notions of interconnectivity, hybridity and superdiversity (Blommaert & Rampton, 2011). The advent of digital communication has allowed much of what we considered tied to specific locales to be encountered in deterritorialised online forms, extending communicative practices over time and space (Jacquemet, 2005).

The argument that I make in this book begins by grappling with the notion of immersion and its effect on the way digital communications technology has been conceptualised in research on language learning abroad. Then, by examining the experiences of Japanese adolescents in depth, we see that the 'abroad' in study abroad has not somehow been diminished by digital communications technology but broadened, complexified and become more nebulous. Language learning abroad in an era of social media still involves important questions of identity and belonging, yet sojourners' responses to those questions may also involve online communication – complementing, contesting, multiplying and extending face-to-face interactions. Digital communications allow the work of learning and community interaction to begin before one sets foot upon distant shores, and continue long after farewells have been exchanged. It is important to note, however, that even as digital communication continues to reshape the ways we relate to each other, the act of studying abroad still involves a physical relocation to unfamiliar or differing social, cultural and geographical contexts. Sojourners' use of digital technology doesn't take place in intangible, online spaces, but is reflective of, and situated in, lived offline realities.

Beyond this though, I wish to make a broader point about the way that study abroad exists, not in an isolated way, but within and as part of the flows which Appadurai (1990) identified. That is to say, experiences of language learning abroad are not wholly experiences of host contexts, but are emergent of, and negotiated through, tensions between localised and globalised imaginaries of language, identity and place.

## About this Book

This book draws its insights from an investigation of the rich personal, social and geographical factors that supported and inhibited the development of a group of Japanese adolescents' multilingual repertoires during both a year abroad, and in the year that followed their return. The participants in the project were drawn from a cohort of almost 300 high school students who, through the organisation AFS Intercultural Programs Japan, studied in over 20 different nations located across North and South America, Asia and Europe from mid-2016 to mid-2017. Of the 100 students who responded to an initial survey of their experiences, 14 completed a set of interviews conducted a month after their return to Japan and 12 of these again one year later. The majority of those interviewed provided access to the social media accounts they had used while abroad, primarily on the platform Instagram. Weaving together the multimodal narratives they created online with the stories they related to me through their semi-structured interviews and following Barkhuizen *et al.* (2013), I developed narrative case studies of each of these adolescents. The case studies explore how the informants negotiated high school life in unfamiliar contexts, renegotiated their lives on returning to Japan and the way this intersected with language learning and use. Interestingly, for a project on language learning, many of those interviewed did not initially participate in the programme with strong intentions of learning language. Instead, its importance became apparent as they began navigating relationships in the host families and school communities in which they spent so much of their time, seeking to perform identities tied to these communities, in person and online.

This book focuses on five of those participants, each travelling to separate locations with differing linguistic ecologies in Brazil, Canada, Germany, Hungary and the United States. While I detail the selection process for these cases later, they represent both a broad cross section of the experiences contained in the project and demonstrate the various ways that language learning and social media use intersect in study abroad. Taken together, their experiences paint a picture of study abroad in an era of ubiquitous social media use and intensified human movement. Drawing on the resulting insights, this book makes the following contributions to our understanding of language learning abroad.

The first is to detail the way that each of the featured informants' experiences is shaped by tensions which emerge from intersecting local and global forces across differing locales. In doing this, we observe the multifaceted ways that digital communications, in particular social media, intersect with language learning, identity and belonging. The informants' accounts reveal how digital communications technology is part of the social fabric of their lives, both abroad and upon return. It influenced how they perceived, engaged with and invested in the cultural and linguistic practices they encountered even as the affordances they perceived it offering were transformed while moving across geographical and linguistic borders.

This view is enhanced by a focus on the perspectives of non-Anglophone students studying abroad in a variety of non-Anglophone destinations, at a moment when English(es) have become predominant in international communication. In this project, the informants needed to negotiate environments where English was often part of diverse, multilingual ecologies that reflected both historical and recent flows of people and information. Thus, their experiences were mediated by local instantiations of English and the identities and communities indexed by those instantiations. The informants' accounts show that parochial views of study abroad contexts – as delimited contexts of target language learning – are no longer relevant (if indeed they ever have been).

Finally, the book presents an extensive account of the effect of study abroad on adolescents' language learning. As I detail below, research on language learning abroad has almost exclusively focused on those in higher education despite significant numbers of secondary school students electing to spend part of their high school life living and studying abroad. By neglecting these perspectives, we limit our understanding of what language learning abroad entails and how a sojourn during adolescence fits into the picture of lifelong language development.

## Study Abroad as a Scalar, Translocal Process

There is an imperative to view experiences of mobility as dynamic processes that transcend and interconnect across multiple locales rather than being situated wholly within an imagined monolithic territory. Indeed, as a sojourner arrives in their host location, they bring with them repertoires of linguistic and cultural practices connected to the locations and communities they have previously inhabited. Drawing on the insights which emerge from the foci described above, I argue for a view of study abroad that recognises it as structured by tensions that emerge at the intersections of local and global forces and imaginations; as translocal, transnational and viewed productively through a metaphor of scales.

### Translocality

*Translocality* is a concept that allows us to move beyond traditional notions of static territoriality, recognising that movements of people and information are multidirectional and transcend conventional spatial and temporal constraints. Defined by Kytölä (2016: 620) as 'a sense of *connectedness* between locales where both the local and the global are meaningful parameters for social and cultural activities', a translocal perspective emphasises the interactions and convergences of global flows with localised realities. Although sojourners occupy specific physical spaces while abroad, they also maintain connections to individuals and communities located in other physical and online spaces. They have access to communications and media that extend beyond those traditionally available in the host community, even as they remain tethered to its local realities. Moreover, host communities exist at different intersections of global flows, with individuals and communities maintaining their own connections that extend outside of their immediate locales. Therefore, all experiences of study abroad are, in effect, translocal.

This translocality can manifest in different ways in experiences of academic mobility. Hasnain and Hajek (2022), for example, identify translocality as a vital part of international students' sense of connectedness while abroad, as they bring with them online attachments to different communities. Indeed, the social support identified by Mikal and Grace (2012) as available to sojourners through social media for dealing with issues of adjustment during study abroad is an example of the way translocal connectedness functions. However, the translocal nature of digital communications technology during study abroad is not simply a matter of personal networks. In a study in which Martin and Rizvi (2014: 2) explore the online media habits of international students in Melbourne, they show that while access to media and engagement with people online can reflect practices at home, this engagement itself is 'one of the embodied practices of habitation through which the meaning of place is accomplished'. In effect, media and interaction provided by online networks contribute to and are interwoven with their experience of Melbourne as a place, shaping their imagination of the city.

We can also see translocality at work in Kinginger's (2008) account of American students studying in France during the US invasion of Iraq, as the participants needed to navigate the sociopolitical tensions which manifested within interactions with their hosts. This in turn led to implications for the way they sought to position themselves in relation to American national identities. While the conflict itself was taking place far from their host families' homes in France, it had immediate and significant ramifications for their experience of study abroad.

The notion of translocality is vital for conceptualising sojourners' experiences of study abroad. In essence, a translocal perspective recognises that local places and communities are shaped by and, in turn, shape larger regional and global dynamics. In order to understand what takes place locally we must consider how it relates to wider processes and networks. It also recognises that sojourners necessarily engage with multiple localities, geographically and virtually, during their study abroad experiences. There has been a tendency to overlook these processes when considering the language learning abroad, conceiving of study abroad contexts in more demarcated terms.

## Transnationality

As the above examples show, experiences of translocality become highly salient for mobile individuals as relationships, activities and the value of linguistic and cultural resources shift across localities. Alignment with specific identities can become less distinct as individuals negotiate these shifts while maintaining active and often interactive connections with the places they departed (Bauman, 2000; Jacquemet, 2005). Thus, the related concept of *transnationality* is often invoked as a way of conceptualising the ways in which individuals negotiate identity alignments to geographically disparate locales. In developing a definition of transnationality, Ong (1999: 4) points to states of cultural interconnection that reflect the 'the *horizontal* and *relational* nature of the contemporary economic, social, and cultural processes that stream across spaces'. In effect, the notion of translocality emphasises dialogical flows between the local and the global while transnationality conceptualises the way that ties, relationships and interactions extend across geographical space.

The practice of studying abroad generally involves a limited relocation to a different geographical location, usually a different nation state, for academic purposes. A temporary transnational experience if you will. Through this experience, participants develop connections and ways of being aligned with the places and communities they inhabit; resources that can be combined with those they already possess to forge new transnational identities. They may also experience their time abroad through a sense of detachment to connections and practices they associate with home. Anderson (2019), for example, has shown how Chinese students studying abroad must negotiate various understandings of transnationality, for example, seeking to downplay their Chinese citizenship and opting for practices such as the use of English names while abroad, or alternatively seeing themselves as part of an academic diaspora who continue to remain aligned with China even as they live and study abroad. These processes are also evident in Plews' (2015) study of Canadian university students, who through their study abroad experiences in Germany, found themselves needing to negotiate and dissociate themselves from localised understandings of Americanness even as they came to understand their sense of being Canadian while abroad.

Conceptually, the notion of transnationality allows us to represent and explore the ways that individuals navigate connections, language and identities that go beyond the binary of host and home. Within study abroad, it accentuates the way that mobility involves more than just physical relocation to another country, but encompasses the necessary renegotiations and reimaginations of self and belonging as they exist in broader, interconnected ways.

## Scales and orders of indexicality

As the above discussions indicate, we need to work across ideas of the local and global in order to grasp processes taking place during study abroad. Another valuable concept in this regard is the sociolinguistic notion of scales. This concept helps us better understand how the local and the global become relevant for individuals as they move between different places and communities. Developed by Blommaert (2007, 2010) as a means to grapple with the idea of language as a mobile resource, scales serve as a metaphor to complexify notions of context by highlighting the hierarchical relations which serve to govern the value of linguistic resources at any given point. As Blommaert (2021: 379) himself notes, they function as 'an instrument enabling a fundamental revision of what we believe certain facts to be'. For example, we can observe the inequal relations that exist between different varieties of English. At the local scale of community, certain varieties may be seen as legitimate and those who use them evaluated as English speakers. However, the same varieties may be seen as less legitimate or not even recognised when global scales of evaluation are invoked. Individuals with the ability to do so, may therefore move between scales in interaction in an activity known as *rescaling*, for example, shifting to a register that indicates local solidarity with their addressee or one that indexes their international mobility.

Blommaert (2007, 2010) names these systems of evaluation, *orders of indexicality*. Effectively norms of evaluation tied to specific scales, orders of indexicality dictate what qualifies as language, who has the authority to use it and the specific conditions under which it can be employed. Related to discourse, orders of indexicality are organised differently across scales and contribute to the creation of social categories that impact our understanding of belonging and identity. Thus, the social meanings enregistered to a specific linguistic resource can shift when moving across scales, even within the same interaction. More relevant for this book, the same resource can receive different evaluations across different communities and geographical contexts. This, of course, has implications for sojourners, the linguistic resources they possess and those they seek to appropriate and use.

Turning to investigations of language learning in study abroad, we can observe how different orders of indexicality are at work in the experiences of sojourners. Surveying studies of heritage speakers of Spanish in study abroad, Pozzi *et al.* (2021) note how competencies and practices that had been evaluated positively in the United States could be subject to negative evaluations against localised norms of monolingualism or standardisation when sojourning in Spanish-speaking countries. Viewed through the concept of scales, we can observe how the value of their Spanish repertoires was subject to differing regimes of evaluation as they move across borders and communities. Badwan and Simpson (2022), who directly draw on a scalar metaphor in their analysis of a Saudi student and a Palestinian student studying postgraduate degrees in the UK, note how their participants orient to differing scales when evaluating their own English ability – for example, perceiving the value of their English as high in relation to others at home but low in relation to other students at the university. Importantly, Badwan and Simpson (2022) note that these evaluations are dynamic and interrelated with ecological features such as the topic, speakers and interactional setting. In both of these examples the nature of the participants' competencies did not change; rather it was the way they were evaluated in a given moment or interaction.

We should therefore see scales and their attendant orders of indexicality as a means of conceptualising social processes of evaluation that are instantiated through interaction. These evaluations are tied to the ecological, historical and political realities of a given situation, which are themselves also subject to scaling. For sojourners, travelling to new contexts means encountering and being evaluated under unfamiliar orders of indexicality.

The concepts of scale and orders of indexicality are therefore epidemiologically useful for grappling with the way that the value of sojourners' linguistic resources can shift as they move across borders. They also allow us to engage with the way that highly mobile and widely dispersed linguistic varieties, such as those collected under the idea of 'English', can take on different values and meanings across various settings. Further, they allow us to view the way both the local and translocal can emerge as relevant in a given context or interaction and better explicate processes of language learning as they occur to individuals studying abroad.

## The social imaginary of study abroad

Having now conceptualised experiences of study abroad as involving both vertical and horizontal orientations to social and cultural processes and noting that the value of resources fluctuates through mobility and across scales, we now turn to the way that study abroad is widely understood. Kubota's (2016) identification of a *social imaginary* of study abroad is instructive here. Briefly stated, the concept of social imaginaries was developed by the philosopher Charles Taylor, who built upon Anderson's (2006) ideas of nation states as imagined communities. Taylor (2004) conceptualised social imaginaries as the way that societies construct shared understandings, or imaginaries, that shape their collective identity and practices. According to Taylor (2004), identifying these social imaginaries allows us to gain insight into the functioning of modern societies, their historical development and their evolution over time.

Returning to Kubota's (2016) use of the concept, she positions study abroad within a neoliberal social imaginary, arguing that it exists as part of globalising education policy. Reviewing online materials advertising study abroad, Kubota identifies language learning, intercultural competence, personal growth and identity changes, and increasing career opportunities as elemental to the social imaginary of study abroad. The globalising imaginary of study abroad is, therefore, one that constructs sojourners as gaining globally competitive communicative and intercultural competencies. Kubota notes that international education policies are inevitably intertwined with the global spread of English, since its high-mobility value (as per Blommaert, 2010) is connected to its status as a language of international communication, and so the 'globally competent' individual is also imagined as an English speaker. As touched on above, and as Kubota herself notes, this globalising imaginary of study abroad is complexified and contradicted once the particular realities of sojourners are examined.

Using case studies of five Japanese adolescent sojourners, this book argues that experiences of study abroad and the language learning they entail are structured by the tensions that arise between this globalising imaginary and localised realities. Importantly for this book, the case studies feature informants travelling to a diverse range of locales and therefore encountering vastly different linguistic milieu which come with their own sets of locally enacted norms. Their negotiations of local realisations of these tensions, and their overriding desire to belong, define the linguistic resources they seek to appropriate and the ways they (re) imagine their identities both during and beyond their sojourns.

## Liminality in Life and Research: Reflections on Subjectivity and Life as an Immigrant Worker in Japan

Having outlined the overall approach that will inform this book, it is essential that I describe my own relationship to the project which has informed it, since its origins are entangled with my own personal story. The opportunities that led to the project's formation are a product of experiences and connections formed through my own mobility, in particular, as a teacher at a private secondary school in Kanagawa Prefecture, Japan.

Working there and reading academic studies on language learning during study abroad, I became aware that the experiences of students like those in my classes were largely missing from the literature. Therefore, one of my intentions in developing this project was to foreground the voices of adolescents who made the often-challenging decision to leave behind the familiarity of their families and peers to study overseas for a year. Throughout the life of this project, however, I have been conscious of the way that the processes and culture of academic research have necessitated the appropriation and curation of these voices, subsuming them to processes of entextualisation, analysis and interpretation. Although this occurs with the consent of participants, it is vital that our own role in the production of knowledge is acknowledged. Throughout the development of this book and the project that preceded it, I have attempted to remain conscious of the way that my own subjectivities have impacted upon these processes and driven the research and writing choices I made. What follows is a brief reflection on aspects of my personal history and positionality that I observed as contributing to the way this project took shape. I offer them here as a means of contextualising the form and direction this project has taken and the epistemological position from which the research was conducted.

In 2001, while still an undergraduate at the University of Newcastle, Australia, I travelled overseas for the first time to participate in a three-week study trip of infrastructure projects jointly developed by the Ilocano peoples of Northern Luzon, Philippines, and the Anglican Board of Missions, Australia. In what could be considered my own short-term study abroad experience, I was forced to examine many of the preconceived notions I had held about language, economic opportunity and racialised inequality as I shared meals, interactions and sleeping quarters with our hosts. For a white, monolingual kid who had grown up in a largely white, Anglophone, working-class part of regional Australia, the experiences were pivotal in ongoing examinations of my own prejudices and privledge. During this trip, I was struck by the widespread use of mobile phones in the villages we stayed, something I didn't yet possess in Australia despite their growing availability and affordability. Remote villages that were accessible only via hours of travel on unsealed mountain roads, often had a community device that allowed communication with relatives who had moved to the cities for work. A decade before the advent of the iPhone, it was for me a tangible example of the way that mobile communications technology was already reshaping how a whole generation understood space, time and connection.

In 2003, after an unsuccessful attempt to return to the Philippines with a non-governmental organisation (NGO), I accepted an offer to teach English for a private company in Japan, where I then resided for the next 14 years. In 2008, in what would be a defining aspect of this project, I began work as a teacher at a high school with a significant proportion of 帰国子女 (kikokushijyo[1]), which included taking on pastoral activities as a homeroom teacher and supervision of sporting clubs. Living that role, as a Japanese-speaking member of a secondary school community, informed much of the project on which this book is based. Therefore, I wish to briefly describe certain aspects of Japanese high school life, since my experience as an immigrant worker in Japan forms part of my claim to be able to interpret the accounts of a population from which I stand apart. It also serves to contextualise this project for those unfamiliar with the setting.

## Secondary teaching in Kanagawa

A key role of secondary school teachers is that of 担任 (tannin) or homeroom teacher, which includes the responsibility for the well-being and academic progress of around 30 students each year. As tannin, I had the opportunity to support both local students returning to Japan from life and study overseas and international students who were on long-term exchanges at our school. Witnessing the destabilising effects of this change and the ways they struggled to participate in communities of their peers, I was consistently moved by their attempts to reconcile experiences of life elsewhere with the rigors of Japanese educational spaces. I witnessed the ways they were marginalised by the expectations of conformity placed upon them institutionally and interpersonally, and by the way their multilingual repertoires were simultaneously a marker of difference and a focus of adoration and jealousy. Watching and attempting to support these students, I came to a greater awareness of the sociocultural factors that impacted their opportunities to learn, speak and belong. A desire to better understand and explicate these factors and communicate the stories of young people making what amounted to one of the biggest decisions and journeys of their lives set me on the path to this project.

A vital part of secondary school life in Japan involves participation in extracurricular clubs, referred to as クラブ活動 (kurabu katsudō). Clubs are tied to sporting or cultural activities such as baseball, Japanese archery, orchestra, tea ceremonies and second language use. Importantly, participation in these clubs is virtually mandatory, as it is often where students develop many of their most important friendships and provides socialisation into many communicative and interpersonal norms that carry over into professional life in Japan. Although some students elect not to join a club, generally this needs to be justified as it is considered a fundamental part of secondary education. During club activities, which can take place for several hours after class and, in many cases, during weekends, students train together or participate in demonstrations, practice games and competitions related to their chosen activity. During summer vacation, these clubs may also have 合宿 (gashuku) or training camps to encourage team building and engage in rituals and traditions associated with their club. Gashuku are often attended by 先輩 (senpai[2]) who were previously in the club but have now proceeded to higher education or the workforce. This provides opportunities for current club members to build connections that serve them as they enter university and the workforce. Although much of the activity of the club is student led, high school teaching staff are responsible for the supervision, organisation and sometime coaching of these club activities. This results in many instances of teacher-directed learning and socialisation in spaces beyond the classroom, particularly around morals, behaviour and ways of being in Japanese society. In many instances, students and teachers may spend more time with each other during club activities than they do in the classroom, or for that matter, with their own families.

This brings me to the other part of my claim to be able to undertake this project. Working as a transnational cultural labourer in Japan, I saw shades of my students' experiences in my own. Although I recognise that my subjectivities can be considered in many respects to be in tension with those of the informants, I bring to the project almost two decades of lived experience in, and moving through, spaces where my body marks me as an outsider, albeit often experienced as privilege. Yet, racialised privilege, like other manifestations of ascribed identity, is subject to discursive orders of indexicality (Blommaert, 2010), particularly when it is derived from a position of alterity. In Japanese language spaces, I have often experienced my whiteness as flattening; my role narrowly defined as that of English speaker and language learning resource. My time among Japanese-speaking communities has been marked by an ongoing struggle to be recognised as a legitimate speaker of Japanese, even as my body and its unconscious dispositions serve as visible markers of my otherness. For this reason, my positionality has often been one of *liminality* – of actively participating in the linguistic and cultural practices of Japanese language communities while simultaneously being perceived as a cultural and linguistic outsider. It is from this position that I find resonance with the experiences of those who, through academic mobility, find themselves struggling to be legitimised as members of the communities they inhabit.

### Researching from Melbourne

I have also often found myself negotiating liminal positions in relation to the research itself. Beginning the project while still a high school teacher in Japan, I moved to Melbourne, Australia, initially alone and then bringing family from Japan, in order to focus on the project full time. Although I had returned to Australia, it was a large metropolis more than a thousand kilometres from the area where I had grown up. Even as I was living a translocal experience of academic mobility, I began meeting the informants for this project, first through email and then Zoom and found myself needing to construct my role as researcher – one that was distinct from that of educator and supporter that I had often played when engaging with other adolescent sojourners. With much reflection, my role as I understand it in this project is therefore one of invested observer, as I also experienced the informants' stories vicariously – through repeated listenings of their interviews and analysis of their Instagram posts – seeing echoes of my own experiences in theirs.

Throughout my interactions with the participants, I was conscious of how aspects of my identity emerged and were made apparent to the participants in my communications with them; adult, Anglo-Australian, male, researcher, English speaker, Japanese speaker, former high school teacher in Japan. Recognising that these subjectivities would affect the ways the participants responded to me, I followed the advice of Holliday (2016: 18), and attempted to draw upon them to 'disturb the surface of the culture [I was] investigating... to dig deeper and reveal the hidden and the counter'. Informed by the experiences of liminality discussed above, I positioned myself to the informants as someone who has existed both outside of and within Japanese cultural settings, giving them a brief overview of the history related above and restating the aims of the project to them. By adopting this position, I was also asking them to relate to me as a fellow sojourner and someone who would be able to empathise with their experiences. It is my interpretation that this positionality partially contributed to their decisions to narrate their experiences to me, despite differences in age, ethnicity and gender. The extent to which they shared and withheld their experiences from me is, of course, ultimately unknowable since I only have access to what was communicated in interviews and on social media. Indeed, any interview is 'a product of the interaction between interviewer and interviewee' (Block, 2000: 759); an *account* grounded in the time and place of the interview, rather than an objective record of reality. Any social media post too is inherently a performative act for an imagined audience embedded within the authors' positioning and framing, and so the Instagram data I drew upon remains a differently located but still subjective source. My use of the term *account* throughout this volume therefore reflects these understandings and the limitations it implies.

In saying all of this, I wish to point out that what is contained in this book is ultimately my own rendering of the informants' experiences. I therefore submit to you, the reader, the observations, interpretations and analysis that have emerged over several years of listening to, and then repeatedly revisiting, the accounts gifted to me by the informants.

## The Structure of this Book

Although the aim of this book is to argue for a view of language learning abroad as structured by, and negotiated through, tensions between the local and the global, at its heart are the case studies of five young Japanese people who volunteered to share their stories of year-long sojourns abroad and a subsequent year after returning to Japan. The book is therefore centred around these case studies, with Chapters 1 and 2 serving to frame my approach.

Chapter 1 unpacks the idea of sociality online and the ways that digital communications technology have been understood in relation to language learning abroad. This is used to begin a discussion on the nature of immersion as it is imagined and the implications this has for the way that study abroad is conceptualised and approached. Finally, the chapter identifies key areas that demand exploration in order to better comprehend language learning abroad from translocal perspectives.

Chapter 2 then provides an overview of theoretical and methodological approaches used in the project that informed this book. Reflecting growing recognition that holistic perspectives are needed if we are to better understand how language learning takes place abroad, this chapter briefly outlines the ecological approach that was used. This chapter also underscores the importance of examining the experiences of adolescent sojourners as well as providing contextualising information on the Japanese education system and attitudes towards English learning. I then describe the methods from which the case studies in this book are presented. Significantly, this section presents the methodological innovations used to determine the representativeness of the case studies within the larger cohort from which they were drawn, and the criteria used to select the case studies.

The next five chapters each then cover a single case study. Each chapter presents the account of a Japanese high school student who took a year-long sojourn to a different location. Each chapter provides background on the informants, including the factors that led to their decision to study abroad, their experiences during their year abroad and how they experienced the year that followed. The case studies themselves have been written to trace the narrative of the informants from their initial interest in studying abroad, through their year-long sojourn and then their experiences in the year after returning. I highlight in each the role that the local and translocal played in their experiences and ability to appropriate the communicative practices encountered abroad.

In the final chapter, I survey the findings and what they mean for the way we think about and conceptualise language learning abroad. I also reflect on assumptions of study abroad that require a reassessment in light of what has been presented.

## Notes

(1) Returnee Japanese children who have previously lived with parents on overseas placements for a number of years.
(2) Often literally translated as one's senior, it often represents a relationship whereby mentoring and support is offered by the senpai to junior members (kōhai) of an organisation in return for respect and ensuring that the institution is maintained after their departure.

# 1 Digital Sociality, Immersion and Translocality

### Sociality in a Digital Era

Sociality has long been a driving force in the adoption of communication technologies, particularly among young people. One only has to look at the uptake of ポケベル (pokeberu) or pagers among young people in Japan during the early 1990s, or the development of online registers by young people using the character-limited short messaging service on Nokia cellular phones later that decade. As a teenager in regional Australia during the 1990s, one of the first things I did after obtaining a second-hand 14.4k modem from a friend, was to dial into a local bulletin board system (BBS) to join an online community composed of teenagers from other schools in the area. Once permanent internet connections became more widespread, ICQ became a staple way to stay connected with others outside of school hours, exchanging answers to assessments and communicating without the oversight of parents. Internet use at that time though was far from ubiquitous, instead limited to a cadre of 'computer nerds' with the privilege of a personal computer at home and a basic understanding of networking protocols.

My first encounter with social media was during the mid-2000s while working for an 英会話 (eikaiwa[1]) in Japan. I began patronising a small 居酒屋 (izakaya[2]) by the train station near my house on a regular basis. It was a non-descript place, with only a small, illuminated Asahi beer sign and a fan blowing smoke from grilling 焼き鳥 (yakitori[3]) onto the street marking its presence. It was here that I developed friendships with other locals and first came into contact with social media through an invitation to join the platform ミクシィ (Mixi).

Reflecting on this experience almost two decades later, I can see how my invitation to, and my participation in, the community on Mixi was both a recognition and an extension of my membership in the community that frequented the izakaya. As someone learning Japanese informally at the time, I was often unable to reconcile the ways that people communicated on Mixi with those of in-person interactions. My observations and attempts to interact became an education in the variation of registers and communicative norms across different modalities. As a relatively recent immigrant attempting to negotiate the cultural and linguistic practices of this community, the injection of social media alongside other forms of digital interaction popular at the time (email and short text messages) was often overwhelming. My regular failures to comprehend or respond to interactions that took place on Mixi emphasised my sense of apartness, particularly when opportunities for social engagement beyond the izakaya, such as a barbeque at a local beach, were proposed and planned on the platform. However, what I was aware of was an online dimension to the practices of this community that I could linguistically 'brush against', even as I struggled to fully engage. Since then, a steady procession of new platforms has redefined the affordances available for interaction online and social media has become increasingly ubiquitous, multimodal and complex.

Importantly though, my access to the online interactions of this community was facilitated by in-person interactions that took place over multiple evenings and shared bottles of 焼酎 (shōchū[4]). The community's basis was a shared physical space. With seating for less than 15 people and its proximity to a train station that largely served a coastal residential area, the discussions that occurred were predominately intimate and localised. The nature of members' online interactions therefore reflected the registers and topics of in-person interactions – brief recaps of local surfing conditions, results of a member's son's soccer match or photos of a barbeque. The intertwining of these offline and online relationships illustrates a broader conceptual point advocated by Androutsopoulos (2006) and now widely adopted in studies of language and digital communication: online communication is *situated* in the local contexts of its users. Digital communication is not a wholly online phenomenon. It is bound up in the social, material and historical contexts of its users. Observing the activities that users engage in beyond digital spaces allows us to better understand what is taking place online.

Having said that, online interaction is not simply a mirror of what would traditionally take place in person. The nature of digital communication is that it removes the requirements of physical and temporal proximity for interaction to take place. A message can be responded to almost instantaneously from across the room or many hours and thousands of kilometres away from when and where it was sent. Even as members have moved away or spent less time at the izakaya due to life changes, many (including myself) remain effectively connected to the community, sharing in the lives (and deaths) of members through social media. Even as the community is and remains grounded in the physical location of the izakaya, it also exists partially online as connections, in different configurations, are made, reproduced or extended digitally. Mediated by communications technology, it is effectively a translocal community.

The upshot of this is that social media allows us to rekindle and maintain interpersonal connections with communities we frequented in the past but have since departed. As we progress through our lives, encountering people through family, school, work and play, digital communication makes it possible to build diffuse networks and extend and maintain the social practices of those groups online (Leander & Mckim, 2003). This means that over time, our online networks can contain a diversity of people who would never otherwise have occasion to interact. Social media creates these possibilities, particularly when we elect to post content that is intended to be viewed by all of our contacts, or even online publics more generally.

## The Nature of Online Interaction

Before turning to the role of social media in language learning abroad, there is a need to consider the nature of interaction online, particularly in the ways that it deviates from traditional face-to-face communication that characterises much of the learning that sojourners engage in while abroad. There is a rich literature of socially oriented work that has sought to map the nature of online interaction and its connections to learning and language. Selectively drawing on this literature, I want to illustrate a number of concepts that are vital to understanding the way that sociality takes place online which will inform our analysis.

A logical starting point for thinking about digital communication is its defining characteristics of persistence, scalability and accessibility regardless of geographical location (boyd, 2008). Messages posted online can potentially reach unlimited audiences that are spatially and temporally removed from their originating source. This, in turn, carries with it a number of implications for a user of social media who wishes to post something online. The first of these is the realisation that what is posted online can potentially be seen by a large, diverse audience who may not necessarily share the same values, linguistic repertoire, cultural understandings or expectations of communication. This is particularly prevalent in networks that may be publicly accessible or contain large numbers of people who wouldn't normally interact offline. This effect of social media, termed *context collapse* (Marwick & boyd, 2011), means that those posting online are often required to manage and negotiate these expectations across a potentially diverse array of communicative styles. Following Bell's (1984) insight that audience (real or imagined) is crucial in influencing the language choices that a speaker makes (which he termed *audience design*), Androutsopoulos (2014) observes this process at play when people attempt to negotiate ever-present instances of context collapse when posting online. In his study of the online communicative practices of multilingual young people in Germany, Androutsopoulos showed how his participants selected from among the linguistic resources available to them in order to tailor their message for specific audiences. This could mean, for example, replicating a message across more than one language to maximise their audience. It could also mean choosing a specific language, or using specific terms of address, such as the German 'reunde, familie & der rest "friends, family and the rest"' (Androutsopoulos, 2014: 67) in order to target a particular subsection of their audience. The participants also drew on other forms of semiosis to design the audience for particular posts, such as photos, videos, punctuation and emoji.

This leads us to another important characteristic of digital communication. Underpinning users' ability to negotiate meaning online is the inherent multimodality of modern social media platforms and the way that the architecture of the internet in general affords users the ability to engage in heteroglossic practices of semiotic recontextualisation (Adami, 2014). Effectively, recontextualisation involves taking text and other forms of semiosis and reusing them in a different context, potentially leading to the transformation of their meanings (Bernstein, 2000). Young people in particular have been identified as adept and prolific in their reuse and recombination of various linguistic and other semiotic resources. Rymes (2012), for example, notes how the semiotic elements of viral videos on YouTube are recontextualised into remakes which draw elements from the original but create different meanings. This includes classroom practices which, influenced by these videos, are themselves uploaded and contribute to unfolding processes of resemiotisation across online and offline spaces. These processes have also been noted by Dovchin *et al.* (2017) who highlight how young people draw upon diverse repertoires of linguistic resources to engage in practices of linguistic play and position themselves in kaleidoscopic ways in relation to each other, global pop culture and monolithic discourses of national identity.

In effect, this speaks to the way that social media is used to participate in acts of self-representation. From selecting a username and profile picture, to deciding what images to post and which content to reshare, individuals collate, assemble and recontexualise symbolic resources online in the service of what Potter (2012: 2) has termed a 'new "curatorship of the self"'. The curation of an online persona is subject to practices of concealment and disclosure, as users select which aspects of their social identity to perform, structured and shaped by the architecture of the platform itself. Georgalou (2016) has noted how users adopt combinations of linguistic and sociotechno practices to limit who can read, understand and respond to their messages. This includes encoding posts through oblique cultural references and code-switching, sporadically deleting past posts, suggesting switches to alternative platforms and locking comments. Platforms such as Reddit and 4chan thrive on the anonymity they offer their users; therefore, users may be more likely to participate in discussions that carry greater social risk, such as topics of an intimate, taboo or political nature. On the other hand, with platforms such as Facebook that encourage the use of real names, users are more likely to engage in processes of self-making which align with their 'offline' selves (Barton & Lee, 2013), and the social status they provide encourages many to present their 'best' selves to their audiences (Baron, 2008). For most users, the processes of curation they engage in online are in the service of sense-making identity work, building a coherent narrative of themselves (Potter, 2012).

Added to all of this is the idea that digital communications allow us more discretion about the communities we participate in and who we elect to maintain contact with, rather than simply relying on serendipity. Observing this process taking place in Japanese society with the spread of personal communication devices, Matsuda (2006) termed it *selective sociality*. No longer reliant on physical proximity to determine who we interact with, we can cultivate connections with those whom we wish to maintain contact with, and the semi-private nature of many platforms means that we can pursue those interactions beyond the social, institutional and physical restrictions that would limit them in face-to-face settings. In this too, we see the translocality of many of the interpersonal connections we maintain, their situatedness and connection to place, and the way they also simultaneously transcend it through digital technology (Greiner & Sakdapolrak, 2013).

Yet, this raises an important point about the nature of interaction online. Throughout this section, I have emphasised the agency of the individual to control what and to whom they present online. This is intentional as this volume is primarily interested in considering and exploring the ways that young people use social media and related digital tools in conjunction with their experiences and language learning abroad. However, interaction online is subject to a range of social, material and platform-based structuring forces. One example is that much of the behaviour in social spaces online, particularly among young people, comes with an expectation of *reciprocity* (boyd, 2019). What this means is that online actions such as adding someone as a 'friend' or liking or commenting on a post come with the expectation of an in-kind response, particularly in smaller online communities. Failure to reciprocate can therefore be interpreted as a negative social behaviour with consequences that can be felt in the offline contexts of those relationships. In Ito and Okabe's (2005) study for example, respondents felt the need to engage in acts of excusing or apologising if they did not promptly respond to a message, highlighting how norms of reciprocity create regimes of availability.

As previously alluded to, the architecture of a platform exerts a formative influence on the norms and means of interaction within it. Notably, social media platforms employ predetermined templates that guide user behaviour and prompt certain types of responses, thereby creating an interdependence between the exchange of information and the design of the platform (Jovanovic & Van Leeuwen, 2018). Pangrazio (2019) has noted that young people also respond to the architecture of the platforms they post to, becoming socialised into producing certain content both through observation and responses from peers and through the platform itself, such as gaining more followers and likes when posting certain content. An understanding of what is presented as desirable on a given platform is usually gained 'through observation and trial and error' (Pangrazio, 2019: 1321). As users become more literate in the technological affordances and social norms of a platform, their behaviour can also be shaped through the influence of algorithms which promote certain types of content while supressing others. Thus, algorithmic influence, which is often occulted and unacknowledged, can modify user behaviour and reshape the nature of interactions within the platform.

It is also crucial to acknowledge that the material aspects of accessing content online can have a distinct influence on how a user interacts and what they learn. As scholars such as Kell (2015) and Pennycook and Otsuji (2017) have pointed out, the way we make meaning is indelibly tied to the physical and material realities of how we go about getting things done. Darvin (2023), for example, has pointed out how the device that is used to access information online, as well as the interface and orientation of that device, can shape what information is perceived as pertinent and what affordances are available to access that information. Beyond the device-level influences, there also exist a host of other geographical, institutional and social factors that dictate an individual's access to specific sites or even the internet itself. These include, but are not limited to, the individual's physical location, their ability to connect to local cellular and wifi networks, and the controls placed on their access by other individuals or institutions. In the context of study abroad, when examining the interdependent relationship between social media and language learning, it is crucial to recognise the inherent tensions that exist between these factors and the user's ability to act agentively online.

What I have presented here is by no means an exhaustive look at the nature of online communication. Rather, I have provided an overview of ideas that can guide our thinking about the intersections between social media and study abroad. Online interaction, although situated in and subject to the local contexts from which it arises, can simultaneously transcend those contexts and provide users with affordances to present themselves to audiences located in distant locations and times. For adolescents in particular, its connections with identity and belonging make social media an alluring and powerful part of their social lives. The hyperconnectivity achieved through technological advances is having far-reaching impacts on the ways we understand and interact with each other and study abroad, deeply oriented as it is to fostering social connections across borders, and must account for this complexity and transformation.

## Adolescents and social media

Having noted the ways that sociality is carried out in online spaces, we now turn to the use of social media among young people who make up the bulk of those participating in study abroad. For adolescents in particular, the role of social media is amplified at a time in their lives when identity, belonging and growing independence are of greatest importance. An annual survey carried out by the Japanese Government's Cabinet Office (2021) indicates that, on average, Japanese high school students spend almost four and a half hours a day (263.5 minutes) online, with these numbers increasing steadily over the previous decade. Of this, just over an hour (60.8 minutes) is dedicated to 'communicating with family, friends and others' while more than two and a half hours (164.7 minutes) are spent on 'interests and entertainment'. The remaining time is split between 'studying, learning and mental training' and 'other activities'.

Thus, what can be said about the use of social media, at least among Japanese high school students, is that it is largely driven by relationships and leisure activities. This aligns with scholarship of US youth that has found that a majority of the learning that adolescents are doing is 'situated in the social and recreational activities of youth rather than in contexts of explicit instruction' (Itō *et al.*, 2019: 12). Digital communications technology and its attendant social media platforms are fundamental to the ways that adolescents now understand and construct themselves. Participation in social media has become a non-negotiable part of their social worlds – part of a fully realised social life. We must therefore recognise that digital communications mediate much of the learning that takes place beyond the classroom, including how young people use, understand and learn language.

The importance of informal interactions with peers is correspondent to adolescents' growing desire for independence. However, this desire is often in tension with the reality that most young people, particularly those at high school, remain dependent upon the adults in their lives. The spaces that adolescents generally inhabit, such as classrooms and homes, are largely subject to relations of power controlled by adults. Consequently, adolescents often seek out environments that enable them to engage in social interaction and explore identity and intimacy free from adult oversight. Digital spaces accessible through smartphones provide precisely these types of opportunities. In their study of young people's digital practices in Japan, Ito and Okabe (2005) show that online interaction provides important sites for adolescents to challenge and subvert social institutions that dictate their behaviour and establish their own autonomy. They also note that the affordances of digital communication allow interaction to continue even in spaces where it would usually be subjected to the surveillance and control of adults. All these points apply not only to sojourners, but also to young people in host communities themselves. As prolific users of social media, adolescents, regardless of their linguistic background, may seek to make sense of themselves and their interpersonal relationships through digital communications. Therefore, it is imperative that we take the dynamics of their online and offline interactions into account when seeking to understand how they engage in processes of linguistic appropriation and development.

## Conceptions of Digital Communications in Study Abroad

The expanding presence of digital technologies in the mediation of social interactions has not gone unheeded by researchers interested in the experiences of language learning and study abroad. Indeed, consideration of internet facilities in study abroad programme design was already noted several decades ago (e.g. Twombly, 1995). Despite such recognition, the literature on study abroad has yet to adequately address digital communication in its complexity, particularly its influence on sociality as described above. In my reading of this literature, I have observed two widely used framings of digital communication that have shaped how it has been, and continues to be, approached.

The first of these, I call the 'disengagement perspective', which narrowly conceives of digital communication as a means for sojourners to remain in contact with those at 'home', reducing their opportunities to engage in cultural and language learning while abroad. This view is manifested in Engle and Engle's (2002: 97) reference to the 'umbilical availability of instantaneous electronic communication', an infantilising metaphor that insinuates total dependence on the home connection which was subsequently taken up elsewhere (Allen & Dupuy, 2012; Kinginger, 2008). Drawing on reports of email use by sojourners in Spain and Mexico, Knight and Schmidt-Rinehart (2002: 192) relay the concerns of hosts that the technology stops sojourners from engaging with Spanish, noting that, 'it is more difficult for students to "cut off" than in the past because of technology'. Engle and Engle (2003: 6) return to ask if access to tools such as email are 'depriving [sojourners] of what they really need: in the first case, those key initial interactions, unsettling but rich, with their environment; then later, a rare and valuable emotional space with its potential for reflective growth'. These and the comments of many other scholars (e.g. Coleman & Chafer, 2010; Hofer *et al.*, 2016; Jackson, 2017; Magnan & Lafford, 2012; Ogden, 2008; Wolcott, 2016) frame digital communications technology in terms that place its affordances for maintaining connections with those located at home directly in tension with notions of immersion. This discourse draws its potency from the idea that the language and culture of the 'other', with whom the sojourner is primarily abroad to engage with, exist soley in the territorialised space of study abroad contexts.

To be fair, many of the studies I refer to were completed prior to the development and mass adoption of social media and smartphone technologies. However, this caveat should be tempered with a number of studies that were already pointing to the possibilities of digital communication to engage with the cultural and linguistic 'other' before the turn of the century (e.g. Kinginger *et al.*, 1999; Morita & Nagasawa, 1999). Even in my own experience immigrating to Japan in the early 2000s, the ability to access information online in internet cafés was instrumental in locating Japanese language classes near my workplace as well as local record shops and live music venues, which led to further opportunities to practice and develop my ability to interact in Japanese. Importantly, I'm not claiming that digital communications technology can't be used in part to avoid interacting with local communities or the often challenging linguistic and identity work that accompanies it (as indeed Kinginger's [2008] assessment of Deirdre shows it can and does). Rather, I want to point out how this view takes the effect (using technology) for the cause (avoiding engagement with the host community), ascribing it the narrow function of maintaining contact with home. The fact is that even before widespread access to digital communications technology, individuals studying abroad struggled with the discomfort that emerges from contact with the unfamiliar and sought refuge in communities of co-nationals or their own solitude.

More recently, however, 'instrumentalist perspectives' of technology in study abroad have gained prominence, framing digital communication platforms as tools that can significantly contribute to cultural and language development. This perspective emphasises the pedagogical applications of technology, often overlooking its interdependence with the social and material contexts in which it is used. In effect, this perspective has emerged alongside, and intersects with, the field of computer-assisted language learning (CALL), whose primary concerns have been the applications and mediation of computer technologies in language learning (Lomicka & Lord, 2019). Examples of this approach include Lomicka and Ducate's (2021) demonstration of Padlet as a means to mediate intercultural learning; Dressler *et al.*'s (2021) study on the use of personal blogs as tools for reflection on experiences abroad; and Han's (2019) arguments on the benefits of embedding virtual tours into study abroad programmes.

While exploring the pedagogical possibilities of technology in study abroad is an important endeavour, it is also imperative that we recognise these perspectives align with discourses of tech-solutionism, which position technology as a panacea to stated problems while overlooking the complex social, cultural and political contexts from which they emerge (McQuillan, 2022). In the study abroad literature, the 'problem' is often perceived to be the linguistic and cultural learning of participants for which technology serves as an instrument to improve, augment or otherwise lead to pedagogically preferred outcomes. My concern here is that this perspective is reminiscent of an earlier era of research that focused on the programmatic outcomes of study abroad while neglecting the processual and particular nature of language learning (Wilkinson, 1998b), inadvertently reinforcing the belief that technology serves to resolve the complexities of language learning, rather than existing in complex relationships to it. Therefore, it is crucial to recognise that our understanding of technology cannot be detached from the contextual factors shaping its usage.

What I am arguing for then is a conception of online interaction as a fundamental and inseparable element of sojourners' sociality, part of the ecological whole of their language learning before, during and after study abroad. I argue that an understanding of what is taking place online is not complete without also understanding its intersections with what is happening in person – that these aspects of a sojourner's experience are dialogically connected. Through the affordances of digital communications, processes of language learning, identity negotiation and host community-based interaction are multithreaded affairs extending beyond the time and place of a sojourn abroad.

## Beyond Immersion in Study Abroad

We now return to Kubota's (2016) identification of a social imaginary of study abroad. Given the above discussions, there is a need to understand aspects of the imaginary that sit beyond those of individual outcomes and relate to the way that the activity of study abroad itself is imagined as occurring. Indeed, Kubota (2016: 349) has identified the notion of immersion as 'a major part of the study-abroad imaginary' and it permeates thought on language learning in study abroad.

Looking at both disengagement and instrumentalist perspectives of digital communications in study abroad, an important question emerges: Why have these perspectives taken precedence over a more integrationalist and dialogic understanding of digital communications? In this, I believe they find their genesis in the social imaginary of study abroad, specifically the shibboleth of 'immersion' and its long-standing associations with territorialised views of language and culture. Despite the radical transformations wrought by global connectivity, this imagination of immersion permeates our perceptions of digital communications technology in study abroad.

In framing this discussion of immersion in the study abroad literature, I want to begin with an extract from Japanese novelist (遠藤周作) Shūsaku Endō's semi-autobiographical account in his 1965 book 「留学」 (*Foreign Studies*). Presented in the third person, the book – which is based on his time spent living and studying French literature in post-World War II Paris – is illuminating as it was written at a time when international communication for the individual remained very much limited to postal services and telegrams.

> ソルボンヌのすぐ近くにある学生食堂で、若い連中と一緒に並び、うす肉や馬鈴薯のスープの皿を載せたアルミ盆をかかえて片隅で一人で晩飯を食う。陰気な表情をしたこの日本人には話好きの仏蘭西学生たちも、ほとんど声をかけない。ホテルにたどりつくと、彼は長い間、ベッドにひっくりかえって、雨の染みのついた天井をじっと眺めていることもあった。起きあがって、日本の家族や友人に手紙を書く。下着や靴下を馴れぬ手つきで洗濯し、それを、あまり暖房のきかないスチームの上に干す時はわびしかった　（遠藤周作「留学」1965）

He would head to the student cafeteria near the Sorbonne, lining up with the young people there to be served a plate of weak meat and potato soup on an aluminium tray which he ate by himself in a corner. The otherwise chatty French students said barely a word to this grim-faced Japanese man. After returning to his hotel, he would often just lie on the bed staring at the damp spots on the ceiling for some time before getting up to write letters to family and friends back in Japan. And when he laid out the socks and underwear he had washed with unpractised hands on top of the barely functioning steam heater, he would be overcome with loneliness. (Endō, 1965)[5]

I find this extract encapsulates the inherent tension that frequently defines the study abroad experience: the simultaneous sense of being in a place while being apart from it. A kind of emplaced disconnection. We are acutely aware of our immediate surroundings, while simultaneously yearning for the comfort that comes from recognition and familiarity. Yet, in the Paris of the middle of the 20th century when Endo's story is set, life for his protagonist is steeped in heteroglossia and the negotiation of different linguistic communities encountered while abroad. He writes notes in 'childish' French even as he successfully interacts with French-speaking doctors and scholars. He finds the vernacular language of other Japanese scholars he encounters in a Montparnasse café unbecoming of their positions and uses an intimate register in letters to his wife in Japan. Japanese language is not confined to the territory of Japan, but in part, mediates the his experience of Paris. While fictionalised, the account reflects a reality where sojourners' linguistic and social encounters lie at the intersection of local and transnational forces which carry their own linguistic heterogeneity.

Although the notion that sojourners are 'expected to be completely immersed in the L2 with few opportunities to connect with L1-speaking friends and family' (Salaberry *et al.*, 2019: 10) is pervasive throughout the literature, it is worth questioning to what extent this reality exists (or has existed) in a world where the speed and volume of transnational communication and mobility has only continued to accelerate post-World War II. While there is certainly an argument to be made about the intensification and dynamics of contact following the widespread adoption of the internet and mobile phones, the imagination of study abroad as an experience of a specific target language and culture bounded by place and time requires interrogation.

Although in no way limited to research on study abroad, notions of language and culture as rooted in specific geographies and associated with specific national and ethnoracial identities are deeply embedded in the field. These ideologies have been widely problematised from anthropological (Malkki, 1992), linguistic (Hymes, 1970; Piller, 2016) and cultural (Papastergiadis, 2000) perspectives, particularly in the face of the aforementioned intensifying movement of people and information. Despite this, notions of language and culture as something anchored to specific places have continued to underpin a particular ideological perspective of study abroad with which we are only beginning to come to grips.

Overarchingly, this territorialised perspective of language and culture has informed our understanding of 'immersion'. The imagining of immersion within the study abroad literature intimates that during study abroad individuals are effectively surrounded by the target language. A sojourner's waking moments are filled with opportunities to live, breathe and interact in the target language, beginning as they alight at their destination and concluding as their feet leave the soil of the host nation. This notion of immersion has not been met uncritically by scholars. In the introduction to her influential edited book of study abroad research, Freed (1995: 4) problematised monolithic views of 'immersion language learning environments', observing that 'there are numerous variations of the study abroad experience and it is rarely, if ever, possible to describe with precision the quality and extent of social contact and linguistic variation' (Freed, 1995: 5). Wilkinson (1998a: 124) too, in her oft-cited paper, also noted an 'immersion experience' is one of 'immense complexity and intense individuality'. Yet, even as these views have sought to complexify the notion of 'immersion', they nonetheless continue a tradition of reification, constructing it as an essentialising, qualitative dimension of a study abroad experience. This tendency is present throughout the literature as 'immersion' is described as something which can be 'deeper' (Benson *et al.*, 2013: 106), has 'degrees' (Goldoni, 2013: 366) or can lend its attributes to other situations which then become 'immersion like' (Sanz & Morales-Front, 2018: 2).

The work of anthropologist Neriko Musha Doerr is instructive here in understanding both the ideological motives for this reification and its implications. Firstly, Doerr (2013) locates the discourse of immersion in a need to define study abroad as something distinct from both tourism and traditional classroom language learning. Moreover, Doerr (2016) argues that this discourse constructs study abroad as intense streams of localised learning opportunities, where engagement with even the mundane aspects of the host culture members' lives is construed as crucial opportunities for learning. These notions imbue study abroad contexts with an essence of linguistic and cultural authenticity, sites where those studying abroad are brought into direct proximity with the imagined, and often idealised, local. This discourse is used to construct members of the host community as a static, parochial alternate who can provide the mobile sojourner with an immersive learning experience (Doerr, 2013; Doerr & Suarez, 2018).

This exoticised notion of study abroad contexts as bounded, local spaces of target language learning stands in direct opposition to the flows of people and information that characterise the current globalised era (Appadurai, 1996; Blommaert, 2010). The implicit conceptualisation of study abroad destinations as immersive contexts for monolingual language acquisition has been pervasive in the language learning abroad literature since its inception, and the multilingual corrective is still in its infancy (see Diao & Trentman, 2021). Despite this, it is fair to assume that study abroad contexts have always been linguistically diverse, given the widespread mundanity and 'ordinariness' of translinguistic practices (Dovchin & Lee, 2019). What has changed, as the Douglas Fir Group (2016) acknowledges, is our (Western ontological) awareness and willingness to recognise and account for this diversity in widely accepted understandings of language. Therefore, it is also imperative that we re-examine our understanding of immersion and its grounding in non-existent ideas of language that bind it to specific times and spaces.

It follows then that the linguistic ecologies of study abroad contexts cannot be understood in isolation. The forms and normative hierarchies of language that exist within the *collective consciousness* (Wertsch, 1991) of host communities are dynamically tied to wider social forces. At the levels of community and interpersonal interactions, these ecologies can be unsettled by newcomers who arrive with their own linguistic understandings and practices. The linguistic ecologies that sojourners encounter abroad are indelibly entwined with the cultural, institutional and historical forces present within the host community, yet are also part of wider sets of cultural and linguistic flows. This is why study abroad contexts must be approached not as disconnected bubbles of monolingual linguistic learning, but as interconnected and dynamic zones of multilingual contact and translocal practice.

What is therefore needed is a reconceptualisation of study abroad contexts that does away with reified notions of immersion. One that moves beyond essentialised views of the cultural and linguistic practices of the other and acknowledges the dialogic processes that occur between sojourners and contexts already infused with translocality tied to human migration and communications. Research must recognise study abroad contexts as nodes in larger flows of people and information, bound up as they are in the political and historical circumstances of their existence, yet not wholly and monolithically determined by them. This is not to deny the opportunities they can offer to appropriate the communicative practices of a host community *in situ* as they are encountered through *communicative events* (Hymes, 1967). Yet, host communities and their communicative practices need to be understood from perspectives that recognise they exist within wider, transnational flows. It is within the intersections of the local and the global that sojourners navigate their time abroad and their struggles with language, identity and belonging play out.

A view of study abroad contexts as translocal and interconnected is vital for investigating the processes of language learning that avoid narrow, territorialised or unintegrated understandings of related phenomena, such as the use of online communication. By adopting perspectives of study abroad that recognise the entanglement of social, material and symbolic realities, we gain a fuller understanding of how the processes of language learning function in relation to the environments in which it takes place. Digital communication has been an integral part of study abroad for many years, despite limitations in our ability to fully grapple with its significance. This limitation stems from entrenched notions of immersion that are based on static, monolingual and unconnected views of host communities. What is now needed are conceptualisations of study abroad that seek to integrate the offline with the online, bridging the local and the translocal aspects of study abroad.

## An Integrated View of Social Media and Language Learning Abroad

As argued above, social media use is complex and multifaceted. In the contexts of study abroad, it intersects with sojourners' opportunities for language learning, identity construction and interpersonal connection, shaping and being shaped by their experiences. Sojourners' engagement with social media is therefore entangled with their struggles in the host context and the affordances they perceive it offering them will relate to those struggles. The sociocultural and sociolinguistic perspectives discussed earlier provide essential insights into the complexities that emerge when viewing social media use as situated in the translocal contexts of study abroad. Drawing on broader themes that permeate the socioculturally oriented language learning abroad literature, I identify three key aspects that warrant exploration in understanding the intersections between social media and study abroad.

## Social media as a vector of language learning and socialisation

Language learning is fundamentally a social activity that emerges through participation in communicative events. The notion of learning as situated in the lived over the contrived is commensurable with Itō et al.'s (2019) observation that adolescents' learning is primarily situated in peer sociality. Given that social media now occupies a fundamental role in sociality, mediating much of our interpersonal interaction and recreational attention, it follows that a significant portion of sojourners' learning while abroad will also be mediated through communicative technologies.

Social media is an obvious medium of observation and interaction for those seeking to appropriate linguistic practices associated with the host community. To a large extent, interaction on social media is informed by and contributes to the vernacular practices of specific communities (Barton & Lee, 2013). It serves as an important site for the development of linguistic repertoires that are reflective of specific social and cultural contexts. The persistent nature of communicative events on most social media platforms has frequently been identified as an important factor in the way that it allows users to work with and decode unfamiliar linguistic resources (Warschauer, 1999). For instance, Back's (2013) study found that social media use in the target language increased over time, including vernacular and online-only forms, indicating a clear link between developing linguistic proficiency in the target language and social media interactions. In this sense, social media use can support the development of a linguistic repertoire associated with the host community.

The multimodality of social media cannot be overlooked in understanding its contributions to language learning during study abroad. The highly visual nature of many platforms and the ability to engage in practices of resemiotisation, deploying diverse semiotic repertoires in interactions, mean that users can draw on other literacies to support developing repertoires connected with the host community. This can be seen in Jin's (2018) study of one sojourner's use of video and memes that allowed him to participate in a group chat even with a limited repertoire in the group's Chinese language practices.

The ability of digital communication to transcend temporal and spatial constraints also means that the language learning opportunities available through social media extend beyond the demarcated bounds of study abroad. Similar to the way that I could continue to interact with members of the izakaya community years after my circumstances changed, so too sojourners can remain participating members of the communities they joined when abroad. This follows the findings of Campbell (2011) and Shiri (2015), who observed that sojourners continue using social media as a means of sustaining connections related to language learning and use even after departing the host community. Social media enables sojourners to maintain transnational connections with their host community, extending the interactive possibilities generated by those connections far beyond the demarcated end of study abroad. Indeed, the possibilities for interaction can extend not only to the post-sojourn but also to the pre-sojourn period.

## Interpersonal connections and social media

As discussed above, social media has been narrowly defined by its ability to provide instantaneous connection with those still at home and media in the home language. Yet, there is also a more complex dimension to this particular facet of digital communication that needs to be considered in the context of study abroad. Part of the appeal of social media is the way it allows us to interact with others who are not immediately present, fulfilling various social functions we seek – play, conflict, intimacy, affirmation, adoration. Consequently, it is crucial to recognise that social media also serves these roles within study abroad contexts. The centrality of social media to the lifeworlds of adolescents means that it will undoubtedly feature in the experiences of those travelling abroad while also being an integral part of the social dynamics among their peers in the host community. Moreover, given the importance of social connections to the experiences and language learning of sojourners, the relationship-driven nature of young people's online practices means that they have a significant impact on how the process of language learning takes place. Social media engagement abroad is therefore about doing relationship work that is at the heart of their language learning endeavours.

Recall that for young people, social media is a vital site of peer sociality. In this way, social media has become essential to the way young people engage in and explore practices of intimacy. Sexual and sexualised encounters have been recognised as a key dimension of many sojourners' experiences abroad (Mitchell *et al.*, 2017; Murphy-Lejeune, 2002; Takahashi, 2013; Twombly, 1995), and romantic engagement with a partner can offer a unique set of language learning opportunities. Pascoe (2019: 117) has noted how 'Young people are at the forefront of developing, using, reworking, and incorporating new media into their dating practices in ways that might be unknown, unfamiliar, and sometimes scary to adults'. Social media can therefore mediate the way that sojourners seek, explore and engage in intimacy with others in ways that differ from what has taken place in the past. Returning to ideas of asynchronicity and selective sociality, the affordances of social media offer young people more control over whom they cultivate intimacy and the pace at which such intimacy develops. From the perspective of someone learning the linguistic and cultural practices of a romantic interest, these affordances provide greater ability to reflect on and refine interactions beyond the immediacy of face-to-face interaction. While in-person interactions may require more complex strategies to avoid unwanted attention such as the advances of Russian men experienced by American women in Polanyi's (1995) study, this type of attention can be addressed and disengaged from without needing requisite communicative abilities. The reciprocal expectations of online engagement are tempered by the affordances to ignore or block undesired advances, offering individuals increased control and boundary setting in their intimate interactions.

On the other hand, social and cultural activities promoted through social media can also serve to facilitate opportunities where they can participate and engage with members of the host community face to face (e.g. Seibert Hanson & Dracos, 2019). This can be particularly beneficial for sojourners seeking to engage in specific activities or events that may not be known to their local contacts, such as host families. Although host families have been identified as crucial in providing sojourners with access to a diverse range of interactive settings (Shiri, 2015), social media and other apps can also enable sojourners to identify additional contexts for interaction and learning (Durbidge, 2019). This relationship between social media and in-person interaction points the way these platforms can enable individuals to maintain and regulate existing social connections while also enabling the formation of new networks.

However, as we have already noted, digital communication means that online interactions transcend those immediate contexts, and also provide access to and interaction with home-based networks. Although this function has often been focused upon in studies adopting disengagement perspectives, it again functions more complexly in practice. In their innovative study for example, Mikal and Grace (2012) pointed to the ways that ongoing connection to home networks can help alleviate some of the stress that comes with arrival to the unfamiliar linguistic and cultural contexts of study abroad.

Importantly, this connectivity must be understood not only in its ability to bring 'home' into the study abroad context, but also in maintaining connections and social capital in a community to which the sojourner must inevitably return. While there is a tendency in study abroad research to elevate the learning context above all others, sojourners may also weigh up their future as well as their immediate present concerns. This is apparent in Dawson's (2019b: 129) study in which she observes that a participant from New Zealand studying in France, Persephone, 'opted to refrain from posting in French' despite engaging with content in French on Facebook due to perceptions that she would be negatively evaluated for doing so by her English-speaking audience. Effectively, Persephone's recognition of the scales through which posts in French could be read by those in New Zealand led her to design her posts in a particular way. Context collapse can therefore be a defining feature of sojourners' experiences, shaping how they engage with those located in the host community on platforms where they can also be observed by those at home.

### Identity and belonging

The connection between identity and study abroad has been the subject of a decades-long exploration that has documented the myriad ways that sojourners' performed and ascribed social identities have shaped their language learning abroad (e.g. Alfurayh, 2022; Anya, 2016; Ichimoto, 2007; Jackson, 2008; Kinginger, 2013; Plews, 2015; Polanyi, 1995). Given the affordances that social media provides for the construction, curation and performance of identity online (Blommaert, 2018b; Potter, 2012), it is unsurprising that it also emerges as a key site for sojourners to explore and negotiate new identity positions abroad. The translocal affordances of digital communications mean that sojourners can use them to interact with those they have met locally, or connect with others who share their language learning aspirations. As sojourners connect online with those they encounter abroad, the events and language of the host community can move online altering the nature of their interactions. Messages that are posted on social media may be engaged with by those in both the home and host communities and this may lead sojourners to tailor what they do online to engage with all or a subset of a linguistically and geographically disparate audience. Thus, online spaces afford sojourners the opportunity to practice and participate in complex semiotic practices, including translanguaging and audience design, drawing on the linguistic practices they are appropriating across different contexts. This can afford them opportunities to negotiate and perform transnational multilingual identities that may not be possible in social spaces offline.

As sojourners develop competence in the semiotic practices of the host community, they are able to incorporate these into their communicative repertoires online. However, this incorporation will be subject both to their own competencies and the perceptions of the audiences they are attempting to reach. Therefore, it is vital that we recognise the inherent multimodality of online spaces and the opportunities it affords sojourners to develop and deploy an increased range of communicative practices. There is something to be said for the ways that the distributed and asynchronous nature of social media may be more (or less) conducive to negotiating identities as transnational multilinguals than that of offline spaces.

### Exploring the Relationship between Language Learning Abroad and Social Media

As discussed above, narrow or unidimensional perspectives of digital communications are inadequate for grasping the manifold ways it intersects with sojourners' lived experiences and the way they understand, present and perform themselves translocally. Study abroad language learning involves social media language learning and that learning cannot be detached from the contexts in which it is situated. My argument in this chapter is that translocal perspectives which incorporate the multifaceted nature of digital communications are needed in language learning abroad research. This means re-examining the assumptions that have led to the imagining of study abroad contexts in terms of territorialised and monolithic cultural and linguistic immersion. No longer should these contexts be viewed as isolated and independent, but as nodes within interconnected global flows of people and information. A translocal perspective of language learning abroad recognises the potential of digital communications to transcend geographic boundaries and facilitate the creation of meaningful connections and identities that are rooted in multiple locations.

Online communication, situated as it is in offline realities, presents an important site for the development and deployment of diverse linguistic repertoires. It connects sojourners with communities and resources which transcend those immediate realities. Recognising and accounting for the fact that online spaces are part of language learning abroad increases the methodological and theoretical complexity of research. The reality is, however, that to truly understand the language learning of sojourners, we must deal with that complexity. Academic mobility is enmeshed in digital communication and study abroad research is uniquely positioned to explore the role of communications technology in language learning, particularly when engagement with the host community may require participants to learn new platforms and digital practices in addition to expanding their linguistic repertoires (Durbidge, 2022).

To understand sojourners' social media use, we therefore need to understand the role it plays in the wider social lives they are leading abroad. The perceived affordances of social media are directly tied to the social needs of sojourners abroad – be it social support from networks based elsewhere, a means to perform identities marginalised at home or a way to facilitate participation in host community peer networks. Being both a part of, and apart from, the immediate interactional realities of sojourners means that their use of digital communication can be located in ecological processes occurring both in the spaces they are physically located and in those to which their online networks extend.

Moreover, the points discussed above demonstrate how the affordances that sojourners perceive digital communicative technology offering them can undergo significant change as they move across geographical and linguistic borders. Interaction with members of the host community may become less frequent and detailed as the quotidian concerns of sojourners' immediate circumstances at home, including pressures to study and maintain interpersonal relationships at school, take priority.

On the other hand, they also offer an ongoing link to experiences and identities that may not be valued in those same home contexts. Aspects of the sojourn may continue to be performed and serve to reinforce the individual's sense of connection to places and people beyond that found at home. Although the degree to which online affordances are perceived and acted upon by sojourners both abroad and at home is a function of individual and context-related factors, there is little doubt of the affordances of digital communications technology to qualitatively change their experiences of both.

Although discussions about the role of communications technology in language learning abroad were initially characterised by a pessimism that saw it in tension with notions of linguistic and cultural immersion, I argue that this parochialised view of immersion does not currently exist. The apparatus of digitally mediated communication is now intrinsic to how the majority of human society functions and particularly to the sociality of young people. What the accounts of the informants in this project demonstrate is the multifarious ways that social media and other surrounding digital affordances form part of the complex ecologies that sojourners navigate both abroad and at home.

The rapid churn in the popularity of online platforms, the rate at which they modify their offerings and wider social attitudes towards online communication mean that what sojourners do with social media while abroad will continue to change. Even as I write this, TikTok usage among young people has overtaken platforms popular during this project such as Instagram and Snapchat and questions are now emerging about the role of generative artificial intelligence (GenAI) in language learning. Although the nature of social media engagement and use will continue to change, digital communications are and will continue to be an integral part of the study abroad experience for many participants. It needs to be recognised and studied for the effects it has on the sojourn and its unfolding effects on the trajectories of participants. Moving forward, it will be important to critically engage with the complex and multifarious ways that online affordances are encountered by participants, both linguistically and sociologically, deeply situated as they are in the material and social lifeworlds they inhabit.

## Notes

(1) Commercial English conversation school.
(2) Informal bar that serves small dishes that compliment alcohol.
(3) Grilled chicken on skewers.
(4) A type of distilled liquor.
(5) Translated from the original Japanese by the author.

# 2 Approach and Participants

**An Ecological View of Language Learning Abroad**

Looking over studies of language learning abroad conducted across previous decades, they have been remarkably consistent in demonstrating the extensive variability in individual outcomes and their interconnection with wider contexts. Schumann's (1980) autoethnographic study of learning Arabic in Tunisia and Persian in Iran for example, highlighted how the presence of co-nationals and cultural attitudes towards gender limited her opportunities to interact in Arabic. Spence-Brown's (1993) study of Japanese high school students in Australia and Siegal's (1995) study of Western women in Japan illuminated how participants' and host communities' cultural expectations impact language learning. Emerging as part of what later came to be known as the social turn in second language acquisition (SLA) research (Block, 2003), the complex relationships between sojourners, the sociocultural environment and language learning have come to define much contemporary study abroad research and undercut views of study abroad as a singular, uniform context.

Over the following decades, considerable progress in understanding factors that affect language learning has been made through a wide-ranging orientation towards, and investigation of, the processual dimensions of individuals' study abroad experiences. Part of this has been a move beyond conceptions of sojourners as simply 'language learners' to recognising them as people whose intentions, interactions, histories and lives extend far beyond the period they spend abroad. In acknowledging the multitude of conflicting individual and environmental factors that contribute to the experience and placing greater emphasis upon how the individuals involved are impacted, a more nuanced and multifaceted perspective of language learning abroad has been revealed. There is now growing acknowledgement of the need to approach the processes of linguistic development in study abroad holistically (Coleman, 2013; Duff, 2019; Isabelli-García *et al.*, 2018), recognising and making the complexity and interrelatedness of individuals and their environments part of the investigation. It is within this approach that the role of digital media must be situated and examined.

## Ecological approaches to language learning

Theories drawing on ecological metaphors to apprehend the processes of language learning have come to prominence through the work of a number of scholars, most notably Leo van Lier (2000, 2004) and Claire Kramsch (2002, 2008). Essentially, an ecological view sees individuals as situated within larger social, symbolic and material systems. Language learning emerges through the processes of socialisation as an individual interacts with other people and materials within the ecological system they are situated. Importantly, an ecological view does not see the individual nor the wider systems they inhabit as static, but as historically constructed and developing over time. At its heart, the ecological metaphor is decidedly post-humanistic (Pennycook, 2018) in its outlook, recognising the agency of individuals in their own learning while attending to the ways that agency is constituted by and interrelated with the surrounding environment.

Central to ecological theories of language learning are the notions of *affordance* and *emergence*. The notion of affordance, originally coined by Gibson (1979: 127), is most readily understood in his explanation that 'The *affordances* of the environment are what it *offers* the animal, what it *provides* or furnishes, either for good or ill'. This idea was taken up by van Lier (2000) and developed as an alternative to then-dominant ideas of 'input' to shift the focus of research away from *language as object* and towards *learning as activity*. For van Lier (2000), affordances signal the connection between the properties of a given environment and the individual seeking to learn language. An individual perceiving a particular affordance in their environment may then use it to engage in a desired activity, and so those seeking to learn language may identify opportunities to interact with other individuals or objects in order to appropriate that language.

To understand the processes of language learning, we therefore need to observe the ways that individuals perceive their environments and the way they make use of them to get things done. For example, digital communications offers the possibility for a single message to be viewed by a large, geographically disperse audience almost instantaneously. How an individual chooses to make use of this affordance, as either the originator or audience, may be directly related to their desire to appropriate and use specific linguistic resources.

Having said this, the way that learning actually takes place is related to, but not necessarily determined by, how an individual makes use of affordances. The idea of emergence was therefore adopted by van Lier (2004: 82) to conceptualise the way that 'the result of events or activities may be dramatically different from the initial inputs to those events or activities, and may not be reducible to them'. Similar to the way the functioning of an ant colony cannot be understood by observing the actions of each of its individual members, we cannot predict if or to what extent an individual will learn something when engaging with a particular affordance. In both cases, the resulting effects are considered to be emergent, with language learning dependent upon engagement with, and participation in, the communicative practices of a speech community.

By foregrounding the notions of interaction and participation, we come to the role that language and other semiotic resources play in engendering language learning. As van Lier (2004: 97) explains, 'Language learning, in a Vygotskyan (sociocultural) perspective, is mediated by all the semiotic resources that are available in the learning environment'. Returning to a point made earlier in this book, non-verbal modalities, such as those found in the semiotically rich affordances of online platforms, may be used by individuals to support interaction with and appropriation of unfamiliar linguistic resources. An ecological perspective recognises that language is 'part of larger meaning-making resources that include the body, cultural historical artifacts, the physical surroundings in short, all the affordances that the physical, social, and symbolic worlds have to offer' (van Lier, 2008: 599). Developing competence in the linguistic practices of a community may require sojourners to learn new or different ways of interacting, including turn-taking strategies, gestures and other non-verbal or paralinguistic ways of expressing themselves, which are 'mediated by the opportunities and struggles of their multilingual lifeworlds' (The Douglas Fir Group, 2016: 26). When a sojourner learns language while abroad, not only are they learning the lexis and syntax of a system of communication, they are also learning new ways of being. Language learning occurs through processes of socialisation into the communicative practices of a given speech community. This too means emphasising the role that the materiality of study abroad contexts play in mediating these processes.

The communicative practices each individual develops are therefore predicated upon the environments they inhabit, including those online, emphasising the interrelatedness of context and learning. In this, I follow Dufva (2012) as she applies the Bakhtinian notion of heteroglossia to the practice of language learning.

> Instead of learning one single 'English,' people may learn very different 'Englishes.' Instead of internalizing 'grammars,' they may appropriate situated usages that differ in their modality, register, genre, purpose, and so on. Instead of learning a language in its (supposed) entirety, each learner develops individual competences that vary across purposes, modalities, and situations and that are, by definition, always partial. (Dufva, 2012: 4–5)

In effect, these competencies provide *communicative mobility* that allows individuals to semiotically traverse and transcend the practices of the speech communities from which they draw. Indeed, they allow for creativity as individuals can draw upon their repertoires of semiotic resources to work in, around and across different varieties, noting that 'what is grammatically imperfect, may in fact, be an artful accomplishment of a speech act or evidence of spontaneous problem solving or conceptual thought' (Hymes, 1972: 272).

An understanding of language learning as emergent of context allows us to apprehend the inherent diversity and particularity of individual outcomes instudy abroad. The focus must not rest solely on the individual or on abstracted and pedagogised notions of competence (see Leung, 2005), but on the interactions between the individual and the contexts in which they are situated and the linguistic development that emerges from them. Studies of language learning abroad must account not only for how individuals develop their linguistic repertoires over time, but also for 'the ecosystemic dynamics where agents pick up on the affordances and pressures of the environment, and where the environment in turn changes as a result' (Steffensen & Kramsch, 2017: 7). This is a view of language learning as an *eco-dialogical process* (Zheng, 2012), which in the case of study abroad sees sojourners not as passive learners of static, parochial host language practices, but as agentive interactants who are part of wider transnational flows into, and through, the communities they inhabit.

Reflecting these notions of language learning, I draw on the *bio-ecological model of human development*, pioneered by Bronfenbrenner (1995, 1999) and refined by Bronfenbrenner and Morris (2006) to understand how these processes take place and lead to changes in individuals' linguistic repertoires. Using the Vygotskian-influenced notion of *proximal process*, Bronfenbrenner sees development occurring when an individual engages in regular, reoccurring and successively more complex interactions with the people, objects and symbols they encounter. As Bronfenbrenner and Morris (2006) note, the dialogic and reciprocal nature of developmentally effective processes is emphasised in cases of interpersonal interaction.

Importantly, these processes are dynamically interrelated to *person*, *context* and *time*. 'Person' recognises the role of the individual in initiating, sustaining, preventing or impeding proximal processes from taking place, playing an active role in the direction of their own development. 'Context' reflects widely used notions of this term in language learning research, although this model adopts a scalar conceptualisation of context. In effect, development occurs at the level of individual interaction but is influenced by the variegated social structures that surround it, including the communities, institutions and cultural zeitgeists of the time. This particular aspect of Bronfenbrenner's model forms the basis for the Douglas Fir Group's (2016) Transdisciplinary Framework for SLA in a Multilingual World that has sought to consolidate much of the socioculturally informed research on language learning and teaching from the past several decades. Finally, the model emphasises the way that *person*, *process* and *context* are interrelated parts of the whole system and are all subject to change over *time*, which also occurs at multiple scales. Interaction occurs and is configured moment to moment, yet development is contingent on the regularity and effect of these interactions and the extent to which they are maintained, discontinued and evolve. At a further remove, wider societal changes are seen to impact upon individuals' development trajectories, and these should also be recognised. This is vital since, as Steffensen and Kramsch (2017) have argued, any view of language learning as an emergent process must also recognise its inherent historicity and subjectivity.

Finally, a fundamental aspect of the bioecological model is the way that it conceptualises development as both dynamic and diachronic. This means that when we speak of development, we do not imply 'change for the better or of continuity in the characteristics of the same person over time' (Bronfenbrenner & Morris, 2006: 796). Linguistic development does therefore not imply a process of continued improvement but rather a change in an individual's communicative repertoire over time. Individuals come to language learning with their own histories and socialised epistemologies that become intertwined with desire in the moments of interaction and appropriation that constitute language learning processes. The communicative practices that sojourners seek to appropriate will therefore reflect this rather than some externalised notion of competence. Community and social relations are therefore central to the language learning of many individuals, particularly for those on study abroad who must re-establish themselves in the unfamiliar linguistic and cultural settings of the host community. It is in localised settings, positioned at the nexus of transnational flows of people and information, that language learning abroad emerges through repeated, sustained and increasingly complex moments of interaction, structuring and being structured by the surrounding social, historical and political milieux.

## Identity and Positioning

In any scenario where cultural and linguistic boundaries are meaningfully traversed, an individual will encounter differing patterns of normativity. As they occur at localised scales, these patterns are often unfamiliar and opaque to newcomers. Encountering them through interactions can provoke a realisation that the currency of currently held identities, abilities and linguistic resources is now subject to re-evaluation by a new set of measures, which Blommaert (2010) conceptualised as *orders of indexicality*. The individual is then thrust into processes which entail re-evaluating one's self, redefining one's sense of belonging and navigating unfamiliar constellations of social actions that shape and construct these things. For some individuals, this can present as an opportunity to reimagine their existence and grasp new, powerful identities (Kramsch,

2009). Yet, it can also result in marginalisation or silencing, leaving individuals grieving for a self that is no longer understood and recognised.

Indeed, the salience of identity as a means of understanding the processes of language learning abroad has been continually affirmed (Anya, 2016; Benson *et al.*, 2013; Block, 2007; Jackson, 2008; Kinginger, 2013; Tullock, 2018), precisely because it places participants in environments where questions of identity have an impact on their desire and opportunities to interact and learn. Poststructuralist approaches to identity have been central in the endeavour of documenting and exploring the ways that sojourners negotiate language learning abroad and they underpin my approach to participant experiences in this study.

The work of Bonny Norton (2000) (also writing as Norton Peirce [1995]) on learners of English in Canada has been crucial in setting the terms for how poststructuralist notions of identity are operationalised in language learning research. Drawing on critical feminist scholars such as Weedon (1996) and Luke and Gore (1993), Norton Peirce (1995: 20) argued for a concept of identity as 'as multiple, a site of struggle, and subject to change' to be applied in studies of language learning and acquisition. Embedded in this conceptualisation is an explicit rejection of identity as fixed or essentialised. Instead, it is viewed as processual and discursive, subject to surrounding social and cultural forces. Hall's (1992, 1997) contributions in this regard are particularly foundational as he identifies historical (rather than biological) processes as key in the constitution of identity, which is continuously reformed in response to the culturally infused discursive processes that surround us. Any apparent stability of identity is contingent on its alignment to the norms of a given community, while its instability and contestedness become evident when it transgresses those norms.

This engenders an understanding of identity as discursively constructed, shaped by options that are offered and recognised through the patterns of normativity associated within a given time and place (Pavlenko & Blackledge, 2004). In effect, discourses are the semiotic manifestations of macro-level ideological structures and so from an ecological perspective, identity emerges from 'the interplay between local interaction and large-scale sociocultural and natural dynamics' (Steffensen & Kramsch, 2017: 9). Discourses structure the way we view the world and determine what is important, valued and accepted, and are the means through which relations of power are both enforced and resisted (Weedon, 1996). Therefore, understanding discourse is crucial to understanding why a given individual may choose to adopt (or refuse) a particular subject position at a given time or attempt (or refuse) to invest in academic mobility and subsequent language learning. Although discourses can restrict the potential of an individual by limiting the subject positions available to them in a given time and space, they can also act as resources for imagined identities. As Kramsch (2009: 13) has noted, stereotypical images of a language and its speakers, such as coolness or sexiness, 'fulfil an important emotional function' and grant symbolic value to the linguistic resources that individuals seek to appropriate.

Having noted all of this, it is vital to also theorise the processual nature of identity construction, noting its interactive and negotiated nature. Davies and Harré's (1990) development of *positioning* has proven to be conceptually fruitful in unpacking this process of being discursively constructed by others even as individuals strive to construct identities for themselves. In their seminal paper, Davies and Harré argue that identities are instantiated through the taking up of specific identity positions in interaction, vis-à-vis those categories available to them through discourse. Positioning is achieved through and interrelated with the illocutionary force carried in speech acts, and involves the attending to, and the co-construction of, meaning as it emerges through interaction. Positioning is, as Davies and Harré (1990: 49) put it, 'the discursive process whereby selves are located in conversations as observably and subjectively coherent participants in jointly produced story lines'. In these instances, the individual's agency is crucial as they strive to resolve the tension that ensues through a process of negotiation, contesting the way they are positioned through language or other signs or through changes to their own reflexive self-understanding. Much of the socioculturally informed research into language learning abroad has sought to grapple with these negotiations as taken-for-granted ways of being and doing in the world are unsettled, and their liquidity is made apparent (e.g. Alfurayh, 2022; Anya, 2016; Dawson, 2019a; Jackson, 2008; Kinginger, 2008).

Renegotiations of the self are not internal processes but take place discursively through processes of interaction with others and within the communities that individuals find themselves (Pavlenko & Blackledge, 2004). In study abroad, this may entail negotiations around legitimacy as the sojourner seeks to occupy a position of acceptance and belonging. It may also involve processes of conflict and rejection, as individual and sociocultural dissonances go unresolved. Language is always a part of this experience since it is fundamentally 'a mode of social action rather than a mere reflection of thought' (Malinowski, 1923: 313). Its ties to identity, belonging, acceptance and alienation made even more acute by the power it provides to negotiate positionalities within a given speech community. As study abroad thrusts individuals into linguistically unfamiliar situations, the centrality of the communicative practice to how we interact across and inhabit social space is made more apparent. Language is interconnected with, and inalienable from, the milieu of social existence (Hymes, 1967) and so processes of language learning are necessarily tied to the contexts from which they emerge.

For these reasons, I think that Murphy-Lejeune's (2002) inspired adaption of Simmel's notion of the stranger to the contexts of study abroad offers an important means of understanding sojourners' positionality. Distinct from the 'other', the social category of the stranger as Simmel (1921) defined it, is an individual who exists within a community and yet is not seen as part of that community. Identifying sojourners in Europe as *new strangers*, Murphy-Lejeune (2002) argues that Simmel's concept allows us to better conceptualise their presence in host communities. Crucially, the positioning of the stranger speaks to the notion of belonging.

> On arrival, the predominant feeling is frequently one of exclusion: exclusion from the language community, from communication situations, from media and public discourse, from social interactions, and above all exclusion from the feeling of belonging to a group whose cohesion is based on a past in which the newcomers have no part. (Murphy-Lejeune, 2002: 104)

Across the breadth of the language learning abroad literature, it is possible to identify instances where those who spent time involved with speech communities abroad struggled to be recognised as legitimate members of those communities. This includes Western sojourners in China (Kinginger *et al.*, 2016), Indonesia (Hassall, 2013) and Japan (Cook, 2006; Iino, 1996, 2006; Siegal, 1995), Japanese sojourners in Australia (Spence-Brown, 1993), the UK (Ayano, 2006) and the United States (Wakana, 2018) and Chinese students in the UK (Jackson, 2008).

Although not all sojourners are necessarily interested in achieving a sense of belonging among the host community while abroad (see Lola's account in Wolcott [2013] for an example), for many a key question is: Under what terms does this community accept me and what linguistic resources do I need to do that? The sojourner arrives as a stranger 'afflicted by a socialisation deficit' (Murphy-Lejeune, 2002: 103) and must attempt to negotiate a participatory role in the community. The personal stake that sojourners have in their experience and the way it shapes how they present and reflexively understand themselves are better understood when we look beyond the identity of 'learner' and see the broader, more complex and intersecting ways they project themselves and are recognised by others. Indeed, these questions hold deep significance for adolescents as a sense of belonging among peers becomes paramount. They must also form a key consideration as we explore the ways that their social media use intersects with experiences of host and return contexts.

## Locating the Adolescent Subject in Study Abroad Research

Reading the empirical literature, you could be forgiven for assuming that studying abroad is exclusively the purview of those in tertiary education. Even recent, comprehensive meta-reviews of the literature tie language learning abroad to the internationalisation of higher education (Isabelli-García *et al.*, 2018; Marijuan & Sanz, 2018). Although this focus is understandable given the large populations of sojourners tied to higher education institutions and their accessibility to researchers, it becomes problematic when the circumstances of these populations become taken-for-granted certainties. In analysing the results of the relatively few studies carried out on adolescent sojourners, Kinginger (2013: 351) concludes that '[a]ge clearly plays an important overall role in the process of language learning'. Despite this, age, or the more sociologically aligned notion of *life stage*, remains a neglected aspect of studies of language learning abroad. As we take up calls to understand sojourners' experiences intersectionally (e.g. Ortega, 2021; Willis, 2015), we must also recognise that notions of life stage are socioculturally structured and interrelated with other social categories such as gender, race and class (James & Prout, 2015). The project on which this book is based specifically looked at the experiences of high school students from Japan; therefore, I unpack what that means in the context of study abroad below.

Childhood has been socially constructed as a time when the individual is 'dependent upon and protected by the adult world' (James & Prout, 2015: 205) and this informs conceptions of adolescence and attendant notions of maturity. One of the defining facets of adolescence is that it entails a transition from the strictures of adult control to a state where greater independence and autonomy can be exercised. Broadly speaking, this period of transition is marked by a realignment in adolescents' relationships, as the individual seeks to understand themselves apart from the adults who have responsibility for them (Erikson & Erikson, 1998), and time spent with peers takes priority over time spent with family (Chudacoff, 1989). For this reason, adolescents will seek to appropriate and use linguistic practices tied to the social identities recognised and valued by their peers (Ling & Yttri, 2006). However, beliefs about adolescents, the practices they engage in and the expectations placed upon them are a function of how adolescence itself is conceptualised in a given social milieu. This has particular relevance for investigations of study abroad, since movement across international borders also entails movement into different sociocultural contexts with differing views on, and expectations of, adolescents and their relationship to adult-controlled spaces.

Studies focusing on the homestays of individuals at different life stages have clearly demonstrated how perceptions of independence, control and belonging can vary across populations. University-age sojourners, for example, report tension in homestay settings as they find their independence limited (Juveland, 2011; Mitchell *et al.*, 2017), the arrangement more transactional than personal (Kinginger, 2008; Tanaka, 2007) or positioned ambiguously as a foreign guest (Cook, 2008). In contrast, Kinginger (2015) found that adolescents may be more accepting of the limitations placed on them by host families while also being more likely to be accepted as a member of the host family. Therefore, the notion of independence, as it has emerged in study abroad research, can likely be traced to socially defined ideas of maturity. Those who are perceived to possess the appropriate criteria are allowed, or expected, to operate independent of the family, while others are seen to both need and require boundaries and support.

This idea is supported by research showing that adolescent sojourners' autonomy is diminished by their dependence on the host family. In her study of German high school students in Australia, Grieve (2015: 651) pointed out how 'host parents had the power to set rules and regulations concerning extracurricular activities, including going to parties, going to friends' places and joining organized sporting activities'. This points to a broader issue that differentiates the lives of adolescents from those in higher education; their existence is largely constrained to spaces that are subject to the control of adults (Ito & Okabe, 2005). This lack of control is further compounded by a lack of economic independence, since the financial means of those still attending high school remain tied to the adults in their lives.

School also plays a major role in the patterns of adolescents' waking lives and the degree to which they are confined to particular social spaces, as the regimentation imposed by formal schooling circumscribes the nature of their sociality. As boyd (2019: 82) notes, 'for the vast majority of teens, the relations fostered in school are by far the most dominant in how they define their peers and friendships'. How this plays out during study abroad can been seen in Spenader's (2011) study of American sojourners at a Swedish high school, where the nature of their participation was dependent upon the peer relationships they formed. Therefore, adolescents tend to focus on status relative to their peers, since its effects feel immediate and exist as something over which they can exert control (Milner, 2004). The encompassing nature of secondary schooling can be contrasted with accounts of university-age sojourners whose social activities incorporate shopping (Mitchell *et al.*, 2017), independent tourism (Kinginger, 2008), clubbing (Anya, 2016) and sexual relationships (Murphy-Lejeune, 2002).

What does this mean then for language learning, particularly for adolescents who find themselves attending schools where they also need to learn and navigate unfamiliar cultural and linguistic practices? The prominence of status in shaping one's social position entails a dependency on local allies within the school community who can support the appropriation of local practices necessary for negotiating identities that reflect that status. This involves learning cultural schema that determine the status of particular identities within a given social milieu, as well as the linguistic resources that are indexical of those identities.

Returning to the role of social media in language learning abroad, it is imperative for us to recognise how life stage shapes the needs and desires of sojourners, as well as the means they have to pursue them. Social media is now an integral part of how we interact and do identity and its near ubiquitous use among young people makes it an essential medium for appropriating linguistic practices and performing identities that convey status among one's peers both locally and translocally.

## Japanese high school students and study abroad

Having outlined key aspects of adolescence generally as they relate to study abroad, we turn to the ways that societal norms and educational institutions structure adolescence in Japan. In its most widely understood form, education in Japan takes place across five levels: 幼稚園 (yōchien) or pre-school, 小学校 (shōgakkō) or elementary school (Grades 1–6), 中学校 (chūgakkō) or middle school (Grades 1–3), 高校 (kōkō) or high school (Grades 1–3) and 高等教育 (kōtōkyōiku) or higher education. There are, of course, other variations such as 高校専門学校 (kōkōsenmon gakkō) or technical colleges which are a blend of high school and higher education; however, these are less common and most students in Japan will progress as described above.

Of these demarcations, high school is often considered the most academically intense, as performance in exams at the conclusion of third year determines an individual's placement at university and, ultimately, the opportunities available to them in wider Japanese society. The reputation of a university in Japan is often seen as a proxy for the quality of its graduates and takes on crucial importance in hiring decisions (which are also subject to gender- and ethnicity-based disparities). Final-year high school students (and, in many cases, final-year junior high school students) are therefore labelled 受験生 (jyukensei) or 'students undertaking exams', emphasising their societally sanctioned role of studying to the exclusion of all else. This includes retiring from the previously mentioned kurabu katsudō so they can fully devote their time to exam preparation.

On the other hand, 大学生 (daigakusei) or university students are constructed almost in opposition to jyukensei and this life stage is seen as a time of freedom and exploration, a liminal space between the academic rigors of secondary school and becoming 社会人 (shakaijin), an adult who contributes to society. For many, time at university represents the socially acceptable period when personally affirming, extracurricular experiences, such as a lengthy overseas sojourn, should be undertaken. The structuring of this life stage in Japanese society is crucial for understanding the experiences of the informants in this book, since their decision to undertake year-long sojourns during high school was made within this context. Following this, I want to suggest that within Japanese society, the notion of age, a biological concept that is often seen as an important dimension in studies of adolescents, has limited sociological relevance. I argue instead that school level and grade are a more relevant structuring principle of Japanese adolescence. The expectations placed on an individual, and therefore the types of activities they should participate in, are determined by how soon they undertake university entrance exams (and indeed how they perform on those exams).

Within this project, all the informants were attending high school at the time of their study abroad but in different schools at different grade levels, both prior to their sojourns and in the year following their return. This resulted in diverging ramifications for how their decisions were perceived prior to leaving and following their return, with implications for their ongoing linguistic development.

## Englishes and the Japanese Sojourner

The rise of English, and indeed Englishes (Tupas, 2015), to become the predominant means of transnational communication, and its associations with cultural, economic and political power, mean that its influence has extended beyond its historical coloniality and now appears in linguistic ecologies across the globe. This presence was noted several decades ago by Schumann (1980) during her language learning in Tunisia and has been centred in more recent investigations of study abroad (Diao, 2021; Mitchell *et al.*, 2017; Trentman, 2013a). An ongoing focus on Anglophone sojourners has meant that the presence of English has often been documented as an impediment to language learning. However, its widespread use also alters the dynamics of language learning for those from non-English-speaking backgrounds who encounter and may need or seek to learn Englishes alongside local systems of communication (e.g. Kalocsai, 2013; Llanes *et al.*, 2016). For the adolescent sojourners discussed in this book, their relationship to English shaped their experiences abroad, yet this relationship began before they had decided to spend a year abroad. Thus, it is important to briefly discuss the way that English appears within the social imaginary of Japanese society and its position in the national curriculum.

Japan has a policy of compulsory 'foreign' language education (外国語教育 gaikokugo kyōiku) in high schools and the policy itself has traditionally been agnostic about which languages should be taught. Despite this, less than 1% of all students take the foreign language component of their university entrance exams in a language other than English (0.019% as reported by the National Centre for University Entrance Examinations [2022]). The hegemony of English in Japanese second language education can be traced to a variety of historical, institutional and societal factors. Central among these is its status in the wider cultural imagination where it is inculcated with the symbolic values of internationalisation and whiteness (Kobayashi, 2018). Despite this and decades of compulsory second language education primarily focused on English, most Japanese students graduate tertiary education with limited ability to use English in everyday interactional contexts (Kobayashi, 2018). Therefore, it holds a complex position in the imaginations of many Japanese students, simultaneously desired for its high symbolic and material value but also appearing personally unobtainable.

This tension often manifests in relation to study abroad when Japanese sojourners find themselves in situations where English appears as part of local linguistic ecologies. In these contexts, Japanese participants often encounter differences in their interlocutor's ability to use English as a power imbalance that induces feelings of anxiety. Some authors have pointed to factors such as pervasive notions of native-speakerism (Nogami, 2013) or lack of confidence and feelings of inferiority (Tajima & Cookson, 2011) as contributing to Japanese sojourners' limited language use and engagement abroad. However, I argue that while many Japanese sojourners experience affective reactions to encounters with English abroad, these need to be viewed through the wider social imaginary discussed above.

In my study of the short-term study abroad experiences of Japanese high school students in the UK and the United States (Durbidge, 2017), almost all participants ascribed difficulties communicating in English to being 'Japanese', rather than adopting explanations that reflected the interactive realities they faced, such as limited proficiency or a lack of accommodation strategies by members of the host community. The results point towards an inherent tension between proficiency in English and notions of what it means to possess a Japanese identity. In the introduction to Wakana's (2018: xiii) doctoral dissertation, she relates an incident where, due to her proficiency in English, she felt treated as an outsider by other Japanese in the UK, explaining, 'English proficiency itself could not be a barrier in communicating for us, because we could easily speak in Japanese'. Discussions of contemporary formulations of Japanese identity, such as those of Morris-Suzuki (1998) and Kawai (2015), demonstrate how they are bound up in notions of ethnoracial and linguistic homogeneity, and constructed in opposition to Western alterity. The encompassing and essentialist nature of the notion of Japaneseness is apparent in studies that have examined the experiences of populations that adhere to the ethnic, linguistic and/or institutional requirements of a Japanese identity, yet become the targets of practices of ostracisation or differentiation, as seen in the experiences of kikokushijyo (Kanno, 2003), immigrating 日系ブラジル人 (nikkei-burajiru jin[1]) (Tsuda, 2003) and those of mixed ethnicity (Kamada, 2010). Returning to the notion that internationalisation and westernisation are intertwined with English in the Japanese social imaginary (and indeed the wider globalising imaginary), it follows that the appropriation of English communicative practices stands in tension with widespread notions of 'Japaneseness'. Indeed, studies of Japanese women abroad have repeatedly demonstrated that English is perceived as a means to mediate identities that subvert societal notions of Japanese femininity and obtain positionalities outside of traditionally assigned gender roles (e.g. Kobayashi, 2007; Matsui, 1995; Takahashi, 2013).

Taken together, this demonstrates that English learning and communication during study abroad is a highly fraught experience for Japanese sojourners, involving issues of power, identity and competence that are affectively experienced as anxiety, apprehension and insecurity. Developing multilingual competence may incidentally run counter to broader notions of what it means to be Japanese and therefore involve complex negotiations of identity that go beyond those often dealt with in the study abroad literature. In the present multilingual reality where English is often part of local language ecologies, Japanese sojourners need to continually negotiate their relationship to English and what it means for their 'Japaneseness'.

## Analysis and Case Selection

Adopting an ecological view of study abroad means emphasising the eco-dialogical relationship of an individual to their environment and recognising that research should aim to grapple with the way that this relationship contributes to processes of interaction and ensuing language development. Case study research has proven to be an effective means of contending with the complexity and particularity of language learning abroad, and underpins many highly influential investigations (e.g. Benson *et al.*, 2013; Jackson, 2008; Kinginer, 2008; Takahashi, 2013; Trentman, 2013b), as well as lesser-cited but insightful studies on Japanese populations (e.g. Ichimoto, 2007; Iwasaki, 2018; Morinaga Williams, 2019).

However, as Duff (2008) points out, one of the difficulties in conducting case study research is establishing the representativeness or uniqueness of particular cases from among the wider population from which they are drawn. To that effect, the project that this book is based on used quantitative methods of data collection and analysis to generate a picture of the wider cohort from which the case studies presented below were drawn and produce measures of representativeness. Below, I outline the selection criteria and the methods used to identify the representative cases used in this book.

From a total of 14 cases, five were selected (see Table 2.1) with all cases developed from informants' interviews and Instagram data. Semi-structured interviews were conducted with informants both within a month of returning from their sojourns abroad and one year after returning and were initially subjected to thematic analysis. Instagram posts were collated and each post in an individual's timeline was subjected to multimodal analysis (following Jewitt, 2016) with the intent of uncovering the significance and communicative intent of the images, the linguistic choices in captions and the social networks and identities represented in comments. Insights from social media and the first round of interviews also informed the topics of subsequent interviews.

In order to take advantage of the chronologies that characterised both the interview and Instagram data, narrative analysis (Barkhuizen *et al.*, 2013) was used to develop each case and provide further insights into the ways that the informants' experiences and language learning

Table 2.1 Interview informants

| Name | Gender identity | School year at departure | School year on return | Experience travelling abroad | Experience living abroad | Destination country | Months in country | Languages formally studied | Languages spoken abroad (in order of reported usage) |
|---|---|---|---|---|---|---|---|---|---|
| Takumi | M | 1 | 2 | Guam, Korea | (none) | USA | 10 | English | English |
| Raiken[a] | M | 2 | 3 | Canada, Indonesia | (none) | Finland | 10 | English | Finnish, English |
| Ruka[a] | M | 2 | 2 | China, Korea, Taiwan, Australia, Malaysia, Thailand, England, France | Hong Kong until age 13 | Italy | 11 | English | Italian, English, Cantonese, Mandarin |
| Nagisa[a] | F | 1 | 2 | Brazil, USA, Singapore, Hong Kong, Malaysia, Korea | (none) | Brazil | 11 | English, Portuguese | Portuguese, English |
| Megumi[a] | F | 2 | 2 | Guam, Korea, Hong Kong | (none) | Germany | 10 | English | German |
| Misa | F | 1 | 2 | Singapore, France, Italy, Northern Europe | (none) | USA | 10.5 | English, Spanish | English |
| Karin[a,b] | F | 1 | N/A | Canada, USA | (none) | USA | 10 | English | English |
| Manabu[a] | M | 2 | 3 | (none) | (none) | Canada | 10.5 | English | French, English |
| Iori[b] | M | 2 | N/A | USA, France, Thailand, Canada | (none) | France | 10 | English, French | French, English |
| Narumi[a] | F | 2 | 3 | USA, Canada | (none) | USA | 10.5 | English | English |
| Kina[a] | F | 2 | 3 | Philippines, USA, Singapore, Indonesia | (none) | USA | 10.5 | English | English |
| Nikko[a] | F | 2 | 3 | England, France | Two-week exchange in England | Hungary | 11.5 | English | English, Hungarian |
| Nanae[a] | F | 1 | 2 | USA, Canada | (none) | USA | 11 | English | English |
| Kumiko[a] | F | 2 | 3 | USA, Australia, Korea | (none) | France | 10 | English | French, English |

Note: All names are pseudonyms.
[a]Provided Instagram data.
[b]Did not complete a second interview.

unfolded over time. The resulting outputs were then used in a process of *case selection and sampling* (Duff, 2008) to obtain the cases covered in this book. It should be noted that the decision to focus on only five cases of a possible 14 was driven by the practicalities of providing detailed narratives required for the approach detailed above. In selecting the cases to include in this book from those who had participated in the interview processes, I adopted the following criteria.

(1) *The informant needed to have completed both interviews in the process.* A crucial dimension of the project was gaining a holistic understanding of the informants' linguistic development as it unfolded both abroad and in the year that followed. Two of the informants did not complete interviews in the year following their return and were excluded.
(2) *The selection needed to cover a range of linguistic environments with a focus on destinations where English varieties were not exclusively dominant.* For this reason, only a single case was selected among those who travelled to the United States, despite these cases representing over 40% of those who completed both interviews.
(3) *The sampling of cases needed to be representative of the wider cohort.* This was achieved by measuring the interview informants' responses through the processes described in the next section.
(4) *The selected cases should provide rich data on the use of digital communications technology.* While digital communications technology was used by all informants to some extent, it was important to focus on cases that would specifically address the themes of this book.
(5) *Selected cases needed to represent a range of school environments, both in Japan and abroad.* As argued in Chapter 1, high school contexts abroad are a significant element of adolescent sojourners' experiences and school year is a crucial structuring principle of Japanese childhood and adolescence.

In accordance with these criteria, the cases of Nikko, Nagisa, Megumi, Manabu and Misa were selected for this book.

A crucial structuring factor omitted from the case selection criteria is that of gender. Given that gender has been identified as one of the most salient aspects of language learning abroad, generally (Kinginger, 2013) and in Japanese populations specifically (e.g. Kobayashi, 2022; Morinaga Williams, 2018; Takahashi, 2013), maintaining a representative balance of male- and female-identifying cases was initially included as a criterion. However, throughout the case selection process, I found that it limited the degree to which other criteria could be effectively addressed, and I detail the three major choices that contributed to its omission below. Furthermore, while analysis had identified gender as a shaping factor in some informants' cases, it was largely eclipsed by, or experienced intersectionally with, other aspects of the informants' social identities. Therefore, I provide brief discussions of the individual decisions that prompted my decision to exclude gender representation as a selection criterion.

*Selecting Nikko (F) over Raiken (M)*: Both of these informants had elected to complete their interviews in English which they had used abroad alongside other locally relevant varieties: Hungarian in Nikko's case and Finnish in Raiken's case. Both also detailed romantic encounters with locals that presented opportunities for language learning. However, Nikko was one of the most engaged informants in the project and provided one of the thickest and most insightful data sets, including extensive detail on the facilitating role that social media played in developing connections while she was abroad. Her experience is also valuable for the detail she provided on negotiating different linguistic varieties across multiple communities of adolescents while abroad: her classmates at school and a local exchange student community.

*Selecting Megumi (F) over Ruka (M)*: Both of these informants reported difficulties returning to school in Japan, as their time abroad was not recognised institutionally and they returned to the same grade they had left despite their peers' progression. Ruka's case was also unique because he had lived in Hong Kong until age 13 and often found himself marginalised on this basis even before departing. Megumi, however, changed host schools part way through her sojourn and the contrast between the schools provides a clear illustration of the extent to which high school environments impact adolescent sojourners' experiences and language learning. Her account is also illustrative of the connections between social media usage and processes of racialisation that are also present in other informants' accounts.

*Selecting Misa (F) over Takumi (M)*: Both participants had travelled to the Midwestern United States and their responses to questions of perceived outcomes from their experiences placed them in different clusters from their peers (see Table 2.3). Despite spending a year in English-speaking communities, both opted to complete their interviews almost entirely in Japanese. Both declined to provide access to their social media, with Takumi indicating that he hadn't been active on it while abroad while Misa provided a limited number of screenshots rather than allowing me to follow her. Misa's case, however, offers additional significant contrasts. She was one of only two informants who had changed host family due to difficulties encountered there (the other was Kina). Additionally, she was the only interviewee who reported and provided detailed reasons for her extensive engagement with Japanese language social media while abroad.

## Research Site and Participants

Each of the interviewed informants came from a larger cohort of Japanese high school students who participated in year-long exchanges abroad through the Japan-based partner of the non-governmental organisation AFS Intercultural Programs (hereafter referred to as AFS). AFS is one of the largest facilitators of study abroad programmes for secondary school-age participants internationally (AFS Intercultural Programs, 2022). Although AFS runs various programmes, the standard and most popular programme involves the placement of 'high school students' with host families for around 10–11 months, generally aligning with the school year in the destination country. During their stay, participants may attend semi-regular events with other AFS exchange students in their area; however, most of their time is spent embedded in a host family and attending a local school as a regular student. Nominally, the objective of the programme is to foster cross-cultural interaction and understanding between participants and the receiving communities; however, language learning often emerges as a crucial element of that experience for students travelling from Japan.

The group from which this project recruited consisted of 293 Japanese high school students who had completed homestays abroad from mid-2016 to mid-2017. This recruitment pool was large enough to allow quantitative methods to be implemented and avoid the 'problems of scale' (Kinginger, 2017: 133) from which many investigations of language learning abroad suffer. Potential respondents were initially invited to complete an online questionnaire on their experiences through explanatory statements and invitations, distributed by AFS representatives, at three debriefing sessions held in Osaka, Nagoya and Tokyo. The questionnaire received 100 unique responses and the responses informed the selection of the case studies included in this book as well as providing an indication of their representativeness in the wider cohort.

Those who completed the questionnaire were invited to participate in interviews about their experiences. Of the 38 respondents who initially indicated an interest in being interviewed for the project, 14 completed an initial interview within a month of returning and 12 completed a second-round interview 12 months after returning to Japan. See Table 2.1 for details of these interviewed informants. The names of all informants in this book are pseudonyms.

One potentially problematic aspect of the interview process that I was conscious of was the language used, since 'many researchers collect stories in one language only, the one most convenient for analysis, without thinking through the implications of this choice' (Pavlenko, 2007: 172). Given the deep relationship of language to identity and the particularity of each individual's competencies, I offered the informants opportunities to negotiate the way they communicated with me throughout the data collection process, using both Japanese and English language resources. Another hurdle that the interview process faced was performing interviews with respondents from different geographical areas of Japan, each with busy schedules that included exam preparation and extracurricular activities. To overcome this, all interviews were conducted through Zoom videoconferencing software, which even in pre-pandemic times, the informants had little trouble using.

At the conclusion of each initial interview, participants were asked if they were willing to share access to their social media. Of the 14 informants, 10 agreed to allow me view their accounts. All of these informants had used Instagram while abroad and seven of them had started the accounts they shared just prior to or just after beginning their sojourn. Three of the participants also allowed me to view their Facebook accounts; however, their activity while abroad was limited and, accordingly in the interviews, several of the participants had commented on Facebook's limited use among their peers. As Miller *et al.* (2016) have noted, each social media platform is part of a larger media ecosystem, and the use of a platform generally represents not only part of an individual's interactions online but also a socially mediated choice that takes into account things such as identity and privacy. Notably, many of the participants reported using other platforms such as Messenger, WhatsApp and Snapchat, but the ephemeral nature of some of the content (Snapchat) and issues of privacy meant that this data was largely not made available. Instagram, on the other hand, contained semi-public postings of the participants that had been curated for their audience and were therefore more accessible and less ethically problematic as a subject of investigation. For these reasons and issues of consistency and time resourcing, data collection was largely restricted to Instagram posts.

As I have discussed elsewhere (Durbidge, 2022), the collection and use of social media data for research brings with it many ethical questions. One of the most urgent from my perspective was the possibility that data reproduced in this book could be located online and reveal the identities of the informants. For that reason, I refer to most of the Instagram data indirectly and the few instances I have provided are either no longer available online or limited to avoid identification.

## Contextualising the case studies

One of the objectives of obtaining questionnaire data from the participants was to understand how representative those I interviewed were in relation to the larger cohort from which they were drawn. Although analysis of this data led to insights reported elsewhere (Durbidge, 2019, 2020), my primary objective was to determine if those I had interviewed were broadly representative of those who had studied abroad from the same cohort or whether they represented only a particular subset of experiences. In order to do this, I applied several statistical methods to the data to explore relationships in the responses I received.[2] From a chronological standpoint, these steps were performed long before case selection took place. I offer them now as a means of better contextualising the cases themselves before presenting them in detail.

Although the questionnaire collected data across 19 main questions, two multi-item questions were particularly instructive in illustrating broad differences in the way the respondents had understood and experienced their sojourn. One question measured students' feelings towards a number of statements on their decisions to study abroad in the first place. The other measured their feelings towards statements about the effects of studying abroad. This data was used in an *exploratory factor analysis* (Grant & Fabrigar, 2007), which attempts to identify patterns in the way that questions are answered by respondents, suggesting broader underlying 'components' that account for the response patterns. I labelled the components that underpinned their motivations as follows:

(1) Self-actualisation
    Respondents who demonstrated this component would, for example, agree that 'Challenging myself in a new environment' was a motivation while also disagreeing with the statement 'Being encouraged to go by family or teachers'.
(2) Instrumental gains
    Respondents who demonstrated this component would, for example, agree that both 'Being encouraged to go by family or teachers' and 'Giving me an advantage in university entrance exams and looking for work' were motivations.
(3) Self-discovery
    Respondents who demonstrated this component would, for example, agree that both 'Wanting to live apart from family/school' and 'Having time to think about my future' were motivations.

From this analysis of the first multi-item question on their reasons for studying abroad, Component (1) emerged as the most significant in influencing questionnaire respondents' decision to study abroad. This component was more highly scored among those who were interviewed than a theoretical 'average' respondent (overall scores ranged from 1.23 to −2.73). Interview informants' scores have been graphed in red in Figure 2.1, with 0.00 representing the mean of all respondents. This suggests that those I interviewed had stronger perceptions of study abroad as a site for self-actualisation than an 'average' respondent. The exception to this was Misa, whose score sat just below the mean and this was a consideration in selecting her case.

Looking at the factor analysis on the responses to the multi-part question on respondents' perceived changes from study abroad, I labelled the components that emerged as follows:

(1) Transformation
    Respondents who demonstrated this component would, for example, agree with the statements 'I gained understanding in other cultures' and 'I became more mentally resilient'.

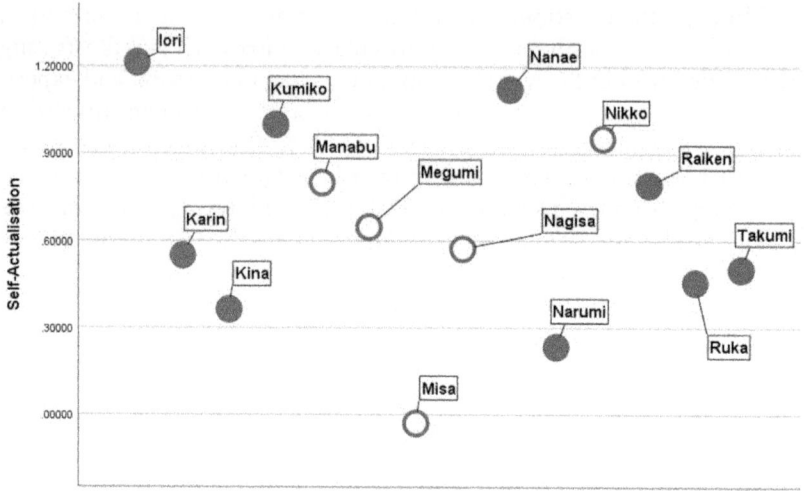

**Figure 2.1** Self-actualisation score across interview informants (cases focused on in this book are shown by points plotted in white)

(2) Decreased affiliation with Japanese identity
    Respondents who demonstrated this component would, for example, agree with the statements 'My ways of thinking no longer match those of my family and friends' and 'I feel less "Japanese"'.
(3) Increased affiliation with Japanese identity
    Respondents who demonstrated this component would, for example, disagree with the statement 'I feel less "Japanese"' while agreeing with the statement 'I became more interested in Japanese culture'.
(4) 'Limited change' or 'not relevant'
    Respondents who demonstrated this component would, for example, disagree with a wide range of statements including 'I became more confident' and 'I have a clear idea about what I want to do in the future'. (This component consisted entirely of negative scores and was therefore difficult to interpret and may simply indicate that a group of respondents didn't feel that the statements related to their outcomes.)

When graphed against the interview informants (Figure 2.2), Component (1) once again demonstrated that those who were interviewed tended to score higher than a theoretically 'average' respondent (overall scores ranged from 1.19 to −2.80). This again suggests that the interviewees represented a subset of the larger group with stronger perceptions of being transformed by their experiences. The key outlier again though is clearly Misa (−1.43), who scored well below that of an 'average' respondent, indicating that her responses pointed to much less individual change than most of her cohort.

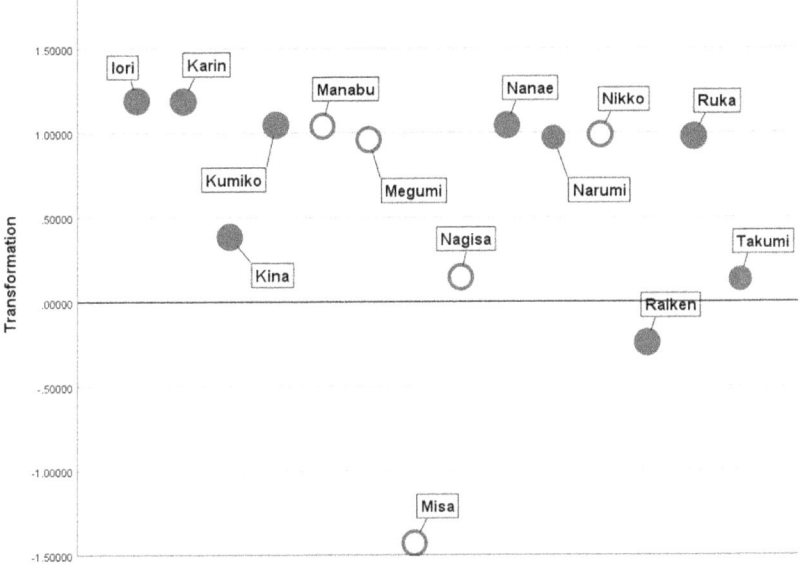

**Figure 2.2** Transformation score across interview informants (cases focused on in this book are shown by points plotted in white)

Taking the analysis of these questions a step further, I used a type of analysis that groups together those who responded to all items in a similar way. This is done by taking the scores for all of the components that emerged from the previous exploratory factor analysis and using them in a machine learning technique known as *hierarchical cluster analysis* (Norušis, 2009), 'clustering' respondents who scored similarly across each component.

For the question on motivations, the largest distance between the scores produced for all respondents (the squared Euclidean distance) was 32.394. However, looking only at those who were interviewed, the largest distance was 6.937. This means that the majority of the interviewees were relatively homogeneous in the way they responded to statements on their reasons for studying abroad. Looking at the clusters in Table 2.2, we can see that all but Iori fall into three clusters and account for 49% of the questionnaire respondents (cutting at 14 clusters with a rescaled distance =5).

For the questions relating to perceived changes due to study abroad, the results of the analysis were more broadly distributed, as shown in Table 2.3. Interviewees fall into five clusters which account for 77% of all respondents (cutting at 15 clusters with rescaled distance =5).

Taking these results together, we can draw some conclusions about the nature of the interviewees and their representativeness of the cohort as a whole. Firstly, we can state that the sample is overtly skewed

**Table 2.2** Motivation clusters

| Cluster No. | Interview informants (+other respondents) |
|---|---|
| 1 | Narumi; Ruka; **Nikko**; Kina (+7) |
| 2 | **Misa**; Kumiko (+8) |
| 3 | **Nagisa**; **Manabu**; Nanae; Karin; Raiken; **Megumi**; Takumi (+20) |
| 4 | (11) |
| 5 | (4) |
| 6 | (2) |
| 7 | (9) |
| 8 | Iori (+9) |
| 9–14 | (15) |

Note: Names represent the cluster that interview participant appeared in. Bolded names indicate the eventual focal participants. Numbers represent the respondents who did not participate in the interview section of the project.

**Table 2.3** Outcomes clusters

| Cluster No. | Interview informants (+other respondents) |
|---|---|
| 1 | Narumi; **Nikko**; **Nagisa**; Raiken (+14) |
| 2 | Kina; Karin; **Megumi**; Iori; Ruka; Nanae (+18) |
| 3 | (8) |
| 4 | (2) |
| 5 | Kumiko; **Manabu** (12) |
| 6 | (2) |
| 7 | (10) |
| 8 | (7) |
| 9 | **Misa** (+7) |
| 10 | (1) |
| 11 | (1) |
| 12 | Takumi (+1) |
| 13–15 | (4) |

Note: Names represent the cluster that interview participant appeared in. Bolded names indicate the eventual focal participants. Numbers represent the respondents who did not participate in the interview section of the project.

towards those who had strong self-actualising motivations for going abroad. Those who may have had other stated motivations such as seeking an advantage in exams or applying for jobs in the future are not represented. Although this is not problematic in itself, it does mean that the overall findings speak to a certain type of sojourner who construes study abroad as an opportunity to obtain identity positions viewed as unavailable within the sociocultural milieux they currently inhabit. The other thing we can state is that based on the responses to outcome statements, the interviewees are more broadly representative of all respondents. The inclusion of Misa as a case study therefore provides needed perspective on the other four cases detailed in the following chapters.

## Presentation of Case Studies

What I have attempted to present in this book are relevant themes that emerged from social media posts and accounts related to me by a group of adolescents keen to talk about their experiences living abroad and returning to Japan. Although this book seeks to understand the experiences of the informants as they relate to the environments they inhabit, it has been written within institutionalised structures of power that has shaped its construction (Steffensen & Fill, 2014). Indeed, working within the bounds of Anglophone higher education, discourses that valorise notions of rigor, sophistication and convention, as well as the need to publicly perform the work of research, have all served to transform the independent voices of the informants into something that carries my name. Therefore, what is presented in the following cases is a subjective interpretation of the accounts and data related to me by the informants. I say all this to make clear the limitations of the production of this research as I see it and emphasise my own role in its construction.

Throughout these accounts and elsewhere, I have tried to acknowledge the heteroglossia found within the linguistic ecologies of study abroad; however, analysis of this is limited by the decidedly monoglossic ontologies that the students themselves used to understand their linguistic environments. I never directly observed the interactions of the informants apart from those that took place on social media and shared with me; therefore, I often refer to named languages as they were described by the informants.

In reporting informant experiences, I also acknowledge that what exists is a partial and interpretive recreation of their accounts as communicated to me. Wherever possible, I have attempted to make the co-constructed nature of the interview apparent by including my questions and responses; however, for reasons of space and readability, this was often not possible. Readability was also a consideration when deciding the way that extracts would be presented; therefore, they have been formatted for clarity rather than to maintain the cadence of informants' utterances. This meant removing disfluencies such as stutters, false starts and repetitions not connected to emphasis. On the other hand, I have tried to preserve the informants' voices where possible and have not modified unusual syntax where I felt the meaning was clear. The English translations that appear after Japanese extracts are all my own and omit hesitation devices that appear in the original recordings.

## Notes

(1) Brazilian nationals who are ethnically Japanese.
(2) For those interested, a more detailed discussion of the data collection and analysis used in the project can be found in Chapter 5 of my doctoral dissertation (Durbidge, 2020).

# 3 Nikko: Translingual Participation In and Beyond Hungary

Nikko's account provides an illustration of the way that locally instantiated configurations of linguistic resources must be negotiated by sojourners as they move in and between communities. Living with a host family in a large Hungarian city for a year, Nikko finds herself needing to manage the learning of both Hungarian and English. The affordances of social media served to facilitate connections in the local community while also supporting her language learning, particularly her appropriation of highly mobile North American English resources associated with teenage vernaculars. While Nikko's experience abroad aligns in many ways with the globalising imaginary of study abroad, upon her return to Japan, her transnational and multilingual identity came into conflict with local discourses which positioned her as an outsider.

Early on a brisk October Melbourne morning in 2017, I cycled to Monash University's Clayton campus for a planned online interview with Nikko, a second-year high school student in the Greater Tokyo region. We had previously set other times to speak, but her busy high school schedule had forced delays and eventuated in this 7.30am Sunday time slot. The campus was almost deserted and the ability to have a shared office to myself was ideal for hearing about the year that Nikko had spent living in Hungary. Speaking with Nikko that morning, I was struck by her confidence and eagerness to recount her time abroad, as she launched into an English language narrative of her experiences almost before I could begin recording. Her keenness to recall her experiences and the detail she went into required us to extend our interview to an additional session the following Sunday.

Nikko's decision to study abroad was rooted in her imagination and the possibilities of transcending her role as the youngest of three children and the only girl in her family. She explained that she sometimes felt patronised and seen as 'young' and a 'little girl' even after entering high school. Although she felt subjected to a gendered positioning of requiring protection, by her brothers in particular, Nikko had already experienced some independence through a previous two-week study abroad programme in England, cultivating a yearning for a longer period abroad.

Ultimately, Nikko located the genesis of her desire to study abroad in romanticised images of Paris she had encountered through media as a child; a city full of beautiful buildings, culture and food. Above all, it was the people in these images who had left the greatest impression on her.

**Nikko:** I saw people and then like, oh my god, they're so beautiful. Then I was like, started to think, OK, I want to be a French girl
**Levi:** What did you imagine being a French girl would be?
**Nikko:** Like, if I were in Japan with [a] French face, then I would be so unique and special and so different from Japanese people, and like, I wanted to be tall. I wanted to have like [a] tall nose,[1] big eyes, those things, yeah. (Nikko, Interview 1.1)

For Nikko and many of the other participants in this project, part of the desire to study abroad emerged through an attraction to the foreign and exotic that manifested much earlier in their lives. As demonstrated through this extract, resources encountered as a child contributed to Nikko's desire to become something different, providing her with a model for reshaping herself into something that transcended her current form. In this case it was an aspiration to physical attributes associated with whiteness, a desire to obtain a different set of racialised characteristics which are valourised in Japanese media discourse (Takahashi, 2013).

Over the years, the practicality of Nikko's desire became more apparent and it matured into something more immediately attainable.

**Nikko:** I was just like OK, I can't be that because I was born here and I'm Japanese, so I can't do that and if I got married foreigner, then I can have half baby between Japan and some country. That was my thought then. Ok, then I started to be interested in another countries, and I really wanted to live in another country or see another culture or just people there, so then I was started to think to be an exchange student. (Nikko, Interview 1.1)

Although on one level this represents a move from childhood fantasy to the expediencies of an adult world, it still carries the idea of transformation, moving from an exotic transformation of her own body to the externalised body of an imagined child, to an embodied experience of transformative exoticness. Importantly, it represents a view of study abroad as a means to obtain that exoticness, running counter to notions of homogeneity and conformity that permeate the Japanese cultural imagination. This counter imaginary of transformation and liberation through transnational and translinguistic mobility is not unique to Nikko, and has been well documented in literature of Japanese women who have sought to transcend locally determined notions of femininity through travel and life abroad (e.g. Ichimoto, 2007; Kobayashi, 2007, 2022).

This can be further seen through Nikko's characterisation of her time abroad as an opportunity to assert her independence from her family by having 'some adventures without them' (Nikko, Interview 1.1). Thus, the act of studying abroad provided an opportunity to redefine her relationship with her family and transcend local gendered norms to which she felt subjected. For Nikko, transnational mobility was imagined in terms of becoming, although language learning did not initially feature as part of that imagination.

## Facilitating Local Connections

Although Nikko was unable to obtain her first preference of a homestay in France, she did receive an offer to study in Hungary. Accessing images of Hungarian architecture and food online after the initial disappointment, she recalled falling in love with the country before departing.

Nikko's host family was located in a metropolitan region of western Hungary. Like other informants, before meeting her host family she underwent a two-day orientation session with other newly arrived AFS exchange students from across the globe. These first few days were formative in the sense that Nikko became immediately aware that the linguistic resources she possessed were insufficient to interact in the same ways as her peers.

Nikko: When I had orientation, people were speaking in English so fluently and volunteers were as well, and I was with Japanese friends, and we were just freaked out […] I was feeling a little bit far from the others because the others were speaking in English, or Spanish even, with the people from another countries. Then I was like, 'oh that's good', but I'm afraid to talk to them because of my English skill. So, at the beginning I was really stressed out because of my language skills. (Nikko, Interview 1.1)

Nikko's encounter with English as a lingua franca reflected the complex circumstances often reported by Japanese sojourners. Idealistically, she understood its use in this context as something desirable, yet her own inability to understand and interact with other exchange students left her feeling anxious and disconnected. Moreover, Nikko and the other Japanese exchange students were in a position to compare their own abilities with those of exchange students arriving from other nominally non-English-speaking backgrounds. This appeared to confirm a discourse she had encountered before arriving that 'Japanese has tough time to talk in

English' (Nikko, Interview 1.1), reflecting wider notions of Japaneseness discussed previously.

However, moving to her host family placement proved to be reassuring, as the linguistic environment she encountered there was more dynamic and accommodating. The host family consisted of two other people, a mother and her daughter who was a similar age to Nikko. Although Nikko's host mother only communicated in Hungarian, her host sister was able to interact through English and, to a more limited degree, Japanese. This meant that their interactions were dynamically negotiated as they each drew on their repertoires of English and Japanese to translanguage shared meaning. As Nikko had no initial competence in Hungarian, she was also reliant on her host sister to mediate communication with her host mother. This meant that her host sister found herself taking on the responsibilities of interpreting, similar to those seen among the *language brokering* done by children of immigrant communities (see Morales and Hanson [2005] for a detailed overview of this phenomenon).

Although Nikko had not initially imagined language learning as a significant part of life abroad, she now realised it would be essential to local participation. Importantly, her account reveals not only the mobility of certain linguistic resources, with English and Spanish appearing as lingua franca in the initial exchange student community, but also the way these resources can be configured differently at local scales. Illustrative of this, in particular, are the negotiated and heterogeneous nature of host family interactions. It also serves to highlight how the linguistic reality of a host context is negotiated; translingual and diversified across communities. Nikko's host sister's use of Japanese resources, alongside those associated with English and Hungarian, must be understood as part of the local linguistic reality and runs counter to territorialised notions of language and immersion.

A reconfiguration of Nikko's home environment occurred approximately three months into Nikko's stay when her host sister departed on her own one-month exchange trip to Japan. Presented with what could have been an alienating experience, given the lack of shared linguistic resources, Nikko sought to invest in both Hungarian and the relationship with her host mother.

**Nikko:** I was thinking like, how can I be good with her then? Because I was at home only with her, and I didn't want to have that time [...] like, silent with her. So, I was thinking like, how I can make it better? [...] I thought maybe I can write, I could write diaries in Hungarian, and she could check it out, and also it's good for studying for me. I started to write really, like, five sentences at the beginning then, but it became one page at the end of my exchange year. (Nikko, Interview 1.1)

Although Nikko appears to have decided on the idea of a diary independent of her host mother, the relationship that had already been mediated through her host sister no doubt contributed to the environment that provided the opportunity. This demonstrates how the proclivities of the individual interface with the social and material contexts in which they find themselves, leading to the emergence of learning affordances that can then, through the agency of the individual, be acted upon. Mutual understanding and Nikko's subsequent linguistic development were mediated in these moments, not only through the affordances of the entries themselves, but also, as Nikko explained, through non-linguistic modes of meaning-making including body language and images located online. We should note too how the daily recurring nature of these interactions fostered the development of Nikko's ability to use Hungarian and demonstrates the key support role that host mothers play, also seen in the informants' accounts in the following chapters.

Nikko's perceived need to nurture the relationship with her host mother also underscores local relations of power present in the adolescent homestay. Although status and belonging among peers are crucial to high school identities, the relationship with her host mother was fundamental to Nikko's ability to exercise her freedom while abroad. As Nikko explained, one of the tensest situations with her host mother occurred when through a miscommunication – she didn't send a message indicating she had arrived at a friend's house for a sleepover – resulting in her host mother becoming understandably upset. In order to restore trust and mend the rift in their relationship, Nikko continued sharing her diary entries with her host mother to reopen a channel of communication and find a resolution. Reflecting perceptions reported in Grieve's (2015) study of German adolescent sojourners in Australia, it emphasises the power that host families hold in regard to participants' activities beyond home and school. In most cases, high school students are dependent upon their adult guardians for things such as local mobility and financial support even as they desire independence, and this applies more to sojourners whose position in the family and lack of social and linguistic resources limit their ability to negotiate. While Nikko's desire to build and maintain a positive relationship with her host mother is obviously built upon more than just this, it is important to recognise how this dependence also contributes to an imperative for the sojourner to align their linguistic repertoire with that of their host family.

During these initial months, Nikko's interactions with her peers at school remained limited. The high school classroom can be a socially fraught environment for any teenager with its own cultural dynamics and evolving sets of social relationships. As Murphy-Lejeune (2002: 104) has theorised, the arrival of the stranger to an established community can destabilise the current social order and 'calls for adjustments on both sides'. Moreover, when the sojourner arrives they do so without social connections, an understanding of local norms and, as in Nikko's case, the communicative resources to negotiate their position in the community. Nikko's host sister, who attended the same school, was therefore an essential source of support, sharing her knowledge of the school system and social norms as well as providing Nikko with access to her social networks. Effectively, Nikko's host sister acted in the role of local expert and initial *key individual* (Durbidge, 2021), facilitating Nikko's knowledge of, and social connections with, the school community. As time went on though, this support also became a source of tension.

**Nikko:** So, my host sister help me a lot in the beginning because I didn't know anything. And she told me about the city or school life and everything then. But she had to learn a lot for the exam at school […] so she didn't have enough time to talk to me or she was just stressed out because she had to, I don't know, like, care about me. And I was kind of depressed, because I could see that she was so tired […] didn't really seem to like to talk to me. (Nikko, Interview 1.2)

This tension proved to be an important catalyst. Although Nikko initially struggled with the attitude she perceived from her host sister, the disruption to her social situation once again provided an opportunity to renegotiate her positionality and take a more agentive role in local contexts of interactions, this time at school.

While Nikko initially had limited interaction with her classmates, she explained that an offer to join their WhatsApp group had been pivotal in redefining her relationship to them and facilitating her participation in their community.

**Nikko:** My classmates send me messages sometimes even [if] we are talking at school, but at the beginning, I wasn't really close to my classmates. But they sent me, like WhatsApp. Then we were talking. (Nikko, Interview 1.1)

It's important at this point to recall the situated nature of online interaction. While the ability of digital communication to promote transnational connections is emphasised, Nikko's statements also highlight how it functions in the establishment of localised connections. The intimacy of the classroom and the community it contained were recreated through the affordances of WhatsApp, with online connections pertaining to interpersonal connections in the physical space of the classroom. As Nikko indicates here, communication that took place online existed simultaneously with, or in proximity to, in-person interactions, demonstrating that it was an additional, rather than an alternative, means of interaction.

Although it could be argued that Nikko's relationships with her classmates would have occurred regardless of whether or not social media had been present in the classroom, this line of reasoning ignores the sociohistorical and material contexts in which her experience took place. Certainly, Nikko herself saw social media as central to establishing connections with her classmates and this is supported by insights in other studies of teenage sociality which have demonstrated that 'an essential step in developing intimacy is being on the same social media platforms' (Pangrazio, 2019: 1320). Given the degree to which social media appears to have been embedded in the localised communicative practices of Nikko and her peers, its importance in fostering interpersonal connections becomes evident.

Recall too that the asynchronous nature of instant messaging means that users, such as Nikko, have time to decode and plan messages, supporting their ability to participate. Being situated in the contexts of classroom interaction, access to online interactions would have supported Nikko's comprehension as topics and ideas communicated rapidly and ephemerally in speech became accessible in persistent forms online. The ability to be part of online spaces where her classmates interacted was therefore an important factor in Nikko's socialisation into their communicative practices and community. All this demonstrates that social media interaction in this instance was a highly localised practice. It served to mediate Nikko's membership of the classroom community across an additional channel, even as it was situated in the contexts of regular, proximal interaction..

These interpersonal relationships took on additional importance when Nikko sought support to deal with a growing divide between herself and her host sister. Bringing the issue to her classmates created an opportunity for interaction with Kristel, a female exchange student from Estonia who was in the same class. During the first few months, there had been limited contact between them and Nikko described being apprehensive approaching her since Kristel 'didn't look like the friendly person' (Nikko, Interview 1.2). When Nikko sought advice from her classmates on the issue with her host sister, Kristel's words resonated with her and provided the impetus for their friendship.

**Nikko:** So [Kristel] told me I shouldn't care about that much and I should live my life. [...] from that time I tried to talk to [Kristel] and she did say really good thing to me. Then I got to know she's a really good person [...] so I decided to take a distance with my host sister and I started to spend more time with Kristel at school. (Nikko, Interview 1.2)

Although Nikko never indicated that their status as exchange students was an important factor in this initial encounter, the events that unfolded as a result of their friendship indicate that their shared identity and lived experiences were uniting factors as the relationship developed.

One factor that strengthened their connection was their shared negotiation of the linguistic environment of the classroom; local students used English as a lingua franca to communicate with exchange students, while conversations with each other and most lessons were conducted in Hungarian. Since Nikko and Kristel had both arrived without prior knowledge of Hungarian, their ability to comprehend and participate in the formal aspects of class was limited and they 'usually didn't have anything to do' (Nikko, Interview 1.2). Instead, they would spend this time together studying Hungarian or interacting through English. They also took Hungarian lessons together once a week at a local teacher's house and began spending more time together informally, going to the movies, shopping or sleeping over at each other's house. At the local scale of Nikko's classroom, both English and Hungarian resources existed as a valid means to achieve interaction with classmates. Yet, outside English classes and in interactions between local peers, Hungarian was needed for full participation. In Nikko's case, a clear tension emerges between the selection of English and Hungarian in language learning and use.

Nikko's relationship with Kristel proved to be influential in this regard, and she ascribed a change in her interactional practices to this, in particular the strategies she adopted in communication. Until Nikko met Kristel, she said that she had been highly conscious of the way that other people perceived her and adopted sociopragmatic strategies intended to avoid conflict. For example, complimenting interlocutors and avoiding criticism. Nikko recalled one episode in particular when Kristel called attention to this strategy.

**Nikko:** [Kristel] told me like, '[Nikko], do you really say what you really think?' Then I was like, 'ye- yeah…' Then like, I was thinking like, 'oh my god, she got to know me' or she just realised, how maybe like, my compliments, what I was saying to her, it was kinda like the same thing […] but I was really happy that she got me then and I wanted to show, my like everything of me to her because I trusted her. (Nikko, Interview 1.2)

By contrasting the sociopragmatic strategy of not saying 'what you really think' with wanting 'to show […] everything' (Nikko, Interview 1.2), Nikko illustrates how, through her interactions with Kristel, she was socialised into different modes of interaction. Viewed from Nikko's perspective, we see too how these practices are evaluated under a different order of indexicality, with the practice of positively complimenting to avoid interpersonal conflict evaluated negatively in relation to 'saying what you think'. Therefore, Nikko seeks to orient towards this norm in interaction as a means of fostering intimacy with Kristel. This orientation was socially vital as the relationship offered affective and embedded support outside of her host sister. Moreover, this incident only emerged as a result of repeated and ongoing interactions, demonstrating the need to see orientations to scale as dynamically unfolding over time.

The degree to which this relationship was mediated through social media is not clear, since it was not directly addressed in our interviews. However, Kristal was certainly part of classroom interactions that took place through WhatsApp and became one of the most prominent relationships featured on Nikko's Instagram in both photos and comments. What is relevant though is that in Nikko's case, her activity on social media was intertwined with the relationships she was forming with other young people in her local community. It was simply part of the way that she engaged with and sought to understand her connection to others, embedded within her everyday practices of meaning-making and identity performance.

## Learning through YouTubers and Translanguaging on Instagram

While social media facilitated interpersonal relationships developing in her classroom, Nikko's account also highlighted its role in mediating the development of her English language repertoire. Although Nikko was able to interact through English with Kristel in one-on-one situations, she struggled to participate when groups of local exchange students met together. As she had prioritised the learning of Hungarian in order to build the relationship with her host mother, development in her ability to use English language resources remained limited. Recalling a specific moment at school, Nikko described being overwhelmed by feelings of disappointment when she was unable to understand a conversation between an American and a Mexican student, who were both 'really good at English' (Nikko, Interview 1.2).

Similar to other instances of anxiety abroad, Nikko sought affordances within her immediate environment for the means to overcome them. In this case, she perceived the video content produced by young English language YouTubers as a resource for developing her ability to communicate with her peers.

**Levi:** So you were studying English through YouTube, who did you use that English with?

**Nikko:** [...] When I was at school I could understand more than before. For example, like when my friends were talking and then they were [using] slangs, I didn't know that [meaning] before, but after I started to watch videos, then I [...] heard that from the videos, [the] same thing what they were saying.

>So yeah, like the conversation when I was at school and also on [social media]. (Nikko, Interview 1.1)

For Nikko, the linguistic repertoires employed by the YouTubers she watched were those she aspired to appropriate, citing their pronunciation and frequent use of vernacular expressions as reasons she had selected these channels.

**Nikko:** Like I watched [a] few YouTubers. Like, they were telling their daily life, like what they did today [...] I was thinking, maybe I should watch the daily, like daily life. How people in [the] USA or Canada do things and they just say daily conversations. (Nikko, Interview 1.1)

Significantly, Nikko targeted specific registers used by young YouTubers based in North America, which she perceived as aligned with the community in which she now sought membership. Practically, this meant spoken adolescent varieties of English, aligned with identities seen as legitimate in a community that included high school students from Brazil, Mexico, Estonia, Italy, America and Taiwan.

Although Nikko was certainly able to engage in English language interactions with her Hungarian classmates and participate in some classes taught in English, she presented these YouTubers as her most essential source of English learning. Certainly, Nikko understood those speaking from the United States or Canada as possessing linguistic resources valued by her international peers. Returning to discussions of scale, these resources were high-mobility forms of English seen as emanating from the Anglosphere. Although the relationships Nikko was forming were confined to a small group of adolescent exchange students in a city in Hungary, participation in this group was partially contingent upon the use of these forms and their indexicality of transnational cachet. Thus, Nikko's account of language learning is demonstrative of how language learning abroad, particularly through online media, is often enmeshed in, and a function of, translocal flows rather than some amorphous idea of immersion. Her ability to appropriate these forms was a function of her mobility and her social desire to become closer to the people she had met.

That is not to deny the situatedness of her language learning. Indeed, the composition and nature of this community were also shaped by local regimes of personal freedom and mobility. Nikko explained that, initially, a group had formed around the exchange students who were attending her school, often gathering during breaks or skipping classes taught in Hungarian to chat or watch Netflix together. This community then grew beyond the school as the members drew on social connections they had formed through the organisations with which they had come to Hungary, including students from neighbouring cities. As Nikko explained, members of these various communities encountered each other and made new friends through social events that were accessible through public transport, within and between cities, allowing them to mutually increase the range of their own social networks.

This process was evident through her posts on social media, which evolved over time to reflect a growing intimacy and sociality with an expanding group of exchange students. Initially, her Instagram posts featured scenery, herself alone or together with her host sister and comments were mainly in Japanese; however, over time her posts began to showcase group activities and experiences with friends. The changes in what was posted online therefore reflected processes that were taking place offline as they also evolved to cater to a diversifying online audience that now included the connections she was making in Hungary. Many of her later posts showed her in urban locations or at restaurants and bars with friends, often after sundown, and included a series that documented a short trip to Italy. Indeed, living in a large European city afforded her a degree of freedom that was often absent from other informants' accounts and her ability to connect with other exchange students both in her city and from other locations nearby was a significant element in her ability to pursue the kind of experiences she documented. Therefore, Nikko's mobility should also be viewed as not only transnational but also local, enabled by the accessibility of public transport within and between cities, as well as the liberty afforded to the exchange students by their host families and schools.

At the intersection of the transnational mobility that had brought these adolescents to Hungary and the local mobility that allowed them to build connections with each other was the variety of linguistic resources that made up their shared linguistic repertoire. While high-mobility versions of English formed the basis for their interactions, posts on Nikko's Instagram revealed their translingual diversity, as comments drew upon Hungarian, Mandarin, Portuguese and Japanese resources mixed with 絵文字 (emoji) and the practice of repeating vowels and other means of representing vernacular speaking practices. For example, one post in which Nikko appears to be hugging a female friend she has captioned 'laotong 👯',[2] to which the friend has replied 'Te amoooo'.[3] In another post that features a large group photo, one poster writes 'Daaaamn I'm awesome 🎰 😎', to which Nikko replied 'hahahah u are undorító666 ♡'.[4] There are also examples of non-Japanese friends writing expressions such as 'Dai suki'[5] or 'kawaiiiiii'[6] using Latinised Japanese.

Moreover, the content Nikko posted online and the ways she engaged with commenters on her posts demonstrated a growing literacy in Instagram posting practices, as she adopted poses used by influencers on the platform and captioned her images with recontextualised motivational-style quotes in English, such as 'Everyone smiles in the same language 😁'. These posts reveal an orientation to values that Nikko viewed as held by her imagined audience, living a glamourous cosmopolitan life abroad that radiates transnational positivity. Importantly though, we can view these posts as emanating from localised spaces in Hungary but performed through translocal practices whose association with global discourses allows Nikko to 'scale up' her post to maximise her audience.

On the other hand, instances of audience partitioning were also visible on her Instagram, as some posts were captioned with references to specific events or used oblique expressions to restrict their ability to be 'read' by specific audiences. One such post of Nikko and Kristel taking a selfie in a mirror was captioned 'Special day for me' without further elaboration. Nikko would also switch into Japanese or Hungarian in response to comments in those languages, reflecting ideas of reciprocity in language use and targeting the response to the commenter. In effect, she engaged in practices of horizontal and vertical linguistic mobility, crossing linguistic varieties as needed to scale her message in relation to her intended audience. Altogether, the images she posted and the translingual interaction and play that Nikko engaged in online worked to perform the identity of a vivacious, multilingual and highly mobile young person.

As Nikko explained, translanguaging was an ordinary part of in-person interactions among the exchange student community, reflecting both their diverse linguistic backgrounds and sense of cosmopolitanism. Most interesting was Nikko's explanation that the only Hungarian language that many exchange students knew was swear words, which interspersed their interactions and served to index informality, solidarity and knowledge of local youth culture.

Together with Kristel, Nikko continued to develop a wider repertoire of Hungarian language practices. Over time, it afforded them the opportunity to begin negotiating Hungarian-speaking identities in the classroom together. Although English had been the language of interaction with their classmates, around this time they began initiating exchanges and responding to their classmates in Hungarian. Although these interactions were limited at first, their classmates were supportive and encouraging. This, in turn, led Nikko to attempt more complex interactions and begin positioning herself as an emerging member of the community, particularly through the use of 'slang in Hungarian' (Nikko, Interview 1.1). Alongside renegotiating the language of interaction, Nikko also felt that there had been a shift in the intimacy she felt with her classmates, stating that 'when I'm speaking in Hungarian, I can get more closer to them' (Nikko, Interview 1.1). At the scale of the classroom at least, English was the language of the exchange student *stranger*, and by establishing herself as a legitimate user of Hungarian she drew on local orders of indexicality to position herself as a legitimate member of that community.

## Ephemerality, Intimacy and Social Media

In the later months of Nikko's time abroad, an encounter with a local led to a connection that held romantic possibilities. While out with friends one evening, she was approached by a local boy.

Nikko: One guy came and sat next to me, and he told me that he was interested in Japanese culture and he knows [a] few Japanese words. We started to talk but I had to leave at that night, like quick, and we could only speak for 10 minutes, or like 15 minutes. And after that day, he sent me a friend request on Facebook and I accepted because I got to know him, and then we [started] talking on Messenger. (Nikko, Interview 1.2)

These interactions on Facebook's Messenger app became more intimate and the following weekend they met again at an event. It was here that she 'got to know him, [and] he told me that he liked me. And I also started to kinda like him' (Nikko, Interview 1.2). Connecting on social media not only allowed them to extend their interaction beyond the immediacy of their initial contact, but it also allowed the couple to develop their relationship and explore romantic possibilities through a medium that held less risk and greater scope for reflection and composition. The ability to reconnect online after that first interaction and in a medium that was facilitative of considered engagement cannot be overlooked as significant in mediating the type of romantic attention that the study abroad literature has pointed to variously as debilitative (Polanyi, 1995), advantageous (Murphy-Lejeune, 2002) or unobtainable (Morinaga Williams, 2018) for those learning language abroad.

As Nikko's account illustrates, through social media a serendipitous meeting is transformed into an intimate possibility that transcends the fleeting temporality of their brief encounter. Messaging became their primary medium of connection and allowed them, despite limited opportunities to physically meet, to become 'really close' (Nikko, Interview 1.2). Importantly too, the nature of the medium enables young people to determine the nature and intensity of their interactions. While online interactions are subject to the norms of reciprocity, their affordances offer individuals a degree of power to ignore, block or hide messages or individuals with whom they no longer wish to engage.

These exchanges continued across several weeks, with online interactions culminating in in-person meetings, usually in the company of friends. Despite a seemingly growing intensity, the impermanent nature of Nikko's residence was experienced as an obstacle to pursuing further intimacy leading to a bittersweet resolution.

**Nikko:** He told me that he knew that I had to leave soon. If we got together [...] then we can't be together like longer, like just few months [...] so we just decided to be a good friends. (Nikko, Interview 1.2)

Nikko regretted that they had not met earlier, saying 'if it was at the beginning then it could [have been] something' (Nikko, Interview 1.2). It is here that we can also see the effect of how time is conceived, with the remaining time constructed as being outside the scale required to have a successful relationship. This sense of ephemerality is a phenomenon that many of the informants reported as a force that influenced the decisions they made while abroad. Authors such as Murphy-Lejeune (2002: 18) have pointed out how sojourners can be 'infinitely sensitive to the richness of a fleeting temporality', finding in it a precarity as relationships can be measured by an approaching departure date and, as Nikko's account shows, this can act as a constraint on their desire to pursue new relationships, even with the transnational connections afforded to them through social media.

This sensitivity to the ephemerality of her experience was also evident as the final weeks of her exchange approached. Seeing her friend Kristel off at the airport during this time signified closure for Nikko.

**Nikko:** I saw the [departure] gate and I saw people who we're going inside, and I started to, like, everything just came back to my mind. Everything I had done with her [...] She wasn't crying, I think, because she didn't get the feeling that she is actually leaving, but I got that feeling. I started to cry a lot then. Yeah. Then I said goodbye to her, and when my turn came, when I was leaving Hungary, I couldn't get that feeling. (Nikko, Interview 1.2)

The grief that Nikko experienced at the airport when she saw Kristel off wasn't present when it was time for her to depart, leaving behind the other places and relationships she had formed while there. Although social media and other communications technology allowed interaction to continue, this episode demonstrates how these relations were also bound up in local realities of shared space. Nikko's relationship with Kristel was situated in the contexts and shared experiences of their time together in Hungary and Kristel's departure reconfigured the nature of Nikko's ongoing experience. It would also reconfigure the nature of the interactions that could take place on social media. No longer could their shared moments and experiences be reflected in their posts and interactions. Instead, the way that social media mediated their relationship was transformed in the wake of this separation even as it enabled them to maintain their connection to each other.

## Return and Renegotiation

Nikko returned to Japan in the final year of high school, several months before taking entrance exams for university. This divided the year after returning into separate phases, with exams functioning as a point of demarcation. Nikko's view of returning to high school evolved in the 10 months between each of her interview sessions, highlighting the instability of sojourners' understandings of their experiences and the structuring effects of return contexts on those understandings.

Despite initially being positive during her first interviews, in her second-round interview a year after returning, Nikko was decidedly more negative of her final months in high school. Her description of that period was characterised by a sense of restricted freedom and choice, both in the way Nikko spent her time and the way she presented herself. Being an exchange student in Hungary had meant that many of the responsibilities that came with being a student, such as sitting exams and participating in classes, were done at her discretion. Returning to high school in Japan as a jyukensei had brought with it expectations and pressure to perform academically. Nikko framed the difference around the issue of choice.

**Nikko:** When I was in Hungary I was kind of like, having freedom to choose whatever I want to do, and [...] when I was in Japanese high school [...] I kind of didn't really have any choice but I have to like, study or be in the class, and having high school life. (Nikko, Interview 2)

One of the more overt ways that Nikko found her sense of freedom curtailed was through criticism of changes in her outward appearance by her teacher. Students' hair is a common area for enforcing conformity in Japanese high schools (Yoneyama, 1999), and Nikko had lightened her hair during her time abroad. This became such an issue for teachers that she was forced to dye it black, which led to further criticism for it being unnaturally black.

Another telling moment came when Nikko described how her friends had defended her in the face of criticism from her teacher.

**Nikko:** The funny thing is that my friends were telling the teacher that [...] '[Nikko] went to Hungary so she's not really Japanese anymore so please, @ forgive her', or something like that. (Nikko, Interview 2)

Although the statements of Nikko's friends appear on the surface to be a light-hearted defence, their illocutionary force resides in an ideological belief that sees notions of 'Japaneseness' as being in tension with spending significant time outside of Japan. The idea that having studied abroad marked Nikko as somehow different among her peers was also evident in the way she now found herself asked to perform.

**Nikko:** I was kind of like, shy to speak in English ((@)) to others because they were thinking that my English got improved or something. [...] for example, a lot of friends asked me like, 'Speak in English' or like, 'Say something in English', and I was like, 'No I don't really want to. Like, why do I have to? You're Japanese ((@)) we can talk in Japanese'. (Nikko, Interview 2)

This vignette offers further evidence for the way that Nikko, as a returned sojourner, was now viewed as a *stranger* in her school, despite having spent the majority of her life and schooling in Japan. Demands to 'say something in English' appeal only to an alterior positioning. It reflects the request to 'say something in your language' that Fisseha (2021) identifies multilinguals as being subjected to, emphasising their difference through requests to perform their perceived alterity. Perhaps realising the othering work that this type of request would do, Nikko rejects the premise through an appeal to her own agency and the ability to use communicative resources that emphasise her legitimacy as a member of the community. English becomes the symbolic language of the outsider, contrasted with that of the Japanese insider.

From a linguistic development standpoint, like many of the other informants, Nikko found the high school context inconducive to maintaining the competencies she had gained abroad and instead had to focus on preparing for university entrance exams. Although the limited opportunities to use Hungarian were to be expected, Nikko also found her English competence unsupported as she spent her English classes just 'listen[ing] to the teacher about English grammar and [...] to the tape as a listening skill' (Nikko, Interview 2). This contravened her experiences of English as a means to interact and perform identities associated with her time abroad.

It shows the complexity of return identities and the ways that they are subject to evaluation against sources of authority that sojourners may not have recognised prior to their departure. By transgressing locally normative patterns of behaviour and interaction through practices they have appropriated under different orders of indexicality, they position themselves as belonging elsewhere. Moreover, it demonstrates the tension that emerges between global and local imaginaries of English. All Japanese high school students are required to study English and, as we have already noted, academic performance carries significant social cachet. However, its performance outside of specific registers connected to academic learning is indelibly evaluated as aligning with non-Japanese identities. Although Nikko's desire for these markers had driven her decision to study abroad and all she had achieved while away, she inevitably found herself struggling to renegotiate this tension once back in Japan.

Throughout her time at high school, Nikko had maintained her connection with Kristel through social media, although she admitted that the intensity of studying for exams limited their ability to interact. However, a two-week visit by Kristel to Japan after university entrance exams was planned through these online interactions. Reconnecting with a key individual from her time abroad felt to Nikko like a return to reality, since it 'didn't feel like anything special. Just like it was [...] back in Hungary again' (Nikko, Interview 2).

Indeed, digital communication also allowed Nikko and Kristel to reconnect with friends from their time abroad, obtaining virtual co-presence through Skype. This ability to re-establish shared connections from their time abroad, albeit in very different geographical locales, demonstrates how the translocality of their social connections and identities was manifested through social media. While previous studies have emphasised the importance of interpersonal connections within the context of a host community in sojourners' language development (Dewey *et al.*, 2013; Isabelli-García, 2006), Nikko's experiences show how those connections continue to be mediated, invoked and experienced beyond the traditionally demarcated bounds of study abroad. In Nikko's case, the linguistic existence that comes with being a member of this community is extended beyond the classrooms and cafés of Hungary and into different moments and spaces. Although communications technology can provide a means to maintain contact beyond the bounds of study abroad, the experiences of the informants in this study, including Nikko, indicate that physical proximity in many ways drives the frequency of online interactions. It was the local presence of Kristel which served as a catalyst for re-invoking connections that were now geographically disparate.

After graduating high school, Nikko enrolled at a university known for its high enrolments of international students which allowed Nikko to recreate some of the conditions that she had known in Hungary, living independently in a highly international and multilingual community of her peers. During her first summer vacation from university, she returned to Hungary to reunite with Kristel, friends from the class they had attended and her host family. It was during this time that the effect of her lack of ongoing contact with Hungarian, apart from messaging her classmates on social media, became apparent as she struggled to engage with the spoken language even as her ability to interact in English had improved. For Nikko, Hungarian remained largely connected to the local contexts of her year abroad, and indeed it was important in maintaining her connection to people she had met; however, the utility and links to transnationalism she imagined in English magnified its importance for her future.

| | |
|---|---|
| Levi: | So, for your future, do you see yourself mainly just using English then? Hungarian is not that important for your future? or do you want to have both? |
| Nikko: | Um, for the future, I'm not thinking to, like, for example, to like live in Hungary, or get a job in Hungary, so I don't think that Hungarian's gonna be so useful. Like, more like, I feel like English is really important, so like I want to improve it more. But I want to visit Hungry like, continuously. So like, still my Hungarian is important when it comes to talk to friends and family ((hmm)), so I don't want to lose my Hungarian, like knowledge. (Nikko, Interview 2) |

Putting aside the instrumental nature of her comment, it highlights the impermanence of the competencies that Nikko had developed abroad and the effects of returning to an environment where the opportunities to use Hungarian were not readily available. Importantly, Hungarian is imagined as a low-mobility language, tied to the space and communities of Nikko's homestay which are no longer relevant in Japan. English exists as a high-mobility language and, as previously discussed, its translocal value is defined in contrast to the local value of Japanese.

This underscores the importance of engaging with the longer trajectories of sojourners' language use, since linguistic development does not end at the conclusion of the sojourn. Indeed, processes of globalisation entwined with the hegemony of English as an international lingua franca shaped Nikko's language learning abroad and in the year after her return. Although sojourners may maintain an affective connection to the localised communicative practices of their host communities, Nikko's case demonstrates that the social and communicative realities of their lives may lead them to adopt different linguistic priorities, even with the translocal affordances of social media.

### Reflections: Negotiations across Local and Global Imaginaries

Examining the social, material and symbolic dimensions of Nikko's account provides us with a compelling illustration of the different factors that worked to structure her experiences, both abroad and upon return. Importantly, observing how these factors were stratified allows us to complexify notions of mobility, online interaction and imagination and their effects on her language learning and use.

Beginning with the idea of mobility, it is commonly understood in the language learning abroad literature as something that occurs at a transnational scale. While that is certainly the case with Nikko's relocation from Japan to Hungary, recognition of her mobility at local scales is also productive in understanding the affordances for sociality and associated language learning that became available to her. Being located in a large European city was a significant influence on her experience. A large international exchange student population was present – a function of their own transnational mobility – providing opportunities to diversify her linguistic repertoire beyond varieties commonly associated with Hungary, while access to public transport afforded this community to meet beyond the bounds of their immediate schools and neighbourhoods. The students themselves appeared to be offered a significant degree of freedom to socialise beyond their host families which also contributed to their local mobility.

This brings us to the imaginaries of language and place and how they were understood by Nikko throughout her stay. Initially, Nikko conceives of Hungary in aesthetic terms and commensurate with her long-held desire to appropriate the exoticness she associated with becoming 'French'. Upon arriving in Hungary, she is met with the practicalities of interacting with others and the importance of appropriating the linguistic resources required. Given that English and Hungarian linguistic resources were both viable targets for language learning and use, Nikko necessarily needed to make choices about which resources she would focus on at any given time. While at home, the distribution of linguistic resources meant that Hungarian was prioritised in order to communicate with her host mother, in the communities of her classroom and local exchange students however, she needed to continually assess the value of Hungarian and English. For non-Anglophone students such as Nikko who find English an important part of local linguistic ecologies, processes of language learning involve considerations which go beyond the communities of which they seek membership, to include the mobility of linguistic resources at translocal scales. While the presence of English as a lingua franca during study abroad may be seen as an impediment to language learning for those coming from Anglophone backgrounds (Mitchell *et al.*, 2017), Nikko's account accentuates how transnational English-speaking communities also contribute to complex negotiations of language learning.

What is important to note, however, is that while this analysis takes a structural view of the linguistic resources that Nikko sought to appropriate, the measures by which she evaluated their relative value fluctuated in relation to the social connections and identities she prioritised throughout her time abroad and even in the year after her return. Although the first languages that Nikko encountered upon arriving in Hungary were the lingua francas of English and Spanish, it was Hungarian that she decided to prioritise for the first few months, highlighting the importance she placed on the relationship with her host mother. As other studies such as Grieve (2015) and Yashima *et al.* (2004) have demonstrated, stable relationships within the host family are often a prerequisite for adolescents to develop peer relationships outside of the host family. This shows the importance of viewing language learning not only through the metaphor of scales, but also through other epistemological constructs such as social networks, to understand why and how they focus on specific forms and varieties. Nikko's relationship with Kristel is a case in point as it demonstrates how a relationship, mediated through English language resources, became instrumental in their ongoing learning of Hungarian, which was then used to renegotiate the language of interaction, and thus their positionality with their classmates.

What we can also observe through Nikko's account are the ways that online interaction served to facilitate and mediate processes of language learning, belonging and identity negotiation in both Hungary and Japan. Connecting to others through social media in ways that transcended face-to-face interactions was, by Nikko's account, a vital part of the way that she built connections with peers while in Hungary. Interacting online served to compliment, support and contribute to interactions that took place in person. However, social media also served to mediate transnational connections with friends in Japan while in Hungary and then with those she had connected with abroad once back in Japan. Therefore, it operates as both a site for the production and maintenance of identity and social connection across local and translocal scales.

YouTube, acting as part of the global cultural flows that Appadurai (1996) identified, is also perceived by Nikko as an affordance for appropriating the highly mobile varieties of adolescent English. This contrasts with the localised practice of learning Hungarian through conversations about diary entries that she pursued with her host mother or attending Hungarian language classes with Kristel. Therefore, we can also understand Nikko's language learning as a practice that is scaled, not only by the contexts in which she is able to effectively deploy the resources she appropriates, but also by the learning affordances available to her.

The presence of globally mobile English alongside other locally available linguistic resources, enabled through online communications, has implications for how sojourners are able to engage with language abroad. The varieties that sojourners choose to pursue are mediated by their orientations to scale, identities and the norms and values of using specific varieties in a given context. It should also be noted that the linguistic reality of Nikko's time abroad was decidedly more heteroglossic than it would appear on the surface. Japanese was part of the communicative melange of host family interactions, and its presence on social media both in the interactions of Nikko's friends from home and in Latinised comments made by others who followed her demonstrate its translocal value. Nikko's own admissions about the prevalence of swearing in Hungarian among her exchange student friends demonstrate how localised linguistic resources could be appropriated and used in acts of translinguistic downscaling to index localised identities.

Tullock (2021: 208) has observed that, 'encountering societal multilingualism in a new context, such as [study abroad], fuels numerous discoveries of multilingualism, language diversity and the politics of language choice'. Nikko's account demonstrates how these discoveries are not limited to the host context but extend into return contexts. While she had appropriated the markers of a transnational identity, they were evaluated within her high school in Japan as incompatible with a Japanese identity. Moreover, institutional norms which valorise academic achievement assessed against national standards also constrained her ability to maintain connections with friends from abroad and the linguistic competencies associated with them. However, upon entering a university which prioritised international interactions, access to markers of transnationality, including the use of English, functioned as affordances for a plethora of new opportunities. By becoming daigakusei, Nikko was freed from many academic expectations and experienced greater independence to pursue activities and relationships conducive to language learning and development. It underscores the significance of assigned life-stage identities in Japan and the institutionalised orders of indexicality associated with them. Thus, it is crucial to understand sojourners from a life-stage perspective, considering the societal institutions that shape expectations and the implications for sojourners' reintegration upon return.

Finally, in Nikko's account we see the inevitable contradictions that arise between the globalising imaginary of study abroad and the localised realities of host and home contexts. While Nikko's year abroad would be conceived of as a means for her to obtain skills relevant to international labour markets, a point that Nikko herself gestured towards, upon returning to high school in Japan the linguistic resources of Hungarian and English held little value. Indeed, despite the relevance of Hungarian to her experience, Nikko noted its lack of value in relation to her aspirations of joining the global labour market. Further, her multilingual identity and the changes to her appearance marked her as an outsider within the orders of indexicality present at her Japanese high school, forcing her to renegotiate her positionality with her teachers and peers. Yet, the ability to also exist outside of these contexts, through the temporality of social media and travel, and by simply transcending them when she moved to an internationalised university meant that Nikko also experienced fluctuations in the value of these resources. Altogether we can say that Nikko's language learning and her understanding of her time spent abroad emerge among these tensions. Negotiations of language and identity unfold among, and are configured by, orientations to both global and local imaginaries of language, place and ethnicity. Nikko's study abroad experience transcends a reductionist image of learning Hungarian (or English) in Hungary and instead must be conceived of as an ongoing translocal negotiation of these imaginaries, both within and beyond the host context.

## Notes

(1) Japanese–English expression that refers to a high nasal bridge.
(2) Mandarin meaning 'sisterly bond' or 'friends for life'.
(3) Portuguese meaning 'love you' with the final vowel elongated.
(4) Hungarian meaning 'disgusting' or 'gross' with the final vowel elongated.
(5) Japanese meaning 'really like/love'.
(6) Japanese meaning 'cute' or 'adorable' with the final vowel elongated.

# 4 Nagisa: Translocal Ties and Online Identity in Brazil

Nagisa's decision to learn Portuguese in Brazil, influenced by family connections there, is conceived in contrast to the imaginary of study abroad as a means to gain proficiency in English. As a prolific social media user, Nagisa uses online platforms to mediate her experience even as she finds her ability to participate in local scales of interaction hampered by limitations on her connectivity. Engaging with Japanese diaspora in Brazil and navigating localised discourses of Japanese identity further complicated her experiences. Upon returning to Japan, Nagisa finds that social media allows her to transcend restrictions placed on her multilingual identities even as she must orient to local scales of interaction and behaviour.

It's almost unremarkable now to say that one of the things that makes a study abroad so compelling is the way that it can upend presumed norms and call into question things we had previously taken for granted. What remains remarkable is the way that this process takes place in highly particular ways and the effect this has for language learning. In Nagisa's case, she encountered ethnicity, language and race in Brazil in ways that made complex and salient her understanding of what it meant to hold a Japanese identity. Her experiences moved the idea of Japanese identity from the mundane and abstract to the personal and embodied.

Due to Nagisa's busy extracurricular schedule, she was only available for interviews late in the evening in Japan, which given the time difference meant that our interviews began in the early morning Melbourne time. She Zoomed me from her room on a laptop computer rather than a smartphone as many of the other informants had done. The role of digital communication in her life was prominent in interviews, as she periodically interacted with her smartphone and would occasionally show me things on its screen during our interviews. Nagisa was clearly digitally literate and was the informant most active on social media while abroad, sometimes posting to Instagram multiple times a day as well as cross-posting to other social networks such as Facebook and Twitter.

Nagisa was also unique among the informants as her mother was involved in study abroad associations and they often hosted a number of high school exchange students from organisations such as AFS and Rotary. Nagisa explained that in the year after she had returned from her sojourn to Brazil, they had four or five exchange students stay with them, from between a month to a year. Therefore, her decision to study abroad was one that had the full support of her family. Her mother's expectation was that she would spend a year abroad in an Anglophone community. However, Nagisa explained that her decision involved more complex calculations.

ナギサ： 私も、最初は自分の学校の勉強とか、成績のために英語圏に行くんじゃないかというふうなことを考えたんです。なんですけど、よくよく考えてみて、ここから大事な話なんですけど、私の母方の親戚がブラジルにたくさんいまして、お母さんの親戚がいっぱいブラジルに移民でいて。その人達はもうほとんど日本語は話せないブラジルにいる日本人なんです。日系ブラジルの人達とポルトガル語でちゃんと会話をできるようにすれば、これからも、もっとその交流とかコネクションが続いていくんじゃないかと思ったんです。

**Nagisa:** I was also thinking at first that I would probably go to an English-speaking country because it would help with my schoolwork and grades and so on. But when I really thought about it, and this point is really important, I have a lot of family on my mother's side who are in Brazil. A lot of my mother's family emigrated there. They are mostly [ethnic] Japanese in Brazil who can't really speak Japanese anymore. So, I thought that if I could speak Portuguese with Japanese Brazilians then I could maintain that connection and increase interaction between our families. (Nagisa, Interview 1)

Nagisa's decision, as she indicated, must be read as taking place in an environment where English held a hegemonic position in discourses of language learning. Therefore, her desire to study abroad sat in tension with the imaginaries study abroad as a means of granting academic and career-based advantages through interactions with English-speaking ネイティブ (neitibu[1]), based in predominantly white Anglophone nations. Thus, this decision represented an exercise of Nagisa's own agency and she emphasised to me that she had sought out and applied for her programme in Brazil herself in contrast to these expectations.

Unlike many of the other informants in this study, Nagisa's primary motivation for studying abroad was tied to developing a linguistic repertoire that would grant her the ability to interact with Japanese Brazilians and forge transnational ties between family members. While Portuguese language resources hold limited value within the national scales of education or the wider Japanese society, it was perceived by Nagisa as possessing translocal value, connecting her to diasporic elements of her family residing in Brazil. Nagisa's awareness of this value had been cultivated through trips that she had made with her immediate family to visit relatives in Brazil during the second year of elementary school and the second year of middle school.

Throughout our interactions, I noted Nagisa was consistently translanguaging and regularly used uncommon Japanese expressions. Combined with her almost constant use of 丁寧語 (teineigo[2]) during our interactions, Nagisa demonstrated an ability to wield a vast array of linguistic resources unusual for her age and education. Throughout our communications it became clear to me that this repertoire reflected the diversity of her social networks, which included students and professors at a university affiliated with her high school.[3]

During our second interview, I asked her about these practices in her speech and her answer once again pointed to the influence of her mother.

| ナギサ: | うちのお母さんもそういう人で、昔からなんか、英単語すごい、会話に挟んでくる人だったんですよ。で、「私、送り迎えに行くよ」と言った時は、「ああ、じゃあ、何時に[ナギサ]をPick Up しに行くからね」とかと言うんです。 |
|---|---|
| **Nagisa:** | My mother is that type of person too. For a very long time, she's been the type of person who will just drop English words into her conversations. So, when she would drop me off somewhere she would say things like 'So I'll come and *pick* you *up*[4] at this time, Ok?' (Nagisa, Interview 2) |

Nagisa explained that the ongoing presence of exchange students in her house meant that she was constantly adjusting her language to accommodate their abilities, often including English expressions in place of more difficult Japanese expressions. Nagisa's home was, therefore, a continual and dynamic site of language contact where English served as a lingua franca that could be substituted for Japanese when limitations in interactants' Japanese linguistic repertoires were observed or anticipated. She could effectively engage in processes of rescaling both within and across linguistic varieties, adopting varieties which she perceived as appropriate to the context and audience, including our interview.

The picture I was able to draw of Nagisa's linguistic home life was one infused with translanguaging practices deployed both in the service of the interactional realities of housing multiple exchange students and deeply woven into the day-to-day communicative practices of the family unit. Thus, Nagisa's communicative repertoire already afforded her the communicative mobility to traverse liminal transglossic spaces and was something she readily applied upon arriving at her host family's place in the south of Brazil.

## Negotiating Linguistic Environments In and Beyond the Host Family

Nagisa's host family situation was one of conflicting emotional experiences that she described at times as alienating and at other times as deeply loving. Linguistically, interactions in the host family were fundamentally translingual as the repertoires of Nagisa and her host family were navigated and renegotiated across her stay. Two months prior to departure, Nagisa received contact details for her host family and sent them a message introducing herself. Demonstrating how digital communications stretches the typically demarcated bounds to the start of a study abroad experience, this initial communication began to define the linguistic terms of interaction during her homestay.

Assumptions about intercultural communication, built through Nagisa's own experiences living with exchanges students and reinforced through globalising imaginaries, led her to send this inaugural message in English despite her own stated desire to travel to Brazil to learn Portuguese.

ナギサ： 　向こうのホストファミリーが can't speak English だったんですよ。何もわからなくて、で、私が一回英語を書いた文を、não sei、だから、can't understand と言ったんですよ。

**Nagisa:** My host family in Brazil couldn't speak English. They didn't understand anything, and when I first wrote them a message in English they replied 'não sei', which means I can't understand. (Nagisa, Interview 1)

Viewed through a scalar metaphor and given the context that Nagisa's host sister possessed the ability to communicate in English (which we will return to in a moment), this response offers an important insight into the functioning of language and imagination in Nagisa's experience of study abroad. Nagisa composed the message at a translocal scale in line with her preconceptions of international communication, adopting English as the *de facto* medium for that message. The utterance *não sei* rejects this assumption and positions Portuguese as the variety that will be prioritised in interactions with the family, pointing to a localised linguistic order which will be in place once she joins the family in southern Brazil. In this way, Nagisa was oriented to a local linguistic imaginary, through digital communication, before arriving in Brazil.

However, after meeting her host family, the heterogeneous distribution of linguistic resources across her host community was made apparent. Nagisa's host sister was proficient in English and, as in the cases of other informants, needed to perform the labour of language brokering (Morales & Hanson, 2005) for the first few months. Nagisa reported that during these months, she devoted several hours at home each evening to language study. Like other informants, the dyadic relationship between Nagisa and her host mother proved to be a crucial aspect of her linguistic development.

| | |
|---|---|
| ナギサ: | 話しながらお母さんの仕事の愚痴、大変なことを聞いたり、そのお母さんのお母さん、おばあちゃんの話を聞いたりとかっていうことを、ずっと学校帰ってから勉強して寝るまで過ごしてっていうふうにしていました。 |
| **Nagisa:** | We would be talking and she would complain about her work, talk about things that were bothering her, also about her mother, she would tell me about things like that. We made a habit of spending our time together this way from the time I got home from school until I studied and went to bed. (Nagisa, Interview 1) |

The recurring nature of these interactions, enabled through the availability of the host mother as well as the quotidian nature of the content, was pivotal and also reinforced the support offered by the relationship.

As in Nikko's account, tension soon emerged between Nagisa and her host sister, yet in this case it appeared to be due to significant differences in values. In one episode, Nagisa arrived home from school sometime after her host sister and boyfriend and found a used condom lying on the floor of their shared bathroom. This and other incidents contributed to Nagisa's perception that the friendly, caring image her host sister performed hid a more self-serving and irresponsible side.

| | |
|---|---|
| ナギサ: | 最初は host sister のボーイフレンドや、その友達たちと遊んでいましたが、だんだん私が、その人たちのことをあまり良いと思わなくなって、[…]学期の変わり目で違う友達と付き合うようにしたら、もっと(友達が)増えました。 |
| **Nagisa:** | At the start I spent time with my host sister's friends, her boyfriend, people like that, but gradually I realised that they weren't very good people. […] at the start of the next semester I made more friends and I started spending time with different friends. (Nagisa, personal communication) |

Nagisa reported that through ongoing practices of self-study and interactions with her host mother, she largely ceased using English after a month abroad and gained the ability to exercise greater independence, both within the household and with her school peers. Like Nikko, developing competence in the communicative practices of the host community allowed her to expand her social networks independent of her English-speaking host sibling. This underscores the connection between language learning, agency and the structure of peer networks. Importantly, Nagisa's account illustrates the dynamic nature of multilingual home environments and the way they are renegotiated over time in response to developments in personal relationships and linguistic repertoires.

For Nagisa, Portuguese resources were the medium and means to deepen relationships with those around her and pursue her goal of forging stronger transnational family ties. Although English existed within the linguistic ecology of her host family, it served a transitional role while she built her ability to interact with, and embed herself into, that community. While English had afforded her the ability to interact with exchange students who had stayed in her house in Japan, she understood that she needed to orient towards local norms that valued Portuguese as the dominant variety for interaction and therefore the formation of social connections.

### Encountering Japanese Identity in Brazil

A crucial aspect of Nagisa's experience was the presence of ethnic Japanese populations in Brazil who largely migrated there in the first half of the 20th century. Brazil has one of the largest populations of ethnic Japanese outside of Japan, with those who identify as Japanese making up almost 1% of the total population (Ministry of Foreign Affairs of Japan, 2022). With her family connections, Nagisa arrived in Brazil already possessing an awareness of the history and presence of these communities. Therefore, from early in her stay, she sought to made contact with local Japanese through local community events, which led to a growing awareness of their contributions to wider Brazilian society.

| | |
|---|---|
| ナギサ： | びっくりして、その人達と、日本語やポルトガル語というふうに話してるうちに、「ああ、ここに住んでる日本人もいっぱいいて、そういう交流たくさん生まれてるんだ」ということ思って、で、「じゃあ日本人もう受け入れられてるし」ということを考えたときに、いろんな、その日本人に対する印象、ブラジル人から聞いたりとかしたときに、日本人が作るパステルという、ブラジルの揚げ物があるんですけど、(はい)そんな揚げ物は本当に美味しいから、絶対に間違いはないということ言ってくれたりとか |
| **Nagisa:** | It was surprising, as I was talking to these people in Japanese and Portuguese I thought 'Oh, there are a lot of Japanese people living here and there is a lot of cultural exchange taking place'. And then I thought, 'Well, Japanese people are already accepted here'. And when I heard Brazilians' |

different impressions of Japanese, they told me that there is a Brazilian fried food called pastel, that is made by Japanese people (right), and that this fried food is really delicious, and you can't go wrong with it. (Nagisa, Interview 1)

Nagisa made friends with several people through these events. One was an ethnic Japanese who lived a 15-minute walk from Nagisa's residence, and she was sometimes invited to visit his home for meals.

| | |
|---|---|
| ナギサ： | その、日本人の、働いてる家族は、お父さんが日本人で、その現地の人と結婚したんですよ。だからお母さん、お嫁さんは、ポルトガル語しか喋れないんです。しかもポルトガル語の、南のポルトガル語じゃなくて、北のポルトガル語で、発音が全然違うんですよね。だから、たまに聞き取れなくて、これは確か親戚が喋ったポルトガル語だということを思いながら、その違いも考えて、で、一生懸命ポルトガル語喋るようにして |
| **Nagisa:** | So, this Japanese family who is working in Brazil, well, the father is Japanese and he married a local woman. And so, the mother, his wife, speaks only Portuguese. And it is not the Portuguese of the South, but that of the North, and the pronunciation is totally different. So, sometimes I couldn't catch what was said. And I thought about those differences while thinking that this was the Portuguese spoken by my relatives, and so I tried really hard to speak Portuguese with them. (Nagisa, Interview 1) |

This relationship afforded Nagisa important insights into the cultural and linguistic context of her host community, initially by exposing her to the heteroglossia of Brazilian Portuguese. It also provided her with a better understanding of the ways that populations of ethnic Japanese were invisible to the wider Brazilian society. Although demographic studies of the Japanese diaspora in Brazil have previously indicated that around half of the population is concentrated in the south-eastern state of São Paulo (IBGE, 2008), Nagisa explained that she encountered widespread ideas, including from her relatives in the north, that Japanese populations simply didn't exist further south where she was located.

An awareness of the history of immigration from Japan to Brazil and her own interactions with local Japanese communities were important resources in Nagisa's understanding of her own identity abroad, as she related to me with pride the contributions they had made to the economy and culture of Brazil. The local presence of this population, their enduring social, economic and cultural connections with Japan, were instrumental in Nagisa's understanding of herself and her relationship to the

Portuguese language. In this diasporic population, Portuguese was the language of the other, but constituted part of their cultural consciousness, thus providing a model of the Portuguese-speaking Japanese to which she could aspire.

Outside of these diasporic communities though, she often found herself confronting essentialising attitudes that further complexified her understanding of what holding a Japanese identity in Brazil meant. One aspect of this was the hurled comments of passers-by, similar to those experienced by Megumi (covered in Chapter 5).

| | |
|---|---|
| ナギサ： | 道を渡ろう、普通に歩いてたら、急に「ありがとう」とか、「かわいい」とか、「こんにちは」と言われたりとかして。日本語でですよ。 |
| **Nagisa:** | When I was crossing the street, just walking along like everyone else, people would suddenly say things like 'arigatō', 'kawaii' or 'konnichi wa' at me. They said it in Japanese! |
| リーバイ： | えー。そう言われたら、どう思いましたか？ |
| **Levi:** | Oh wow. So, what did you think about having that said to you? |
| ナギサ： | 多分、向こうは意味わかってないんですよね。「ありがとう」なんて。そんな、何もしてないのに言葉じゃないので。なんですけど、日本人を見つけて、そういうことを言おうというふうに考えてくれるということが、すごい嬉しくて。 |
| **Nagisa:** | I guess maybe they didn't know what it meant. Because they used 'arigatō', even though I wasn't doing anything. So, it wasn't a word for them. It was just because they saw a Japanese person and thought to say something like that to them, so I was really happy. (Nagisa, Interview 1) |

Nagisa perceived this type of attention as affirming since it aligned with a growing sense of pride in her Japanese identity. Something she felt was understood positively in the social milieu of her host community.

Nagisa also explained that members of her community positively viewed Japanese cultural exports such as television, and people she interacted with, including classmates and her teacher, made a point of learning expressions in Japanese to use with her. Although the Japanese language learning that took place was certainly not equivalent to that being done by Nagisa herself, it again demonstrates how Japanese linguistic resources carried translocal value, and the bidirectional appropriation and use of a sojourner's linguistic resources also noted in Nikko's account.

Nagisa's experience of Japanese identity in her communities was also complexified by local attitudes that Nagisa herself labelled as 「自分の都合のいい日本のカルチャー」, a 'self-serving idea of Japanese culture'.

ナギサ： 例えば、アニメ作品とか、日本の漫画とか、寿司とか、ブラジル人が好きなふうに改造された寿司とか、みたいなだったので、もうそれは、日本のカルチャーっていうよりかは、日本のカルチャーの中であなたたちが好きなふうにしたもの…本物の日本人が、日本人として築き上げたものではないっていうのことも、分かってもらいたいな〜

**Nagisa:** Things like, anime, manga, sushi. Sushi changed for Brazilian tastes. So, it wasn't really Japanese culture anymore, it was just Japanese culture changed to how they wanted it. I wanted them to understand it wasn't something that real Japanese had created for other Japanese people. (Nagisa, Interview 2)

What Nagisa was describing was the repackaging of Japanese cultural exports, that are stripped of their nuances and, through their exoticism, rendered quintessentially Japanese. She locates the authority for evaluating notions of Japaneseness with the scale of 'Japanese people', rejecting the indexicality ascribed locally and associated imaginations of what Japanese identity entails.

This was encapsulated through an episode that occurred when she went with her host family to a local sushi restaurant one evening. After waiting an hour to be seated, the food they were served didn't reflect Japanese ideas of sushi and was, in both Nagisa and her family's estimation, terrible. The situation was made worse as the family ridiculed the meal and bought a large serving of hot potato chips on the way home instead.

ナギサ： もう、本当に、その時に、すごい悔しくて、「こんな寿司食べないといけないんだぞ」と思って。「こんなんだから美味しくないんだ」と思って。それ見たときに、「[ナギサ]は食べるでしょ」って言われて、「食べるわけないじゃん」って言って、すごく怒って。で、ブチギレて、家帰っても、大泣きして[…]日本に住んでて、寿司を馬鹿にされるとか、なんか、変なもん、変な日本のカルチャーを押し付けられて、日本人が、私に向かって、「それ変じゃん」っていうことは絶対ないので[…]自分の誇りで持っているものとか、大切にしていることを、あの、意図せずとも、なんか、軽く見られたとか、馬鹿にされたとか、そういうようなことを思ったっていうのがやっぱり、一番悔しかったですね。

**Nagisa:** I was really just so frustrated then and thought, 'I'm going to have to eat this sushi'. I thought, 'This is why it doesn't taste good'. And when they saw it, someone said, 'This is what you eat, right?', and I said, 'There's no damn way I would eat that!' and got really angry. I was just so upset.

And even after we got home, I was bawling my eyes out. [...] Living in Japan, Japanese people would absolutely never come up to me and be like making fun of sushi or forcing strange Japanese culture on me or saying 'That's so weird' [...] It was the most frustrating thing, even if it was unintentional, for something that I'm proud of, something I valued, to be looked down on and ridiculed. (Nagisa, Interview 2)

Even over a year after it had occurred, Nagisa described it as the most difficult experience of her time abroad. As explained earlier, Nagisa views the culinary contributions of Japanese communities as emblematic of the value they contributed to Brazilian society. Nagisa expressed a strong personal and cultural connection to food that she constantly affirmed through posts on Instagram. Moreover, sushi was an important 名物 (meibutsu[5]) in her hometown and therefore represented a particular point of pride. To encounter iconic Japanese food in an unflattering way while with her host family, and have it, from her perspective, become a means to characterise Japanese culture as 'weird' was highly confronting. Although this incident stood out to Nagisa, she encountered similar attitudes throughout her stay.

| | |
|---|---|
| ナギサ： | やっぱり、日本よく知らない人で、中国とか韓国とか、アジアの方の国と、日本と一緒にするんですよ。だから、日本は忍者とか侍とか、なんか目はこうつり目で、すし食べて、ラーメン食ってて、でなんか、こんなことしだす[合掌ジェスチャーしながら]みたいなことばかり言ってる人いっぱいいたんです。あたしの、なんか、留学している友達にも、で、なんか、「カエルを食べるのは日本でしょう」とか、「カラス食べるんでしょう」とか、「犬食べるんでしょ」。 |
| **Nagisa:** | People who don't know much about Japan tend to compare Japan with other Asian countries such as China and Korea. So, in Japan, there are things like ninjas and samurai, with slanted eyes like this, eating sushi and ramen noodles, and doing things like this [performing a wai gesture]. I met a lot of people who said things like that. A friend of mine who studied abroad said she had been asked, 'Japanese are the ones who eat frogs, right?', or 'They eat crows, right?', or 'They eat dogs, right?'. (Nagisa, Interview 2) |

These discourses rely on exoticised and racist tropes of Japanese culture, and as Megumi's account in the following chapter shows, involve conflation with larger orientalist discourses. By proxy, Nagisa found herself essentialised and ascribed identities connected to these discourses. Like Cook's (2006) study of Americans staying with Japanese host families, family spaces were the main site for confronting and attempting to renegotiate these perceptions. These interactions held a realisation for Nagisa that despite her personal awareness of extant local populations of Japanese, they and their cultural contributions appeared to be invisible among the wider community. In effect, Nagisa was the only Japanese person many in her networks knew and as such felt seen as an embodiment of Japanese exoticness and weirdness. This identity, as it intersected with gender, also led to attention from a subset of young men while she was abroad.

| | |
|---|---|
| リーバイ： | ブラジルの男性はどういうふうに[ナギサ]見てたんですか？ |
| **Levi:** | How were Brazilian guys seeing you? |
| ナギサ： | なんか、私のことを好きって言ってくれる子もいたし、あと、日本人だから日本のオタクカルチャー交流できる友達として |
| **Nagisa:** | There were some who told me that they liked me, and also because I'm Japanese, they saw me as a friend who they could talk with about Japanese otaku culture. (Nagisa, Interview 1) |

However, Nagisa explained that she often felt uncomfortable with this attention, as even those she saw as male friends would 「いつもお腹触ってきたりとか、首触ったりとか」 'Always be like touching my stomach, or touching my neck'. Although Nagisa understood from her experiences that physical contact between people was much more common in Brazil than in Japan, she also identified that most of the unwanted contact she experienced came from young men.

This also illustrates how ethnoracial identities are not encountered independently but intersected by other categories such as gender. Here and previously in Nikko's account, being identified as a young Japanese woman drew romantic attention from local young men. Although Nikkoreciprocated the attention she received, along with Nagisa's case, it highlights how the informants were compelled to experience their physical presence in the world as an exotic Japanese other. As Morinaga Williams (2019: 62) has argued, intersections of gender with Japanese ethnicity exist within a 'hierarchy of desirability' that, among some groups of heterosexual males, favour Japanese women. When this attention is undesired and/or harassing, as in Nagisa's case, it can negatively impact language learning, as has been highlighted predominantly in studies of American women abroad (e.g. Polanyi, 1995; Talburt & Stewart, 1999; Trentman, 2013a). However, Takahashi (2013) has shown that these 'hierarchies of desire' also exist among Japanese women, with white English-speaking men highly placed. Intersecting matrices of ethnicity, race, language and desire may therefore underpin the interactions of individuals abroad and their desire to engage in romantic interactions that also function as sites for the appropriation of linguistic resources.

It speaks to the multifarious and contradictory ways that identity, particularly in this case ethnoracial identities, can be experienced and performed by sojourners abroad, particularly as they move through spaces where they are subject to differing orders of indexicality. Nagisa often found herself defined by her Japanese identity, in how she was viewed by strangers and within the communities she was known, including school and her host family even as she aligned more strongly with that identification. A disjuncture emerges when this identity is subjected to essentialising and negative cultural representations even as Nagisa ascribes to it her own set of related positive cultural representations and appears to appreciate the limited celebrity it provides. A newly heightened awareness of what being Japanese meant simultaneously became a source of pride and a site of othering.

## (De)Connectivity and Participation

Throughout Nagisa's time abroad, she posted on Instagram almost daily, sometimes several times a day across multiple platforms. This is in contrast to the other informants who posted from between a few times a week to a few times a month. The majority of Nagisa's posts centred on food and connected to her experiences in the host context. She explained that the types of aesthetic experiences she was used to encountering regularly in Japan, for example artistic and appealing arrangements of food, weren't available to her abroad. Therefore, she set about creating her own dishes at home, photographing them and posting them to her Instagram account, often with detailed narratives about how she had obtained the ingredients and the steps she had taken to prepare the dish.

This is an important demonstration of how social media use by sojourners is situated in, and constructed by, their experiences in local, material contexts. For Nagisa, food culture was a vital part of her lifeworld and, as indicated in the previous section, connected to her understanding of a Japanese identity in Brazil. Struggling with challenges to her values and the lived actuality of the food culture in her host family, social media became a curatorial space where she could exert her power to emphasise and reinforce these closely held values.

Over the course of her stay, there was also a marked change both in the way Nagisa constructed her posts and in the nature of the comments she received. In the first month abroad, many of her posts contained a single word or phrase in Portuguese, such as *feijãos*, which simply repeated the idea of beans contained in her photos. Over time, however, she began giving more detailed descriptions of the food she had prepared and translanguaging became more prevalent. For example, in one post she wrote:

...Pode ser... é queijo eu sei 🧑‍🤝‍🧑💡
Ganhei! ✉️ 今日は海岸近くのスーパーで
輸入チーズゲット！
...It might be... I know it's cheese 🧑‍🤝‍🧑💡
I got it! ✉️ Today I went to a supermarket near
the sea and got this imported cheese!

Her posts also began to include hashtags in greater numbers in Japanese, Portuguese and English. The frequency with which these occurred, even when posting entirely in Japanese, suggests that hashtags with their limited syntactical complexity were an effective and easily appropriated means of upscaling her posts, maximising her potential audience and demonstrating her translinguistic and transnational affiliations. Comments on Nagisa's posts also started to reflect her developing social networks as the comment sections contained interactions taking place in both Portuguese and Japanese. In effect, they demonstrated that Nagisa was learning not only how to communicate in Portuguese but also how to engage in practices of translinguistic audience design through which she sought to appeal and respond to her diversifying audience. Like Nikko, her social media activity was situated in the translocality of her experiences and the localised events and practices she shared were curated and recontextualised for an audience located in and beyond Brazil.

Despite her social media activity while abroad, Nagisa reported being limited in her ability to be online. While living in Brazil, Nagisa had her own device but lacked a cellular connection, relying instead on local wifi connectivity, which her school did not offer. This posed a number of problems, since her peers had access to local cellular networks there was an assumption that students had online connectivity at school. One outcome of this was that Nagisa was reliant on the generosity of other classmates for online functionality such as using Google Translate when struggling to comprehend the teacher or other classmates.

Nagisa's ability to function in the host school classroom was therefore a product of both her local material circumstances – lacking connectivity that her classmates possessed, and her social circumstances – the ability to negotiate access to her classmates' devices. This also meant that her communication was limited to face-to-face interaction with those in her class even as interaction was also taking place between them online. This indirect exclusion led to a number of instances where she found herself alone at school, unable to receive last-minute notifications about her teacher being absent from class.

ナギサ：　　先生も「今日は気分悪いから休むわ」ということを授業始まる30分前に言ったりして、それを連絡がソーシャルネットワー

|  |  |
|---|---|
|  | クサービスで回ってくるので、私は wifi 持ってなくて連絡も貰ってなくて、一時間とかずっと待ってたりしていて |
| Nagisa: | 30 minutes before class started, my teacher would say 'I don't feel well so I'll be taking the day off'. That would go around on social media, so because I didn't have wifi, I wouldn't get the message and would be just waiting there for an hour or so. |
| リーバイ： | 一人で？ |
| Levi: | By yourself? |
| ナギサ： | そうです。もう大変でしたね。で、その後、あの学校にいた他のクラスの友達に「ねえ今日授業ないの？」と聞いたら「えー？そのクラス今日もうみんなとっくに帰ってるよ」とか言ったりして。そういうことは二週間に一回ありました。 |
| Nagisa: | Yes. It was horrible. And then, afterwards, when I would ask my friend from another class 'Hey, don't we have class today?' they would say stuff like, 'What? That class went home ages ago!' That would happen like once a fortnight. (Nagisa, Interview 1) |

Looking at this episode ecologically highlights how the social environments that sojourners navigate while abroad are intertwined with the materiality of their surroundings. Despite being digitally literate and engaged with translocal networks online, Nagisa was connectively impoverished during the hours she spent at school. On the one hand, this may have prompted her to engage in more co-present interactions with her classmates since this was her only means of interaction. On the other hand, she was dependent on the support of her classmates to access resources that required connectivity such as translation technology, and was unable to participate in, or even view, online interactions that took place while she was at school. Therefore, Nagisa was restricted to proximal forms of interaction while at school, with implications for her learning and participation.

The material barriers that Nagisa faced in accessing digital communication at school, a location central to her social being and language learning while abroad, illustrate how the prominence and ubiquity of an always-online youth culture can act to exclude those who lack the means to participate. As Nikko's account demonstrated, being able to connect with peers online can be a fundamental part of forming adolescent relationships. There were ways to circumvent some of these issues, and indeed Nagisa did so through a friendship with owners of a bakery she frequented near the school who offered her access to their wifi. However, the reality was that Nagisa's lack of connectivity impacted her ability to fully participate as a regular member of her classroom community and reinforced her status as *stranger*.

## Complexities in Returning to Japan

Although living with exchange students in Japan meant that Nagisa had a deeper understanding of the difficulties sojourners face than many of her peers, her own experience abroad had complexified what she had taken for granted about herself. The identity work she had done and the speech communities with which she could now interact were reshaping how she saw herself and the positionalities she sought to occupy upon returning. This sense of difference was experienced as not only a psychological phenomenon, but also a physical one.

ナギサ： 人とこう触り合うとか、誰かを好きになるっていうのは、なんかブラジルの方が、すごく優しい、なんか自分に合ってた感じがしたので、それはブラジルの方でいいかなと思ってます。

Nagisa: I felt that touching each other and liking someone in Brazil was much gentler and suited me better, so I think I'll stick to the Brazilian way. (Nagisa, Interview 2)

Her body had been both a site of exoticised attention and part of her socialisation into local cultural practices. The physicality of Brazilian cultural practices now became explicit in their absence and an embodiment of her transnational connections to host and blood relations in Brazil.

Although this sense of exceptionalism and hybridity might be understood as an asset in globally applicable, neoliberalist notions of linguistic entrepreneurialism (De Costa *et al.*, 2016), homogeneity and conformity tend to be more highly valued and deviations receive negative moralistic evaluations within Japanese high school contexts. Reflecting the experiences of Nikko, deviations from the perceived norms of behaviour and appearance at school were called out, by both teachers and fellow students. Nagisa reported struggling with verbal evaluations from both of these as she tried to reconcile new ways of being and doing with expectations that she understood were reapplied upon returning to Japan.

ナギサ： 留学の時の常識があまり通用しないから、「あんまり好き勝手やってると、嫌われるよ」ってわざわざ言われたりとか。そんなつもりないのになと思って。別にいいし。自分が好きなことやってるしと思ったんですけど。でも、嫌われるとか、嫌われないうんぬんの前に、ちゃんと日本での生活だったら、日本での生活に合わせておかないと、日本でいい具合に、うまくやっていけない

Nagisa: What had become common sense for me while abroad no longer applied, and people went out of their way to say, 'If you just act however you want too much, you aren't going to be liked'. It's not like I meant it that way. Whatever. I knew I was doing what I wanted to. But, before people could make up their minds to hate or not hate me for it, I knew that to live in Japan, I needed to adapt to the way life is lived here otherwise it wouldn't go well. (Nagisa, Interview 2)

It demonstrates again how a desire to inhabit identities formed abroad can make them a site of contestation, as they clash with pressure to demonstrate behaviours associated with Japaneseness. The social costs of non-conformity are high and can lead to exclusion and marginalisation. In Japanese high schools, these pressures are combined with expectations around academic performance, limiting the types of activities that students can pursue. Once again, we see how resources deemed to hold value at transnational scales come to be re-evaluated at local scales. Sojourners' experiences are therefore structured by these tensions as they struggle to reconcile positionalities developed abroad with those deemed appropriate when back at home.

This can be seen further in the way the linguistic resources that Nagisa had appropriated while abroad complexified her high school life. From a practical standpoint, it led to increased ambiguity in second language classes as her linguistic competencies were embedded in practices of translanguaging rather than the pedagogised forms taught in those classes.

ナギサ： 英語で言いたいときにポルトガル語しか出てこなくて、なんと言うんだっけとなったりとかして。学校の英作文書くときに、テストで、「これは多分英語じゃん、英語だと思うけど、ポルトガル語 かな」みたいなことあって、怪しくて、たまにポルトガル語と同じ単語があるので、それをちょっと賭けに入れるのは危険すぎるから、「ああ、じゃあ、また別の言い回し考えると」

**Nagisa:** When I'm speaking English, I can only think of the Portuguese word and I'll be like, 'How do I say it?' When I'm writing an English essay for school, on a test, I'll be uncertain, like 'I guess this word is English. I think it's English, it might be Portuguese'. Sometimes there are words that are the same as Portuguese, so because it's a bit too risky to just gamble and put them in the sentence, I'll be like 'Oh, well, I'll think of another way to say it'. (Nagisa, Interview 2)

Nagisa's multilingual identities also raised a set of complex issues as she had valued and sought to obtain them for the purpose of building connections, yet found they now set her apart from her peers, with implications for her sense of belonging. Demonstrating multilingual abilities within the Japanese classroom would be considered egotistical and evaluated negatively. Encounters with Japanese identity as they were reflected back to her by members of the host community, both Brazilian and Japanese, constituted an act of becoming. Her understanding of what a Japanese identity entailed was made both more salient and complex, even as she appropriated the interactive and cultural practices of the local Brazilian community. Upon returning to Japan, this complex, multilingual understanding of being Japanese was incompatible with localised orders of indexicality.

Nagisa struggled with this because of the way the school positioned itself. The Japanese government offers funding incentives for high schools that incorporate particular curricular objectives related to internationalisation, called スーパーグローバルハイスクール (Super Global High School). Nagisa felt that this was an important aspect of her school environment and therefore struggled with attitudes that emerged from a subset of students who would intentionally try to devalue the experiences of those who went abroad.

ナギサ： そういう人に限って「ああ、私は別に留学に行かないから」とか、「いや、なんか、留学行ったって、そんなもんでしょ」みたいなことわざわざ言いたくてくるんですよ。

**Nagisa:** These types of students would go out of their way to come up to you and say things like, 'Oh, I'm not going to study abroad' or 'Studying abroad? Nah, it's not that special'. (Nagisa, Interview 2)

It highlights a conundrum that exists within the wider contexts in which the informants found themselves. The Japanese government has put much stock in efforts of internationalisation across the education sector, particularly in secondary and tertiary contexts. Moreover, as noted, social imaginaries linked to westernisation and internationalisation in Japan value the ability to interact across international borders. On the other hand, these abilities are not afforded value within the scale of the high school. Therefore, this environment becomes a complex place for those such as Nagisa who perceive the value of multilingual and intercultural abilities as they apply in higher-order scales yet find these dismissed by teachers and peers. Despite its proclamations of being a Super Global High School, Nagisa encountered her institution as flattening and confining – she needed to perform the identity of a Japanese high school student in Japan in order to be seen as a legitimate member of the community. This type of experience thereforehas ramifications for sojourners' ongoing desire to maintain multilingual repertoires and their own sense of belonging.

However, Nagisa relished opportunities to transcend local scales of interaction. She recalled in great detail an episode where, around three months prior to our second interview, a Brazilian relative and his girlfriend came to visit her in Japan. Nagisa took them around her city, interacting in, and translating to, Portuguese throughout.

ナギサ： 「他の子は出来ないだろうな」っていうところはやっぱりあって、そういうのを1回経験してしまうと、これはあまり良くないことなんですけど、自分ができることは、他の子と違うことで、だったら、「じゃあ、私は皆ができることを別にしたくない」と思うふうになっちゃったんですよ。で、これはやっぱり日本でいうと、あまり良くない考え方で

**Nagisa:** There was a moment where I was like, 'Other students can't do this' and once you experience that, and this isn't good, you start thinking what you can do is different to other students so then you think, 'I don't want to do the things that everyone else can do'. And this isn't the right way to think in Japan. (Nagisa, Interview 2)

Her success during this time, particularly in communicating to them about places and practices of cultural significance, reignited a sense of exceptionalism she had sought to suppress in her first few months after returning. Her reaction to these accomplishments is therefore emblematic of the struggle that sojourners can face; they return with highly mobile, transnational resources to a social milieux that constructs itself in opposition to their transnationality.

## Affirming Multilingual Identities through Social Media

There was a sense of resignation in Nagisa's second interview to those factors that limited her ability to function in the same capacity as she had in Brazil. Struggling with locally situated expectations, she sought comfort and acknowledgement through transnational connections.

ナギサ： なんかちょっと寂しいときとか、ホストファミリーに電話したりとかするんですよ。(うん)その時はやっぱり、日本の親に相談する前に、ブラジルのホストファミリーに連絡するんです。その方が明るくなれるんですやっぱりなんか。[…]インスタグラムとか、Twitter とか、たまにポルトガル語で投稿したら、それ読んでくれる友達が「いいね」とか、なんか、「面白い」とかって言ってくれたりとかして、だから、ポルトガル語、英語、日本語は、英語はちょっとたまに時間があるときで、なんかよく Facebook に投稿するときは、Facebook に一番ブラジルの友達がいるので、日本語とポルトガル語両方書い

て投稿してます。やっぱりおじいちゃんとかおばあちゃんとか、以外にも、なんか、友達、向こうの友達、学校の友達も、さらっと読んでくれて、ちょっとなんかコメントしてくれたりとかっていうこともあって、学校の先生とかも。それが凄く嬉しいなって思うので、なるべく頑張ってますね。

**Nagisa:** When I feel a bit lonely or something, I call my host family ((uh-huh)). I call my host family in Brazil before I talk to my parents in Japan. It makes me feel more cheerful [...] I post in Portuguese on Instagram and Twitter sometimes, and my friends who read my posts 'like' them or comment 'That's interesting', so I use Portuguese, English and Japanese. I occasionally use a bit of English when I have time. When I post on Facebook, I post in both Japanese and Portuguese because I have the most Brazilian friends on Facebook. So, apart from people like my Grandma and Grandpa, my friends, friends over in Brazil, also friends at school here, they read it and sometimes they comment a little bit, even school teachers. I feel really happy when that happens, so that's why I try as hard as I can to do that. (Nagisa, Interview 2)

Social media afforded Nagisa opportunities to draw on the range of her linguistic repertoire to communicate with the diverse groups found in her online audience. Although her study abroad experiences and associated multilingual positionalities were marginalised in local contexts, she continued to find affirmation online. The context collapse present in Nagisa's online audience meant that she was able to deploy translinguistic practices to rescale her interactions for the different communities with which she was affiliated.

**ナギサ：** 自分の周りでは、やっぱり、自分だけ話せるっていう、なんか、こういう、優越感っていうんですか？もあるんですけど、でもやっぱりそれよりかは、なんか、自分が作ってきた関係が今も生きているとか、今もそういうのが、自分の生活に影響しているっていうこと、influence を感じてるってということを思うと、やっぱりなんか、ああ、なんか、頑張ってきて良かったなぁってことも思いますし、今までの、自分の、一年間っていうのはまだまだ消えるもんじゃないなぁってことを思って、大切にしていきたいなぁってことはすごい思いますね。

**Nagisa:** Because I am the only one around here who can speak Portuguese, I already have, I guess you could say, a sense of superiority? But more than that, when I think about the fact that the relationships I built are still alive, that they still continue to influence my life even now, and when I think about the influence I feel from them, I just feel so glad that I worked so hard. I also feel like that year I spent there is still lingering on, and I really want to just keep on cherishing it. (Nagisa, Interview 2)

Freed from the need for in-person proximity to maintain relationships that existed across cultural, geographic and linguistic spaces through social media, Nagisa found herself able to transcend the constraints placed upon her as a Japanese high school student. The ability to present these aspects of herself online meant that she was able to maintain and even extend the opportunities she had to perform them. Indeed, Nagisa explained that her online presence offered up new opportunities to broaden her Portuguese-speaking networks with others interested in her experiences.

ナギサ： ソーシャルネットワーキングサービスがあるから、それのおかげで、なんか、学校に行っても、ブラジルの友達と連絡取ったりとか、ホストファミリーと連絡取ったりとか、なんか、そういう事を知ってる、ポルトガル語を話せるんだって、知ってる人から、たまになんか、「どういう経験したの？」、全然知らない人から声かかったりとかして、そういうのを応える時間はやっぱり「ああ、自分留学行ってて良かったな」と思いますし、「友達作ってて良かったな」っていうふう思って

**Nagisa:** So, because social media exists, I've been able to stay in contact with friends in Brazil for example, or my host family, even while I am at school. And I've had people who know that about me, that I speak Portuguese, who are otherwise just complete strangers sometimes reach out online and ask, 'What was your experience like?' and when I'm replying to those sort of things I think 'Yeah, I'm glad I went abroad' and I think 'I'm glad I made friends there'. (Nagisa, Interview 2)

Effectively, the affordances of social media enabled Nagisa to continue to affirm, invest in and perform the multilingual identities she valued. It provided access to communities in which orienting to the translocal was not in opposition to being seen as Japanese. This, in turn, continued to give meaning to the year of her sojourn, even as she felt the need to de-emphasise these aspects of herself in the context of the classroom.

## Reflections: Transnational Identity Negotiations and Orders of Indexicality

Nagisa's account further details the way that sojourners' negotiations of identity and the associated processes of language learning are structured by local and translocal imaginaries. In Nagisa's account, her understanding of Japanese identity was complexified by her engagement with the local diaspora and intersecting discourses of Japan and Japanese culture. Her account reflects the experiences of other sojourners in the literature, such as Beatrice in Kinginger's (2008) study who was forced to confront different imaginings of American identity while abroad in France, or the Chinese participants in Hail's (2015) study who were regularly confronted with combative views about China in the United States. Importantly though, Nagisa also felt an affiliation with Brazil through relatives who resided there and her knowledge of, and contact with, local diasporic communities. In this sense, it was possible for Nagisa to imagine a Japanese identity that was not wholly external to Brazil but located in the scale of wider Brazilian culture.

Ortega (2021: 216) has observed that 'study abroad can spawn positive as well as negative renegotiations of racialized identities by language learners', and Nagisa's experiences demonstrate how this is realised through encounters with differing orders of indexicality. Encounters with local diasporic communities provided the resources to imagine a Japanese identity that existed beyond territorialised ideas of Japan. Simultaneously, Nagisa grappled with localised discourses that exoticised and stereotyped Japanese culture as weird. In response, she actively sought to challenge and resist these essentialising perspectives through her developing competence in Portuguese.

This complexification of racialised identity positions parallels the work of Anya (2016, 2021) on African American women's experiences of Blackness in Salvador, Brazil. As in Anya's work, language learning abroad is a lived, embodied experience where the instability and constructed nature of racialised identity can become highly salient. Just as Nagisa's experiences of Brazil were shaped by the way her body was perceived and interacted with, so too was her return to Japan as the strictures she encountered were not only behavioural but also physical. In Brazil, this meant being subjected to hurled expressions in Japanese from passing strangers and objectification as a potential love interest by those interested in Japanese pop culture. However, Nagisa was also socialised into local practices of physical expression and affection in Brazil, which she was unable to participate in upon returning. Possessing a Japanese body in Japan, it was subjected to differing expectations that compel her to supress particular behaviours and desires, including participating in physical displays of affection with those around her.

These experiences of identity are made more illuminating for the ways they intersected with Nagisa's use of social media both abroad and back in Japan. In Brazil, social media served as a curatorial space to performing values she held as important while bracketing out the parts of her experience that conflicted with these values. By doing so, she sought to operationalise the affordances of social media in order to be 'apart from' the practices she observed in her immediate context, reimagining her experience for a translocal audience. This was not a practice of disengagement, as her posts were firmly situated in the local activities of food purchasing and preparation, often framed through Portuguese. Nagisa demonstrated to her online audience that she was 'a part of' her immediate community. This again illustrates how social media enables and accentuates the translocality of study abroad, in terms of both the individual movement to a different sociocultural locale and the ability to share and make sense of their experiences with others, independent of geographical location.

The social affordances that Nagisa perceived social media providing were transformed once she returned to Japan, serving to maintain connections to Brazil, particularly with her host family when experiencing feelings of loneliness. Indeed, Nagisa's admission demonstrates how social connections formed abroad can extend back into home contexts and provide ongoing social support where it may be lacking or unavailable in the culturally appropriate forms experienced abroad. As the transnational identity positions that Nagisa had developed abroad came into conflict with local imaginaries of Japaneseness, social media served to mediate and affirm this identity even as it was denied to her locally.

Nagisa's experiences were also structured by her acknowledgement of, and resistance to, imaginaries of study abroad. Nagisa imagines study abroad as something beyond of the hegemonic discourse which centers the value and importance of English language learning. Noting her mother's desire for her to travel to an Anglophone location and the instrumental role of English both within the national scale of Japan's educational system and as the *de facto* means of transnational communication, she consciously elected to pursue linguistic resources that held value within the scale of her family. Effectively, Nagisa was already negotiating the tensions which emerged from globalising imaginaries of study abroad before she had decided upon her destination, cultivated perhaps by her family's transnational connections and the diversity of her home life.

## Notes

(1) Native speaker.
(2) A formalised register in Japanese that emphasises power and social distance in relationships.
(3) There are many private universities in Japan that operate subsidiary high schools which offer preferential placement to matriculating students to their programmes.
(4) Italicised words originally spoken using English forms.
(5) A local speciality for which an area is famous.

# 5 Megumi: Racialisation and Marginalisation in Germany

Megumi's account provides an important perspective on the way that translocal flows intersect with locally instantiated orders of indexicality and the resulting tensions this has with monolithic immersive imaginaries of study abroad. Her experiences studying at two different schools in Germany highlight the significant variations that can occur in the symbolic value of specific language varieties in geographically proximal yet socially distinct communities, with profound implications for a sojourner's positioning and access to language learning opportunities. These experiences also shed light on how racialisation is manifested through multilingual repertoires and how social media participation is situated within localised contexts of belonging.

When I first met Megumi, she was attending a high school in the Kansai region of Japan and spoke to me one evening after school. Connecting through Zoom, Megumi appeared in the long-sleeved white blouse and blue vest of a school uniform and a distinct set of white, Apple earbuds. Throughout our first conversation she alternated between holding her smartphone in one hand or resting it against an object on her bed while gesturing as she recounted her experiences living and attending high school for a year in central Germany.

Like the other informants in this study, Megumi's motivation to study abroad emerged from a complex array of desires and experiences across family and school environments. Megumi had been a keen soccer player for most of her life, first joining a team during her second year of elementary school. In 2011, during her final year of elementary school, Megumi had witnessed Japan's momentous win in the Women's FIFA World Cup in Germany and the poise and even-handedness of the referees left a deep impression on her. Upon entering Junior High School, she began taking on refereeing duties and went on to receive accreditation to referee sanctioned youth matches.

Stories of travel and foreignness were woven into the fabric of Megumi's family interactions. Megumi explained that her grandmother often recounted her experiences of travelling throughout Europe, inculcating an imagination of, and a desire to, travel there herself. Megumi also connected her participation in English language classes at school to her motivation to study abroad. Megumi recalled the enjoyment she had interacting in an unfamiliar language in a class led by a non-Japanese teacher during the final year of junior high school. She explained that this experience had sparked in her a desire to relate to others outside of Japan.

Upon entering high school, she began encountering exchange students who had come to study in Japan, and interactions with them began a process whereby her previous abstract desires coalesced into a concrete, attainable goal. This was brought a step closer when Megumi became aware of short-term study abroad programmes organised through her school and was encouraged by her teachers to participate. When speaking to her family about these programmes, this idea transformed as her mother argued for the benefits of pursuing a year-long programme over something that lasted only a few weeks. Although this idea excited Megumi, when she expressed this intention to her teachers it was met with ambivalence.

| | |
|---|---|
| リーバイ： | 行く前に、先生反対してたんですか？ |
| Levi: | Was your teacher against [your decision] before you left? |
| メグミ： | 留学についての反対は、まあ、なかったんですけど、あまりいい顔して、「じゃあ、行ってらっしゃい」っていうふうじゃなく、[…]うちの学校の先生、長期留学よりも、短期留学をすごい勧めてきて「…」[長期留学は]あんまりするって言って、いい顔はされなかったです。 |
| Megumi: | They weren't really against me studying abroad, but it wasn't like they reacted positively and said, 'Have a great time!' […] The teachers at my school strongly advised us to go on short-term rather than long-term programs […] when I said that I was planning to do (a long-term program) it didn't get a positive reaction. (Megumi, Interview 1) |

It is important at this point to highlight that the teacher's opinion carries significant authority in Japanese educational contexts, and Megumi's decision, while not unheard of, would be considered unusual given that the advice was pointed towards short-term programmes. From an institutional perspective, the appeal of short-term programmes comes from the way they provide students with 'intercultural experiences' without creating significant disruptions to the educational regimen that characterises secondary education in Japan. It exemplifies a feature of some of the informants' accounts whereby a decision to take a year off to study abroad was met with indifference or disapproval by teaching staff. Crucially though, Megumi had the support of her family which weighed heavily on her ultimate decision to pursue a year-long programme through AFS. She had wanted to study in a non-Anglophone country, seeking an experience to live with different linguistic and cultural practices to those taught through English classes at school. Her desire to travel to a European country which had a strong football culture informed her preferred destination of Germany, which she successfully obtained.

## Encountering Racialisation Abroad

In the middle of her first year of high school, as summer break began, Megumi left Japan to live with her host mother in central Germany. Megumi's host mother was central to her experience and the person she interacted with most during her stay. Megumi described how they would work through German textbook activities together at home, as well as spending most evenings watching the news on television. Initially these interactions occurred in English, but by the fourth month Megumi described transitioning to mostly using German. Megumi explained that these interactions were her main source of German language learning during the initial months.

Despite the support and stability she experienced in her home life, high school quickly became a source of distress. Megumi had been placed in a local gymnasium[1] and described standing out as a visible minority among a student population of white Germans. This almost immediately became an issue as she encountered discriminatory attitudes towards non-white populations and became a target of racialised positioning herself.

めぐみ: 私の友達なんですけど。駅とか、街とか行った時に、その外国人の、その移民の人とか見ると、「あまり良くないよね」って言ったりしているような人たちで。学校でも、あの「你好」って言われ、知らない人とか「你好」って言われたりとか。そういうのがあったりしてて、[...]普通に「中国人と日本人ってすごい似てるよねー」とか。言われたりして。

**Megumi:** So, when my friends went to the station or into town and they saw foreigners, immigrants, they were the type of people who would say things like 'They're not very nice'. At school too, people would say '*ni hao*' to me. People I didn't know would just come up and say '*ni hao*'. That kind of thing happened [...] people would say 'Chinese and Japanese really look alike don't they' and things like that. (Megumi, Interview 1)

The apparent casualness and widespread nature of the racism that Megumi experienced is perhaps the most salient feature of her account and contrasts with less overt experiences of racialisation that other participants reported. Ortega (2021: 216) has pointed out that 'Race is all-important in understanding the emic experience of language learning while studying abroad' and the ties between Megumi's experience of race while in Germany and her ability to form connections within the host community were made explicit throughout her interviews. Importantly, Megumi's experiences took place in 2016 against a backdrop of around half a million Syrian citizens seeking asylum in Germany. This influx of refugees and the resulting social tensions during that period added a layer of complexity to Megumi's journey, illustrating how study abroad contexts are intrinsically intertwined with broader global flows and emphasising how sociopolitical events at wider scales can shape the day-to-day interactions of sojourners.

Megumi's account is also important as it clearly reveals how multilingualism in the host community was operationalised to enact practices of racialisation and exclusion, particularly in the local interactional contexts of casual school talk. The first illustration of this is apparent in the above extract whereby the Chinese greeting *ni hao* was used to perform acts of 'drive-by' racialisation. It is worth spending a moment to unpack the type of speech act taking place here, since it was something Nagisa and other informants also reported experiencing and presents an example of how linguistic resources can, through their mobility, become enregistered (Agha, 2003) with ideological notions of race within local orders of indexicality.

The first thing to observe is that while this type of speech act appears as a greeting on the surface, it was not intended as such, deviating from the normative ways of performing greetings in the community. This is evident when locating it in the predominantly German-speaking environment in which it took place and the virtue of it being deployed by people Megumi recognised as strangers. The intended effect or illocutionary force of this utterance is to racialise the target and call attention to their embodied otherness for bystanders to observe. The target experiences this force, or the perlocutionary effect, as racialisation into the identity of an Asian other, particularly in Megumi's case since the speech act denied her even the possibility of inhabiting a Japanese identity. Furthermore, the act is made more insidious by the way it also offers the utterer plausible deniability through the speaker's ability to point at the normally accepted meaning of the utterance – a friendly greeting – while ignoring the fact that its markedness in this situation allows it index other possible meanings. It demonstrates the racialising potential of multilingual practice, where in this case, the hurler appropriates a linguistic resource from Mandarin to index ideas of Asianess within a German-speaking milieu.

This type of racialising speech act is not an uncommon phenomenon. Another informant in this project whose account is not included in this book, Kumiko, also reported being subjected to cries of *ni hao* from strangers while living in France. Misheila in Talburt and Stewart's (1999: 168) seminal paper reported being targeted by hurled expressions that were both racialising and sexualising – 'I'm little morena, or I'm little negrita, or chocolate'. Furthermore, I can anecdotally report experiencing similar hurled speech from strangers that drew attention to my whiteness such as 'Hey Joe!'[2] while travelling in the Philippines and 'This is a pen'[3] while living in Japan. Although these expressions carry different significance given the histories of colonisation, immigration and linguistic hegemony from which they emerge, they still serve as a means to draw attention to the observed phenological difference of the target and articulate widely recognised racial categorisations for those in earshot to collectively observe.

Megumi indicated that racialisation occurred not simply through these specific acts, but also through an accumulation of other comments and questions intended to draw attention to her alterity.

めぐみ: なんか、すごい差別されているような 気がして、それか、普通に、日焼け止め塗ってるときに「あっ、 アジア人も日焼け止めを塗るんだ」って言われて。それも、どういう意図で言ったか分からないんですけど。なんか、私からすれば、「えっ？」て思って

**Megumi:** You know I really felt like I was being discriminated against. Or like, when I was putting on sunscreen as people normally do, someone would say 'Oh wow, Asians use sunscreen too!' I don't know what their intentions were in saying it, but like from my perspective I just though 'What the hell?' (Megumi, Interview 1)

Those who Megumi was most able to relate to were other exchange students, including a friend from China who was having similar experiences at a different school. At one point, Megumi recalled attending a Bundesliga football match with this friend, something for which she had been excited. Yet again, it became a place where they were subjected to hurled acts of racialisation.

めぐみ: 私、よくサッカー観戦によく行ってたんですけど。やっぱりそこでも、あの、結構差別されたこととかもありましたし。でも、そのサッカーの文化自体は、すごいいいなと思ったんですけど。一回、中国人の友達と一緒にサッカーを見に行ったときに、フランクフルトだったんですけど。そこで、 フランクフルトとハンブルグの試合で、 ハンブルグのサポーターから、「ああ、あの人たち中国人」と言われて、その後に、私たち、ホットドッグを食べたんですけど。「ああ、犬の肉食べてる」っていうふうに言われて。 いや、何も言い返さなかった

んですけど。「やっぱりそれもあるんだな」っていうふう [思いました]。

**Megumi:** I went to soccer games a lot and I was discriminated against there a lot too. Even with that, I liked the culture around soccer itself a lot. But once, when I went to see a soccer game with a Chinese friend, we went to Frankfurt. The match was between Frankfurt and Hamburg and a Hamburg supporter said to us, 'Oh, they are Chinese'. After that, we were eating hot dogs and they said something like 'Oh, they are eating dog meat'. I couldn't, I didn't say anything back. But I thought, 'Yep, they'll even say things like that'. (Megumi, Interview 1)

When sojourners find themselves racially positioned, it can negatively impact their desire to learn and participate in the communicative practices of the host community (Goldoni, 2017; Jackson, 2008; Talburt & Stewart, 1999) and Megumi was no exception. More psychologically damaging though, from Megumi's perspective, was the deliberate exclusion she faced. Megumi often spent lunch by herself, even as her classmates congregated and interacted with each other. One excursion in particular stood out in this regard.

**めぐみ:** 一回クラスで、あの、旅行に行ったんですけど[...]そのときにずっと一人で、バスの中一人で。行ってからも、先生が「[メグミ]と一緒にいてあげて」と言って、その何人かが一緒にいてくれるけど、その全然、あの、ほったらかしみたいな感じで、だったので。そこでも、何回か学校で、もうすごい、心の中ですごい、なんか色々圧迫しちゃうこととかあって。二回ぐらい、もう学校で泣いたことありました。

**Megumi:** One time the class went on a trip [...] and I was alone the whole time. I alone on the bus by myself and after we got there I was alone too. So, the teacher says 'Make sure you include [Megumi]', and some people came over and were there with me but they didn't do anything, they just neglected me. So there and many times at school, I really had this sense, deep inside my heart, of being overwhelmed. Twice at school I just cried. (Megumi, Interview 1)

More than simply being ignored, Megumi's exclusion was amplified by the way the German students in her class deployed their multilingual repertoires. As Megumi explained, this was manifested through the use of English in what was an otherwise German-speaking environment. When I asked Megumi about her language use at school, she indicated that when she tried to initiate interactions in German, many of her classmates would respond in English. This had the effect of highlighting Megumi's perceived alterity, as all other interactions in the classroom took place through German, denying her opportunities for linguistic development. Megumi explained that she had attempted to renegotiate the language of interaction by continuing to use German even when they spoke English to her, but these attempts were ignored.

As Megumi further elaborated, practices of responding in English were part of wider patterns of exclusion.

めぐみ： やっぱり、そういう子が多くて。私がドイツ語で喋りかけても、英語で返ってくるような子が多くて。あと、やっぱりその、休み時間とかも、あんまりいっぱい喋らなくって。私が勝手に思ってたのが、やっぱりちょっとアジア人に対して、あんまり良いふうに思ってない　のかなと思ってたりもして。態度とか、そのことを見てた時に。

**Megumi:** Definitely, there were a lot of those types of students. There were a lot of students who, when I spoke to them in German would respond back in English. Also, as you can probably guess, during breaks they wouldn't really talk to me either. It might just be me, but the way they acted and the attitudes they had gave me the impression that they didn't really have the best view of Asian people. (Megumi, Interview 1)

In some ways, Megumi's account can be seen to reflect the experiences of Anglophones found elsewhere in the literature (Brown, 2021; Mitchell *et al.*, 2017; Trentman, 2013a) whose interlocuters continue to use English despite the sojourner's insistence or desire to use other local varieties. However, there are many important distinctions that highlight the value of examining intersections of identity, language and belonging ecologically.

Although Megumi, like all Japanese high school students, had taken compulsory English classes and possessed some ability to communicate in the language, she did not view herself as a proficient speaker. Moreover, she had made a conscious choice to travel outside of the Anglosphere and spent time conversing and studying German with her host mother with the intention to develop her ability to interact using these resources. This dimension of Megumi's account is therefore instructive in showing how the linguistic diversity of a given community can be operationalised to perform the work of othering and exclusion. By choosing to use the normative means of interaction found in the scale of her classroom, Megumi sought to position herself as a member of that community. When her classmates selected non-normative means of response, they effectively denied her legitimacy to speak as a member of their community and instead repositioned her utterances as emitting from an outsider.

While global imaginaries of English conceive it as a means to engage in intercultural interaction, that value shifts as it is evaluated against norms at the scale of the school community. Indeed, in Megumi's case, English resources were not used in the service of engendering intercultural communication, but as a means of denial and exclusion.

Descriptions of language learning abroad as acts of socialised becoming, such as those found in the work of Cook (2008), Kinginger (2008) and Anya (2016), have captured the centrality of communicative participation to linguistic appropriation. Therefore, sojourners who find themselves separated from meaningful participation in host communities will struggle to appropriate that community's interactive practices. Megumi continually attempted to resist and renegotiate the language of interaction and her account demonstrates how the potency of these attempts are subject to relations of power held by ingroup members of the community. The ability to rescale interactions and dictate the linguistic resources that Megumi could legitimately use was restricted to her local peers who shared cultural and linguistic affiliations. In some ways, these episodes reflect the migrant experience of Eva in Norton (2000) where deliberate exclusion from local speech communities deprived her of language learning opportunities and reinforced perceptions of incompetence and alterity. Like Eva's Canadian co-workers, the privileged insider status of Megumi's classmates granted them power to deny her access to the interactional opportunities vital for both language learning and obtaining membership and belonging in the community.

Megumi's account also provides a compelling example of what Blommaert *et al.* (2012: 1) have termed *dangerous multilingualism* whereby 'Not all forms of multilingualism are productive, empowering and nice to contemplate. Some – many – are still unwanted, disqualified or actively endangering to people'. Although the Chinese expression of *ni hao* was clearly used to racialise Megumi, her peers' use of English was more insidious. This is because their familiarity with the communicative resources of English allowed it to be recruited to a larger degree to position Megumi as an 'Asian' outsider. When viewed through an ecological perspective, Megumi's account demonstrates how English, a language associated with whiteness and cosmopolitanism in a Japanese context, is enregistered with ideas of non-whiteness when used towards her in a German high school, serving to enforce her marginalisation.

## Multilingual Participation in a Migrant Community

The culmination of these experiences meant that three months into her sojourn, Megumi sought and obtained permission to transfer to another local Gesamtschule.[4] However, this school had a dubious relationship among the students at her first school.

めぐみ： その白人ばかりの学校の方に行ってた時は、なんか、「あっちの学校はよく警察が来るらしいよ」、とか、「あんまり治安がよくないらしいよ」っていう風に言ってたりしてたんですけど。

**Megumi:** When I was going to the all-white school, I was told things like 'The police often come to that school' and like, 'It's not very safe there'. (Megumi, Interview 1)

As Megumi explained, the school that she applied to transfer to had a large proportion of students from migrant backgrounds and therefore the comments made by students at her first school drew upon discourses of immigrant populations described earlier. The prejudices of the students at her first school became more apparent once Megumi began attending the new school as she found the community to be welcoming and supportive. In fact, her experience here was so positive that she admitted not wanting to return to Japan at the end of her stay.

めぐみ： 実際行ってみると、もう今までの学校生活と、本当180度変わるぐらい楽しくて、[…] みんなとすごい仲良くなって、色々、日本のことについても聞いてきてくれたり（うん）、そのドイツ語しゃべったら全然ドイツ語で返してくれるし。休み時間も一人じゃなかったし。その、私がすごい印象的だったのが、この、お手洗いに行く時に一人で行こうとしたら、その友達が、「いや、一人で行かなくていいんだよ」言ってくれた。「いつも一緒に行ってくるから」と言ってくれて。それがすごいその心に残りました。

**Megumi:** When I actually went there and experienced it, it was so fun, like a 180-degree turnaround from my previous school life […] I got on really well with everyone and they would ask me all kinds of questions about Japan ((uh-huh)). And when I spoke German to them, they would reply back in German to me. I wasn't alone during breaks. One thing that left a big impression on me was when I went to go to the toilet alone, my friend says, 'No, you don't have to go by yourself. Just ask, and I'll always go with you'. That left a really strong impression on me. (Megumi, Interview 1)

The new social environment translated into plentiful opportunities for interaction, and Megumi found that the presence of English and German as lingua francas afforded her opportunities to translanguage with resources from both. With her peers, English was not a language of racialised exclusion, but part of the communicative melange. Thus, she was able to quickly build multilingual social networks, including friends from Turkish and Syrian backgrounds.

The upshot of this was that as Megumi's in-person connections flourished, so too did her online connections. At her first school, Megumi's exclusion from in-person interactions in the classroom had also meant that connections with local peers online had been virtually non-existent. However, she described how at her new school she was part of ongoing German and English interactions through Snapchat. This demonstrates the way that sojourners' participation in online communities can be commensurate with their local inclusion with direct implications for their opportunities to engage in the community's linguistic practices. In her move to a new school, Megumi's account serves to highlight how the indexical value of particular linguistic resources is also tied to local orders of indexicality. The heterogeneity of the linguistic backgrounds among students at her new school and its location in a large German city meant that practices of translanguaging were commonplace. Unlike her previous school, where demarcations of insider/outsider were enforced through monolingual practices, such divisions were absent. Rather than index her alterity, English was part of the multilingual fabric of this community and took on a more cosmopolitan value, facilitating rather than excluding her participation.

Being legitimised in this new community had an immediate effect on both her mental health and language learning. When asked to describe her best memory of her time in Germany, she pointed to the multicultural community she had become part of at this second school and the opportunities she had to communicate with people from a diverse range of backgrounds. Importantly for Megumi too, soccer was an ever-present topic of conversation during in-season and one that transcended national and cultural backgrounds. This would frequently generate discussions on social media channels among Megumi's peers and provided constant opportunities for her to take part in the social life of this community.

Megumi also elaborated on the prominence of digital communication among students, as people were constantly interacting online even as conversations were simultaneously taking place in person. This was exemplified during evacuation drills, for example, when students would post and comment online even as they were simultaneously participating in the event in person. The transnational affiliations of Megumi's peers were also readily apparent through the way they customised their mobile devices. For example, students would set the Turkish flag as the background for their smartphones or place stickers of the national flag on their phone cases. This indicated the broader way that mobile devices were integrated into the social world of young people, and their customisation performed important identity work (see Hjorth [2003] for an extended discussion of this phenomenon).

While abroad, Megumi made occasional posts on Instagram, largely featuring touristic images of street scenes, the interiors and exteriors of romantic and gothic-era buildings, food and soccer paraphernalia.

Following Megumi's own explanations and the images she posted, the primary audience for her posts were other Japanese speakers in her networks; however, she often tagged her posts using a combination of German, English and Japanese language tags. In one post featuring an image of a German language soccer rulebook, part of her caption read:

Ich bekomme Deutsch Fußball Regeln!!! Ich kann In Deutschland Schiedsrichter sein!!!!
(I got hold of a German soccer rulebook!!! I can become a referee in Germany!!!)

Given that the comments on her Instagram indicated that her audience at this time was primarily, if not entirely all Japanese speakers, the creation of posts such as this allows her to draw on the exoticness that German linguistic resources held for her audience. From a translocal perspective, it exemplifies how social media platforms like Instagram enable the enactment of locally aligned identities for audiences back home, functioning as digital postcards that can accrue symbolic capital with those audiences.

### Return Identities and Multilingualism Online

A year later, I met Megumi again on Zoom to speak about her experiences after returning to Japan and she had become nostalgic for her time abroad. Despite the initial difficulties she had faced, she explained that she had felt freer at school in Germany and now framed the struggles she had initially faced in terms of resilience. Megumi's ongoing revaluation of the year abroad and its effects on her identity now took into account the realities of the returned school environment.

Despite a focus on the events at her first school during our initial interview, her ongoing understanding of her year abroad appeared to be shaped more by the time she spent among the diverse communities of her second school. This, in turn, meant that like other informants, Megumi struggled to reintegrate into high school in Japan and the constraints she felt it placed upon her. This was compounded by the requirement that she return to the same grade she had departed from and therefore needed to recreate school-based social networks with her 後輩 (kōhai[5]), even as her previous classmates were preparing to graduate. These struggles were further exacerbated by her teachers' attitudes to her year abroad, including forbidding her from interacting with friends and classmates in what was now the grade above.

めぐみ: 夏休み開けたら、すぐテストだったので、まあ、授業の事とか、色々聞きたいなと思って、夏休みとか学校行ったりしたんですけど、なんか、先生が忙しかったりして、あんまり相

|            | 手にしてくれなくて。で、帰って来たばっかりで、本当に夏休み前は友達を作る機会もなく、［…］まあ、そこですごいしんどかったもありますし。なんか、自分が、元々いた学校、元々いた学年、友達とあんまりしゃべるなって言われて、その、まだあんまり友達ができていない状況なのに、［…］ 先生の配慮、配慮というか理解というか、が足りないなと感じました。 |
|---|---|
| Megumi: | We had a test as soon as school got back after the summer break, and I wanted to ask [the teachers] about what we had done in class and things like that. So, I kinda went into school during the Summer but, like, the teachers indicated they were too busy and stuff, they didn't really give me any time. And I'd just got back [from Germany] and so there were absolutely no opportunities to make friends before the Summer Break had started […] yeah, so it was really rough. And I was I was told [by teachers] not to speak with the friends I had from my previous year group, even though I hadn't been able to make any friends in my new year group yet. […] I felt like the teachers were lacking compassion, or you could say lacking understanding. (Megumi, Interview 2) |

Similar to other participants, the linguistic and cultural abilities accrued through her year abroad were not attributed any significant value at the scale of her high school. Megumi's sense of being treated coolly by her teachers, along with restrictions on interaction with her peers prior to her time abroad, further emphasises this disconnect.

Social media also played a crucial role, both in facilitating ongoing use of German resources and in maintaining the social networks she had developed while abroad. Central to this online engagement was the weekly interactions that continued between her and her host mother through WhatsApp. They discussed everyday happenings, life events like birthdays and engaged in collective recollections of things they had shared in the previous year, for example discussing summer in Germany that year and recalling the heat they had experienced together the previous year. Megumi also continued to maintain the peer networks she had developed abroad through both Instagram and Snapchat. Megumi explained that her mode of engagement with these networks had changed from a participatory role to a more passive one of following, where her main activities involved viewing and occasionally liking and commenting on the posts of friends. This was visible on her Instagram account to which she hadn't posted since returning to Japan. This reflects the practice of many of the informants in this study who, upon returning to Japan, reduced the amount of content they posted to social media and therefore the way they engaged with their transnational networks. While the lack of proximity was certainly a factor, many informants pointed to the demands they felt placed upon them returning to Japanese schooling and the expectations and pressure related to university entrance exams as limiting their ability to maintain connections made abroad.

## Reflections: Translocal Flows and Local Linguistic Orders

The significance of Megumi's account lies in the deep contrast offered in her description of her experiences in the two nearby, yet completely different, high schools she attended. While the schools were geographically proximal, their differening populations contributed to very different attitudes towards Megumi and different localised orders of linguistic resources. Megumi's experiences across her two schools complicate the study abroad imaginary of immersive cultural and language learning. While English was used in both schools, the meanings and positionalities it indexes were differently subscribed. In her homestay too, English served to mediate her learning of German, while at her first school it served to deny her this possibility. In effect, the resources and opportunities for language learning are alternatively made available or denied to the individual on the basis of identity and power held by dominant groups (Norton Peirce, 1995), instantiated through localised orders of linguistic indexicality. In the context of language learning abroad, access to linguistic markers of identity and belonging become contingent on local populations seeing sojourners as legitimate users of these varieties, or alternatively ascribing to them an alternate set of resources which signal their alterity.

The depictions of racism that Megumi faced point to the way a sojourner's arrival is situated in, and shaped by, overarching sociopolitical circumstances. It demonstrates the importance of viewing sojourners' experiences and the interactions they engage in as situated in wider historical and political contexts, the language they encounter and use 'indexical of patterns and developments of wider scope and significance' (Blommaert, 2018a: 7). Tensions that emerge at wider political scales reverberate in the interpersonal interactions sojourners must negotiate, serving to structure their experiences and language learning.

For many of the informants, the time they spent abroad was their first experience as a visible minority. The lived reality of many high school students in Japan, and indeed much of the population more broadly, is as members of a majority where questions of race remain abstract, if considered at all (Kawai, 2015). Bauman (2004: 24) has noted how processes of identification increase in significance for the individual, 'once identity loses the social anchors that made it look "natural", predetermined and non-negotiable', and upon entering host community spaces while abroad, informants, like Megumi, began encountering their bodies as sites of racialised difference. This phenomenon has been captured throughout the sociologically informed study abroad literature and many studies have demonstrated the unequivocal connection between ethnoracial identity positionings and language learning (Anya, 2016; Brown, 2021; Goldoni, 2017; Jackson, 2008; Talburt & Stewart, 1999).

Megumi's case represents an important touchstone in this respect, since she experienced racialisation in highly overt ways with direct implications for her language learning, participation and associated social media use. Her exposure to monocular racialising practices that equivocated Chinese with Japanese mirror those of Ada in Jackson's (2008) study of sojourners from Hong Kong, who found herself consistently misidentified as Japanese. In both cases, terms such as 'Japanese' or expressions such as *ni hao* serve simply to index a homogenised Asian other. Megumi's account is illustrative of the way local multilingual repertoires can be operationalised to do the work of racialisation and marginalisation. The aforementioned use of *ni hao* can be seen as one example, as the greeting is appropriated by local students from Mandarin and through a process of semantic racialisation, deployed to index the target's alterity. More pervasive though, was the use of English among her peers to position her as a racial and cultural outsider, denying her both opportunities to be seen as a legitimate member of the community and engage in interactions vital for her linguistic development. It underscores again the tensions that emerge between global imaginaries of English as indexical of transnational interaction and localised imaginaries in which it comes to index outsiderness and alterity.

Megumi's account illustrates the structuring impact that high school has on adolescent experiences of study abroad. Subjected to local instantiations of exclusion, Megumi's use of German online before moving schools was largely limited to performative expressions used to add local flavour to Instagram posts for a Japanese-using audience. However, at her second school, Megumi found belonging among a community with a large migrant population, and it was here that she learned how to draw on the various linguistic practices she was appropriating in both German and English as in-person connections translated into connections online. The interactive affordances available to sojourners through social media are therefore contingent on, and situated in, local realities. Although Megumi encountered racism in the wider community, when spectating at soccer matches for example, at her second school her difference and identity as a Japanese exchange student was something to be valued and shared with others. The translocality of the student population of this school, their mutual status as strangers (Murphy-Lejeune, 2002) in the wider German society with national, ethnic and linguistic links to communities elsewhere engendered Megumi's acceptance as part of their community. Thus, Megumi's account highlights how the sojourner's relative status in relation to members of the host community is instrumental in determining the opportunities to learn and use different linguistic varieties.

The contrasts offered by her two schools also emphasise the ideological nature of language and the importance of using ecological approaches to understand the symbolic value attached to linguistic resources as they move across scales. As Blommaert (2010) has pointed out, the value of language shifts as it crosses cultural and ideological borders, which in Megumi's account is evident in the way that English and Mandarin are enregistered with ideas of race and alterity in her first school, while English and German are seen to index cosmopolitanism at her second school. This analysis is reliant upon Megumi's observations and additional complexity most certainly would have been present. However, there can be little doubt that, through the broad strokes of her retelling, the symbolic value of language in its diverse forms as encountered and negotiated by sojourners abroad has implications for what they can legitimately appropriate and use as they move through different communities. This also includes return contexts, as Megumi's account also shows, where the symbolic value of communicative repertoires is transformed through mobility and evaluated through differing social imaginaries of language and their attendant orders of indexicality.

## Notes

(1) A form of secondary school in Germany that prepares students for higher education.
(2) I was informed at the time that this was a reference to 'GI Joes' or American servicemen.
(3) This is a reference to the first English expression that was traditionally introduced to students in Japan.
(4) Combined high school.
(5) One's junior. The other part of the senpai-kōhai relationship described earlier.

# 6 Manabu: Negotiating Multilingual Identity in Francophone Canada

Manabu's account demonstrates how, despite the perceived value of English, its use may need to be resisted even by non-Anglophone sojourners in order to gain access to non-English resources and identities. Manabu's engagement with digital communications demonstrates the role of technology in informal learning abroad and how online language use comes to reflect that of identities and investments in communities where participation is sought. Manabu's experience also illustrates how processes of language development are embedded with the values, attitudes and identities of the communities in which individuals reside, subjected as they are to translocal flows of people and information.

I first met Manabu on a Saturday morning in November when warmer weather had finally arrived in Melbourne. Located in the Chubu region of Japan, Manabu, however, appeared in a grey hoodie and white earbuds. A row of competition bibs for ski tournaments hung along the wall behind him were an immediate point of interest for me and led to a discussion on his participation in national-level ski tournaments, which he tied to his desire to choose Canada as his destination for study abroad.

Manabu was unique among the informants interviewed for this project in that he had chosen to attend a five-year 高校専門学校 (kōkōsenmon gakkō) or college of technology focused on engineering rather than the traditional three-year high school. Manabu had made this decision because it offered a less demanding path into higher education and provided opportunities to study abroad that would be accredited as part of his secondary education. Due to the distance required to commute from home to school, he had already lived independently for a year in a dormitory and therefore had experience living away from home prior to studying abroad. He was a second-year high school student when he left for his sojourn.

Manabu recalled first hearing about study abroad from a friend of his older brother and being attracted by the idea. The symbolic value he attributed to the experience was indicated in his characterisation of participating in study abroad as かっこいい 'cool' (Manabu, Interview 1).

Important too was Manabu's admission that 「僕があんまり人と同じというのはいやだったんで」 'I didn't really like being the same as other people' (Manabu, Interview 1). Like Nikko, he conceived of study abroad as a means to access an identity that differentiated him from his peers. For Manabu though, the desire was not for an aesthetic exoticness, but an internal sense of exceptionalism. He determined that Canada would be the place he could achieve this while fulfilling other goals, such as skiing in the resort area of Whistler.

| | |
|---|---|
| マナブ： | 僕の留学の目的自体が言語ではなかったので、ただカナダの文化とかが知れるなら、それはすごいでもいいかなっと思って |
| **Manabu:** | The reason I had for going abroad wasn't language, I just wanted to know more about Canadian culture. If that had been all I learned, then that would've been great. (Manabu, Interview 1) |

For this reason, he placed English-speaking Canada as his first choice and French-speaking Canada as his second choice when selecting destination preferences. He then accepted an offer to homestay with a white Francophone family.

## Encounters with Identity through Language

By Manabu's own account, one of the most formative events of his time abroad was also one of the first. Attending the AFS in-country orientation session shortly after arriving in Canada, he immediately began to grapple with issues raised by the linguistic repertoire he possessed and the value it held in these new surroundings.

| | |
|---|---|
| マナブ： | オリエンテーションしてる、がいきなり英語で始まって、で、僕だけ理解しなくて。で、他の子は皆「は〜ん」って感じ理解して、で、ディスカッションとか始めちゃうんですよ。で、僕だけもう[...]「こいつ何やってんだ」みたいな、なんか全然分からなかった、[...]なんかそれが悔しくて。 |
| **Manabu:** | The orientation suddenly began in English and I was the only one who couldn't understand [what was being said], while the other exchange students were going like, 'Uh-huh', just understanding. Then we started discussions and stuff like that and I was the only one [...] who was like 'What is this guy doing?' I couldn't understand a single thing [...] It was frustrating. (Manabu, Interview 2) |

While finding himself seemingly the only exchange student struggling was a shock, this was compounded by the reaction of others towards him and the disconnect he experienced with his own self-image.

| マナブ: | 自分、日本だと、絶対、周りに友達がいる人間なんですよね。(うん)絶対、誰かと一緒に、ワイワイ楽しむし、何でもしている人だったのに、[…]AFSの、コミュニティとか行くと、日本人、「あの日本人しゃべれんから、いや」みたいな、「ちょっとあっち行って」みたいな、そういうのもあって、それできついじゃないですか？(うん)今までは、何なら自分はその、友達と一緒にいる中の中心人物だったかもしれないのに、除外されてしまった、そんな経験が初めてあって、でもそれが辛いことなんですけど |
|---|---|
| **Manabu:** | If this had been Japan, I would have been the type of person who was surrounded by friends. ((mm)) I was the type of person who would always be with people, having a great time, doing everything. But when I was with the AFS community, it was like 'That Japanese can't speak. I don't like him' and 'Just go away' and things like that. That's hurtful, right? ((Yeah)) Until that point, whenever I wanted, maybe you could say I was the centre of attention in a group of friends. But I was excluded [in the AFS community]. That was the first time I had ever experienced something like that. It was hard. (Manabu, Interview 1) |

What Manabu describes here suggests that he was experiencing a threat to what Giddens (1990: 92) calls *ontological security*, 'the confidence that most humans beings have in the continuity of their self-identity and in the constancy of the surrounding social and material environments of action'. Perceiving himself as being actively excluded, Manabu found his identity as a popular and gregarious person surrounded by friends replaced with a sense of helplessness in a location where the linguistic resources he possessed lacked the mobility of those possessed by his peers. The experience left a deep impression on Manabu and brought into sudden focus the acute importance of language to agency and belonging.

Early posts on Manabu's Instagram also underscore his limited local network during the first several months of study abroad. In the month before leaving for Canada, he posted two images, both of himself surrounded by friends. For the next several months, the images he posted were almost all of himself or cultural items such as tinned escargot and hockey jerseys. Yet, even in these early posts, he began captioning his posts in French using his truncated but developing repertoire. This is exemplified in a post that contained an image of himself dressed up in academic regalia for his graduation album with the caption 'j'aime ça #l'école#afs (I like it #school #afs)'.

While linguistically French, these posts performed different types of semiotic labour for different audiences. His Japanese-using audience primarily understood the language as combining with the images to symbolise a sojourner identity which they commented on with expressions such as 'もうかえってくるん？ [sic] (you already coming back?)' and 'え、ドイツ語?? (Huh? Is that German??)'. Through both the selection of images and the truncated use of French, Manabu's posts are read symbolically as 'abroad' by users of Japanese in his audience. On the other hand, local friends in Canada responded to the semantic content of the post. For example, this post received the playful English comment, 'stop lying, everybody knows you don't give a shit about school'. Manabu's posts change meaning as they are read by different audiences, locally and translocally. In this example, Manabu performs both the localised identity of the Francophone high school student and the transnational identity of the Japanese student abroad simultaneously, with the way it is read changing depending onthe contexts and repertoires of the audience.

Although Manabu struggled to form personal connections over the first few months, he was able to rapidly adjust to life with his host family. Similar to Nikko, he found himself living with a Japanese-speaking host sister who was instrumental in facilitating interaction with the rest of the host family.

マナブ： 最初のなんか、何も伝わらないという、[…]普通のことに関する[…]そういうことのストレスはなかったのだから、最初はすごい、助けていただいたので、スムーズにスタートが切れたのかなと思います。

**Manabu:** Even from the start, I didn't have any of that stress not being able to communicate […] about regular stuff […] because [my host sister] really helped me with that from the beginning. So I think I got off to a smooth start. (Manabu, Interview 1)

The support and stability this provided were crucial to his opportunities to appropriate local French-aligned linguistic practices. Firstly, it allowed him to forge connections with the rest of his host family at an early stage that would later provide affordances for language learning. Secondly, it provided an opportunity to join a local amateur ice hockey team.

The interactions that occur over the dinner tables of host families have long been recognised as an important site for language and cultural learning (e.g. Cook, 2006; Iino, 1996; Kinginger & Carnine, 2019; Kinginger & Lee, 2019) and this became the main context in which Manabu attempted to learn French during the early stages of his time abroad.

マナブ： ご飯中は家族同士がみんなしゃべるので、でその会話についていくの最初はなかなか、難しいじゃないですか？速いし（うん）方言もあるし（うん）あと、だからご飯中ずっと耳を澄

|  | まして、どういう会話してんのかをずっと聴きながら食べて、でごはんが終わって、ゆっくりしてきたら、ママと喋って |
|---|---|
| Manabu: | During dinner everyone in the family would be talking to each other, and keeping up with those conversations is pretty hard, right? It's fast ((Yeah)), there is dialect too ((Yes)). So, throughout the meal I had to listen closely, while eating I would be listening and trying to work out what the conversation was about. Then when dinner was finished, when things had settled down, I would speak to [my host] Mum. (Manabu, Interview 1) |

These interactions not only served as a means for Manabu to appropriate the linguistic resources needed to communicate, but also contributed to his growing language awareness. As Manabu indicates, through his interactions with his host family, he became aware of the diversity of linguistic practices subsumed under the idea of 'French' and recognised the importance of local varieties to interaction.

Again, as in so many other cases, it was the availability of Manabu's host mother in the evenings and her willingness to recognise, accommodate and support Manabu as a user of French that proved crucial to his linguistic development. Manabu explained that discussions with his host mother often ranged across the linguistic and cultural, in particular the differences and similarities between French, English and Japanese. These discussions appear to have helped Manabu shift from a deficit view of his own linguistic repertoire to one of possessing valuable, yet different linguistic knowledge to his AFS peers. This was exemplified in an interaction Manabu recalled in which he related to his host mother his struggles to learn French while others in his AFS cohort from European backgrounds seemed to be picking up the language effortlessly. His host mother helped him to understand how the differences stemmed from the closeness of the languages rather than his own failings and encouraged him not to compare himself with others but to develop at his own pace. The reciprocity of these interactions, characteristic of effective developmental processes (Bronfenbrenner & Morris, 2006), and the value placed on his cultural and linguistic knowledge were vital to Manabu's multilingual investment and sense of value as a member of his host family.

Although Manabu's participation in home life remained relatively stable throughout his time abroad, school life was more dynamic. He explained that contrary to his expectations, French Canadians made up less than half of the student body and a large proportion of the students were of other backgrounds, including migrants from Asia, South America and Francophone African countries. Again, as in the previous informants' accounts, the local presence of others with transnational connections to communities elsewhere was influential in shaping Manabu' experiences abroad. One particular group, which he described as 移民 (imin[1]) noted his presence early on and invited him to join them during breaks.

| | |
|---|---|
| マナブ： | 僕は、フランス語喋れないって分かってたんで。だから最初、そういう子達は、そっちから僕に興味を持って、英語で話しかけてくれたんでそういうグループになりました。 |
| **Manabu:** | They knew I couldn't speak French. So those students showed interest in me first and spoke to me in English, and so I became part of that group. (Manabu, Interview 1) |

There are clear parallels here between Manabu's experience and that of Max in Spenader's (2011) study of American adolescent sojourners in Sweden. In that study, Max found himself alienated from the local Swedish population at the high school he attended and the closest relationships he formed at high school were among the 'immigrants'. Although Spenader attributes the notion of 'separation' to this outcome – centring the Swedish-speaking community – it is clear that Max found belonging among an English-speaking group who shared his sense of outsiderness. In Manabu's case too, it was a smaller English-speaking migrant community within the school that first welcomed him and recognised him as a legitimate member. Later in the same interview, Manabu acknowledged the direct connection he understood between the English language and an immigrant identity.

| | |
|---|---|
| マナブ： | 移民がすごい多くて。で、英語喋れるとか、すごい多くて、ダウンタウン行くと大体英語で話しかけられるんですよ。 |
| **Manabu:** | There were a lot of immigrants. A lot of them spoke English or whatever, so when I went downtown, they pretty much only spoke English to me. (Manabu, Interview 1) |

Manabu went on to explain that English was not the only language with this status, as Arabic could also be widely heard throughout the informal contexts of the school and translanguaging involving French, English and Arabic was common. This translingual diversity was part of the fabric not only of the school, but also of the wider community in the area he lived. The linguistic ecology of the school was therefore a microcosm of what was taking place beyond its walls and was something that Manabu appeared acutely aware. Although he acknowledged the linguistic mobility that English provided, he also implicitly recognised the prestige associated with French, perhaps not least of all because of its local association with whiteness.

Manabu's account also exhibits the tension that sojourners from non-Anglophone backgrounds must navigate between globalising imaginations of English and localised orders of indexicality. While

Manabu recognised English as a marker of translocal mobility, he also noted that its use was indexical of populations he associated with – non-local populations. This orientation to local orders of indexicality informs his desire to appropriate French resources that align with what he saw as local identities, including his host family. When it came to questions of language learning, the translocal value of English needed to be weighed against the local identities it indexed. That is not to say that Manabu could focus on only one linguistic variety at a time, but rather which variety he chose to prioritise was influenced by his orientation to scale.

## Learning Affordances in the Digital Wilds

A defining part of Manabu's developmental trajectory abroad was a transformation in his understanding of language learning from a passive process of immersive 'osmosis' to one that required intentionality and commitment. During his interview, Manabu was able to clearly explicate the factors that had led him to adopt a more passive approach initially. The first of these was that he had no explicit knowledge of how to learn a language, explaining that for the first few months, 「何をすればいいかがわからなかった」 'I didn't know what I should do' (Manabu, Interview 1). Perhaps more importantly though was the underlying idea that the act of living in the host community would eventually lead to linguistic competence.

| | |
|---|---|
| リーバイ： | 留学は想像通りでしたか？ |
| Levi: | Did your year abroad go as you imagined? |
| マナブ： | あ、全然、違いました。っていうのは、よく聞く話だと、3ヶ月いれば、「言葉話せるよ、分かるよ」って。聞く、ことがないですか？聞きますよね？（はい）僕は聞いてたんですけど（はい）［…］で3ヶ月たったのに、僕が全然、喋れてないこととか、に気づいて、そこからエンジンかけて、もう、やり始めたって感じです。 |
| Manabu: | Oh, it was completely different. What I mean is, a thing I often heard was that if you are abroad for three months 'You'll be able to speak! You'll understand!' Have you heard that? You've heard that, right? ((sure)) Well, that is what I heard. ((uh-huh)) […] then three months passed and I noticed that I still couldn't speak or whatever. So that's when I got started, I like, hit the ignition switch. (Manabu, Interview 1) |

What stands out from Manabu's narration of his own attempts at language learning was that his initial struggles did not stem from a lack of access to interaction or learning affordances. Instead, the root cause lay in his assumptions about how that learning would take place. Acknowledging the flaws in his beliefs and deciding to adopt a more intentional and strategic approach to his linguistic investment emerge as a point of inflection in his developmental trajectory.

The excerpt shows how widely circulated imaginaries of study abroad encountered before departing as providing access to almost effortless opportunities to learn language can be directly implicated in the language learning practices a sojourner engages in while abroad. What is also evident is the importance that agency can play in reshaping beliefs about language learning, as Manabu's reorientation stemmed from his own critical self-reflection.

Manabu indicated that a combination of language learning applications on his smartphone was central to his learning strategy: Duolingo to increase his vocabulary and LingQ to listen to audiobooks while also reading the text himself. This was supplemented with other resources such as books in French and watching videos on YouTube. Manabu also reported using an electronic dictionary to enable comprehension during classes at school. 「出来るだけフランス語と一緒の時間長くしたって感じですね。'It's like, I would spend as much time with French as I could' (Manabu, Interview 1). Manabu then directly tied the learning he did using these apps to interactions with his host family, highlighting how these learning processes intersected with in-person interactive contexts.

| マナブ： | 家族とできるだけ多く喋って、あの、で、毎回その、部屋で勉強した、覚えた単語を、できるだけ使うようにして、で、家族と話していました。 |
|---|---|
| **Manabu:** | I spoke with my [host] family as much as possible. Also, you know, every time, I tried to use the words that I'd learned as much as I could, the words I'd studied in my room, in conversations with my [host] family. (Manabu, Interview 1) |

Drawing on what has been referred to as the 'digital wilds' (Sauro & Zourou, 2019), Manabu brought the linguistic resources he encountered online into locally situated instances of interaction. Similar to Nikko's account, Manabu actively sought out these resources online, recognising their value in developing competence in local linguistic practices. In this instance, he works across scales in the process of language learning, assembling affordances available through translocal flows and local instances of interaction. Shifting his orientation from assumed passive appropriation to one of active bricolage, he finds himself making tangible progress in his ability to interact at home. Importantly, this took place in a stable, accommodating and supportive social environment, where unfettered access to the 'digital wilds' was available throughout his stay.

Around the three-month mark, Manabu developed a friendship with Antoine, a white Québécois with whom he shared many classes and a bus route home. This relationship created opportunities to connect with Antoine's friends and extend his network of French speakers beyond that of his family and ice hockey club. In particular, a close friend of Antoine's also became friends with Manabu and the three of them spent much of their time at school together.

Despite Antoine and his friend's Francophone backgrounds, they used English to communicate with Manabu. With Manabu's French competence developing through his interactions elsewhere, he actively sought to renegotiate the language of interaction in this part of his network.

マナブ： フランス語あまり喋れなかったんで、最初英語で喋ったんですけど、僕が1回もう、「フランス語に変えようよ」って。言ってから、たまに英語混じってたんですけど。僕が絶対フランス語でしか話さないで。もうフランス語で。会話しています。

**Manabu:** I didn't really speak French, I was speaking English at first. But at one point, I said 'Let's change to French'. After I said that, sometimes English would be mixed in [to our conversations] but I definitely didn't use anything but French and from then on, I was conversing in French. (Manabu, Interview 1)

Returning to the previous observations that Manabu had made about the indexical values of English and French within this community, this can also be seen as a desire to reposition himself in relation to the identities of immigrant/local. By demonstrating his commitment to speaking French, he also sought to demonstrate his alignment to the local identity he perceived his friends holding. Moreover, Manabu explained that finding himself in this multilingual environment, he had begun to imagine himself becoming proficient in both English and French, associating each language with a different group of friends at school.

Despite this, he saw ongoing interactions as contested since Antoine and his friend had different reactions to his request.

マナブ： ［Antoine］は僕には英語で話しかけて、僕は英語を理解して、フランス語で答えるみたいなことが多くて、その3人いたうちのもう一人の人は、僕にフランス語で、頑張って話しかけてくれて。で僕何回も聞き返してみたいな、そんな感じでした。まあでも、それはどんどん良くなってて。

**Manabu:** A lot of the time it was like [Antoine] would speak to me in English, I would understand the English and reply in French.

The other member of our three person group would try to speak to me in French as much as possible, and I would like ask him to repeat things a bunch of times. It was like that. So, I got better [at French] doing that. (Manabu, Interview 1)

This episode again highlights questions of choice, access and identity that govern interactions in multilingual environments and the way that sojourners' experiences are structured by the complexities that emerge when linguistic orders are encountered locally. In Manabu's case, his desire to develop and perform the identity of French speaker was informed by his association of English with a migrant identity. English was, for him, the means of belonging among the community who had initially welcomed him at school, yet his insistence on using French elsewhere despite English being entirely comprehensible represented Manabu's understanding of its symbolic importance in performing the local identities he desired. Additionally, Manabu noted that demonstrating competence in French took on additional significance in relation to his AFS exchange student peers, given the deficit view he initially had of his English competence. He described feeling at less of a disadvantage when comparing his progress in French with them and perceived it as a language he could appropriate to a similar degree during the time spent in Canada.

### Multilingual Belonging

Looking at Manabu's posting habits on Instagram there was a clear change in the types of photos he posted from the seven-month mark into his stay. Beginning with two shots surrounded by members of his hockey club to mark the close of the season, Manabu posted a successive collection of images that highlighted his growing social connections in the local community; standing with friends at Niagara Falls (Month 9), a group shot with his AFS cohort (Month 10), a group shot with his flag football friends (Month 11), two shots celebrating graduation with his two close French Canadian friends (Month 11) and a final image before departing in a restaurant surrounded by a group of friends captioned 'Quelle surprise ♡ (What a surprise ♡)' (Month 12).

The shift in focus from selfies and cultural items to friends was a visual confirmation of the social network development that Manabu described in his interviews, similar to changes that Umino and Benson's (2016) reported finding in the photographic archives of two international students in Japan. The development of Manabu's local peer networks was made further evident in the growing number of comments that appeared in languages other than Japanese. Although Manabu continued throughout his time abroad to caption his images with short sentences and hashtags in

French, the switch from the touristic and cultural to a more communities-oriented focus demonstrates the audience design at work in his posting, as the imagined audience came to include peers living in Canada. The multilingual nature of this audience is also reflected in the – sometimes playful and obscene – linguistic diversity of the comments on Manabu's posts. For example, a photo of prom received the comments 'J'adore :D (I love this :D)', 'This cutest photo! 😍' and '笑イケメンだね〜〜 🙂 (LOL, so handsome~~ 🙂)', while in another post that contained an image of Manabu with the American football team he played with, a poster commented 'Going to miss your okki chinko[2] 🙂' indicating language learning reciprocity in Manabu's peer groups.

The multilingualism and translanguaging present on his Instagram posts were also present in his own developing communicative repertoires as he learned and practiced ways of communicating common among his peers.

| マナブ： | 英語とフランス語を使って話してましたから（うん）何だろう[…]フランス語と英語が混じって話しているんで。 |
|---|---|
| **Manabu:** | I used both English and French to speak ((mm)) What would you say? […] I mixed French and English together when I was speaking. (Manabu, Interview 1) |

Social media also appeared to be a significant element of his participation in peer networks and, like Nikko, this often took place while at school.

| リーバイ： | [カナダに]いる間、なんか、友達いっぱい作って、どうやって連絡取りましたか？ |
|---|---|
| **Levi:** | While you were [in Canada], you made a lot of friends, so how did you keep in touch? |
| マナブ： | 学校の友達ですか？ |
| **Manabu:** | My school friends? |
| リーバイ： | うん。 |
| **Levi:** | Yeah. |
| マナブ： | 普通のアプリで。Facebook とか。あとは、スナップチャット、とか、で、あのコミュニケーションとってました。はい。 |
| **Manabu:** | On the usual apps. Like Facebook. I also used Snapchat and stuff like that to communicate. Yep. |
| リーバイ： | はい。じゃあ、その時は、普通にインターネットが大丈夫だったんですか？なんかちょっと、問題はなかった？ |
| **Levi:** | OK. So, at that time, was, you know, was the internet okay? Did you have any issues? |

マナブ：　そうっす！学校にインターネット、どこにいても学校の中インターネットがあったので、すごい、いつでも連絡とれました。

**Manabu:** It was fine! We had internet at school, wherever we were at school we had internet access, so we could get in touch whenever. (Manabu, Interview 1)

Like other informants, interaction that took place through social media was situated in the social and material contexts of Manabu's school life. Social media was not simply a means to engage with others when face-to-face interaction was not possible, but an additional channel where interactions with friends could take place wherever and whenever. As described before, Manabu's relationships with the English-speaking 'immigrant' group and the French-speaking network clustered around Antoine had emerged from local, in-person encounters; being visually 'recognised' as an outsider in the first instance and sharing the same classes and bus route in the second. His social media participation with these communities now emerged from and reflected these localised in-person relationships, allowing him to further engage with, and participate in, their communicative practices as they took place online, even as he also shared his experiences with transnational Japanese-using networks.

As Manabu's time abroad headed towards its conclusion, he devoted less time to studying and spent more time out with friends, particularly on weekends. Like Nikko, continuing development of his networks and strengthening relationships with friends were made bittersweet by the knowledge that he would soon leave the very communities he now found belonging among. With developing competence too came a greater contextual understanding of his linguistic knowledge.

マナブ：　自分がフランス語勉強してて、分かってくることが増えるじゃないですか？(うん)でも分かったことが増えると、また分からないことも増えるんですよ。(うん、うん、うん)新しいことを発見しちゃうというか、[...]それできりがないんですよ、言語って多分。

**Manabu:** I studied French, so the things I knew about increased, right? ((yeah)) But as the things I knew increased, so did the things I didn't know. ((yep, yep, yep)) I would like discover new things [...] and there is no end to that. That's what language is, maybe. (Manabu, Interview 1)

Manabu described a great sense of satisfaction in the progress he had made during the final gathering of his AFS community before departing. The community had gradually shifted from using English as the main language to French during their monthly meetings and at the final meeting many of the other exchange students praised Manabu for his French ability. For Manabu, to have his identity as a French speaker recognised by those in the community from which he had initially felt linguistically excluded was a significant validation of his progress.

## Return and Renegotiation

Like the other informants in this project, Manabu struggled with the demands of Japanese high school life after returning. In his second-round interview, he indicated that he acutely felt the strictness of high school in Japan, exemplified by rules he now found to be arbitrary, such as being unable to drink water during class. Like other informants, Manabu highlighted the contestation he faced from others at school regarding the way he now performed his identity. He described how students at his school would react, signalling a disconnect between their expectations and his behaviours.

マナブ： 時々あっち[カナダ]で普通だったことやって、やってしまって、で、こっち[日本]でちょっと引かれてしまうこととかもありました。

**Manabu:** Sometimes I would do things, go ahead and do things that were normal there [in Canada] and here [in Japan] there were times that people would recoil a little from me. (Manabu, Interview 2)

This was exemplified in the way that other students accused him of performing 留学かぶれ (ryūgaku kabure), which can be understood as 'over-accentuating one's study abroad experience'. Although Manabu felt that this might be considered a compliment and proof that the changes he had experienced were visible to others, the underlying implication was that he was acting in a way that accentuated his difference to them. The behaviour, seen by Manabu as indicative of his transnationality, was evaluated as violating local norms. It reflects again the way behaviour and language are bound up with ethnoracial notions of Japanese identity as they emerge at the scale of Japanese high schools.

Indeed, like Nikko, Manabu's hairstyle became a target of reproval, his non-conformity evaluated moralistically. He was told by teachers that it was ぼさぼさ (bosabosa), a negative evaluation that connotes messiness, even though it was, as he explained, just permed, and wouldn't be considered strange in Canada. He located the criticism he received on his hair in wider societal attitudes.

マナブ： 日本人って結局髪の毛がまっすぐなんで、とか、みんな黒いはずなんで、そういう髪色とか、髪の毛の形とか、多分こだわってるんですよね、めっちゃ、なんか。髪色なんて、関係

|  | ないから、何か、その人の人格に、多分、僕の意見ですけどね。 |
|---|---|
| **Manabu:** | So Japanese people have straight hair and its assumed everyone has black hair, so people are really particular about hair colour and style I guess. It's just my opinion but I don't think it matters what colour your hair is, it's got nothing to do with a person's character. (Manabu, Interview 2) |

These attitudes, which both Manabu and Nikko reported, reflect widespread practices of policing hairstyles in Japanese high schools, documented both in research (Yoneyama, 1999) and the media (Sekiguchi & Kanazawa, 2022). Indeed, as Mercer (1990: 248–249) argued, hair is a 'medium of significant "statements" about self and society [...] constantly processed by cultural practices that thus invest it with "meanings" and "values"'. In the cases described in this study, the informants used it as a site to perform the cosmopolitan identities they returned with and it therefore became a site for teachers, as representatives of institutional authority, to target through value-based statements. The informants' experiences illustrate how hair is discursively constructed in Japan as a proxy for an individual's moral character and a reflection of a student's attitudes towards education. More broadly, it exemplifies how tensions that emerge between local and translocal evaluations of the seemingly mundane shape sojourners' experiences on return. Confronted with consequences such as exclusion or other punitive responses, the informants find themselves needing to rescale their ways of being and interacting to align with school-based norms. In effect, the transnational resources appropriated abroad become a liability when understood locally.

The other aspect of high school that bothered Manabu was the lack of support he now found for his linguistic competencies, particularly English.

|  |  |
|---|---|
| **マナブ:** | 学校の英語めちゃめちゃ簡単で、なんか、全部ね、全部寝てるというか@(@@)@「これ英語じゃない」[...] だから本当に英語も、家で、好きな時間、なんか、映画見たりとか、TEDを見たりとか、あとはYouTuberを見たりとか。 |
| **Manabu:** | English at school is so simple, like, the whole time I'm just sleeping through it @ ((@@)) @ 'This isn't English!' [...] So really with English too I watch movies or TED talks at home when I want to. I watch YouTubers too. (Manabu, Interview 2) |

Manabu grapples with the disparity between the English presented in the classroom he has returned to and what he has come to understand as English while abroad. Thus, he agentively seeks out online resources through which he can access translocal varieties that he perceives as aligning with the ways of interacting he had participated in while abroad. Although the literature has primarily and understandably focused on processes of language learning as they occur while abroad, often necessitating the negotiation of tensions between classroom learning and language as it is encountered overseas, Manabu's account illuminates a similar challenge upon his return.

In the year after returning from study abroad, Manabu began a part-time job at the coffee shop chain Starbucks. Among young people in Japan, this is considered to be a desirable position due to the symbolic value associated with the brand and the opportunities it offers to use languages other than Japanese as it is often frequented by international visitors and migrant workers over domestic alternatives. The cosmopolitan image of Starbucks was particularly attractive for Manabu upon returning, providing him with opportunities to perform his multilingual identity.

| | |
|---|---|
| マナブ： | やっぱスターバックスだと結構くるんですよね、外国人の方が。でメニュー、あ、メニューは英語でも書いてあるんですけど、やっぱオーダーは英語になるんですけど［…］ただ昨日、スペイン人の方がいて、日本語ペラペラな方なんですけど、あの僕ちょっとスペイン語留学先で覚えたんですよ。挨拶とか、挨拶程度ですけど。でなんかちょっと話したら、すごい喜んでくれたんで、嬉しかったですね。 |
| **Manabu:** | Of course, quite a lot of foreigners come to Starbucks. We have an English menu. So of course they order in English […] Just yesterday, a Spaniard came in. This person is fluent in Japanese. But I remembered a bit of Spanish from my time abroad. Just greetings. And when I just spoke to them a bit [in Spanish] they were really pleased. I was so happy. (Manabu, Interview 2) |

Another benefit that emerged from this job was that the income provided him with increased opportunities for further international mobility. Manabu saw himself travelling to Australia over the Japanese winter and back to Canada in the following summer. He also saw himself travelling to other places connected with the friendships that he had made with other AFS peers in the later stages of his time abroad.

In the months following his return, Manabu continued to maintain contact with those he had met in Canada, across a variety of platforms including Snapchat, Facebook Messenger, Skype and Instagram. Manabu explained how the translanguaging practices he had adopted in Canada were maintained in written online communication.

| | |
|---|---|
| マナブ： | 僕もフランス語で話すんですけど。ちょっと、あっ、この時フランス語分かんないと思った時でも英語を話せば。伝わる |

とかそういうの、はありました。(うん)で今も、友達チャットとかするんですけど。(うん)すごい、すぐその子も英語が混ざるんですよね。( あー)なんか。ところどころフランス、英語が入ってみたいな(うん、うん、うん)感じが、の文章とか。

**Manabu:** I speak French too, but there are times when I think, ah, wait a sec, I don't know the French for this, and if I say it in English then [the other person] will understand. ((mm)) So now, when I'm messaging my friends or whatever, ((mm)) my friend will just start mixing in lots of English [with his French]. ((ahhh)) So it like this bit of the sentence is written in French and that bit is in English ((mm, mm, mm)), like that. (Manabu, Interview 1)

Like other participants, the translocality of social media allowed Manabu to continue to occupy identity positions and engage in linguistic practices denied to him at school. Along with his position at Starbucks, it afforded him the opportunity to orient to scales where he could perform a translocal identity.

During the year that followed his return to Japan, the strength of the connection he had made with his host family facilitated an opportunity to reunite with them. In Manabu's case, this occurred when his host parents visited Japan as part of a trip to see their daughter who had begun an exchange in Japan just after Manabu returned. Manabu now found himself in the role that his host sister had played, interpreting between his parents and host parents.

**マナブ:** 僕の本当の親と僕のカナダのパパとママだったんですけど。そこは会うことができて、で、お酒飲んだりとかして、僕は通訳するんですけど全部、それでちゃんとコミュニケーションも生まれてたんで、うーん、すごい、[…] 楽しかったし、なんか僕としてはそこに、そこのつながりが生まれたのがすごい嬉しかったですね。

**Manabu:** So, it was my real parents and my Mum and Dad from Canada. They were able to meet each other, and they were drinking. I was interpreting everything and real communication happened between them. Yeah. It was so […] enjoyable. Like, because I was there, a connection happened and I was just so happy. (Manabu, Interview 2)

As in the cases of Nagisa and Nikko, transnational crossings connected to their time abroad presented extended opportunities to occupy positions where the diverse linguistic and identity resources they had appropriated abroad were revalued. The joy and fondness with which the informants recalled these moments underscore the deep sense of affirmation they experienced in these moments. Even though they were physically removed from the host community, connections and understandings forged during their time abroad could be recreated and reapplied in other times and places.

The structure of Manabu's high school required a further two and a half years to complete before graduating. As the year after returning progressed, the pressure of the school testing regime and the need to study for industry qualifications limited the opportunities he had to engage with French and English, as well as interact with friends in Canada.

マナブ： もし僕がこのまま話さなくなって、絶対忘れるので、[…]カナダで、仲良くなった友達とコミュニケーションがとれないってことになるんで、(うん)それは悲しいじゃないですか？(うん)[…]それは絶対嫌なので、そのフランス語と英語は大切にしたいというか、これからも喋りたいですよ。だって損になることは絶対にないし。

Manabu: If I go on without speaking like this, I will totally forget […] it will mean that I will stop being able to communicate with the friends I made in Canada ((mm)) That's sad, right? ((mm)) […] I would really hate that, so I want to maintain my French and English. I want to keep using them. I mean it's never going to be a disadvantage. (Manabu, Interview 2)

The ongoing tension between his desire to maintain the competencies he had developed abroad and the pressure exerted by the institutional situation in which he found himself had come to define his time at school. In the interview, Manabu described how he felt that this way of life, the constant pressure and busyness, was not a stage but a feature of Japanese society;「本当は生きるために働くべきなのに。なんか、働くために生きるみたいな」'It really should be working in order to live but, instead it's more like living in order to work' (Manabu, interview 2). This dissatisfaction combined with the opportunities he felt his competencies provided fuelled an imagined future leaving Japan to live and work in France.

**Reflections: Language Learning Negotiations at Local Scales**

Before encountering the host community, Manabu's desire to study abroad had stemmed from a wish to live in Canada and experience life away from Japan. Like many of the informants though, the connection between language, participation and belonging became palpable after arriving and in Manabu's case, the inability to perform his identity as he had in Japan was a strong motivator to appropriate the language tied to the communities he inhabited. One can also look to accounts such as Bill in Kinginer (2008) who prioritised learning French as he sought to participate in various aspects of life in Dijon, or the Japanese women in

Takahashi's (2013) study who sought to access white Australian society in Sydney, to see how language learning abroad is very often intertwined with a desire to be recognised and accepted as a legitimate participant by members of the host community.

When considering Manabu's account from a scalar perspective though, we gain further insights into how different imaginaries of language and identity come to shape the language learning opportunities that sojourners perceive while abroad. Manabu subscribed to an imaginary of study abroad where through immersive contexts he would soak up language and cultural experiences. Instead, he finds that local realities do not support this and reorients himself to agentively appropriating the linguistic resource he perceives as being most valuable.

At local scales the presence of immigrant communities at school allowed Manabu to be recognised and legitimised through affiliation with their transnationality and use of English. However, his perceptions of the prestige that French held over English in the wider community, particularly its association with localness and whiteness, led to a prioritisation of French resources and a desire to negotiate their use among his Francophone friends. This informed Manabu's use of online language learning affordances which then, in turn, informed his interactions with others including his host mother. Once he returned to Japan, social media was transformed from a means to engage in local interactions and perform his experiences for those in Japan to a means to maintain links to a transnational identity he feared losing among the local pressures of schooling. Moreover, while his ability to use Japanese appeared completely unrecognised among his AFS peers, the use of Japanese among friends he formed within the host community demonstrated the value they saw in appropriating and using the language themselves. Through his transnational mobility, Manabu came to consider the value of linguistic resources across different communities and what they represented as markers of his own identity within those communities. Like Nikko in particular, the decisions he made in regard to language learning were driven by orientations to local contingencies.

As evident from the accounts of other informants, social media interaction with classmates is a concurrent and integral part of their school lives, playing a significant role in their development of social connections. As Manabu described, the presence of wifi access in his host high school allowed students to exchange messages regardless of their location, transcending the limitations imposed by physical proximity. The stark contrast between Manabu's ability to connect to wifi at school in Canada and Nagisa's disconnection at school in Brazil highlights how local material conditions intersect with the social aspects of their experiences as sojourners.

Altogether, Manabu's account further underscores the need for a view of language learning abroad that recognises its inherent multilingual complexity, translocality and extension beyond a demarcated 'return'. His pursual of a part-time job at Starbucks and ongoing connections to the host community after returning along with his ongoing negotiations with the forces he felt at his Japanese high school are a testament to this.

## Notes

(1) Immigrants.
(2) Misspelled Japanese expression 「大きいチンコ」 which is an obscene form of 'large penis'.

# 7 Misa: Social Support and Language Learning in the US Midwest

Misa's account provides a crucial contrast to those of the other informants since issues of belonging led to her disengagement with the host community while social media served as a both a source of social support and escapism. A change in host families part way through her sojourn demonstrates the decisiveness of this social context in study abroad language learning. The circumstances under which Misa disengaged problematises reductionist perspectives by illustrating the complex interplay of social, geographical and individual factors that shaped her difficulties with interacting. It also emphasises the significance of considering localised power dynamics and material realities when investigating processes of language learning abroad.

Misa was a second-year high school student who lived in Tokyo with her parents and older sister before going abroad. Attending a high school that had a large number of kikokushijyo, as well as an active population of students studying abroad at any given time, she would have been exposed to discourses that emphasised the importance of international experience. Her interviews were some of the most challenging I faced during the project in terms of eliciting detailed responses. Reviewing my recordings and notes later, I found that during these interviews, conducted entirely in Japanese, I was continually prompting for further elaboration and detail, something that hadn't occurred to that degree with other participants. This led me to infer that a contributing factor to some the difficulties Misa faced abroad may have been a reluctance to take a more agentic role in interactions.

When asked, Misa did not consent to providing access to her social media accounts as the other informants in this book did, although she did send me a few screenshots of conversations as they specifically related to questions in the interview. Misa's narrative is the sole account in this book of a sojourner who travelled to a predominantly Anglophone community. This makes Misa's perspective particularly noteworthy for the contrast it provides, and its demonstration of how individual factors intersect with material and symbolic contexts to structure language learning opportunities abroad. Moreover, Misa's account also demonstrates the importance of recognising the scalar nature of mobility: a sojourner who has travelled across the globe can find themselves rendered immobile in host community settings.

Misa attributed her initial interest in studying abroad to a talk given by one of her senpai on their first-hand experience participating in an exchange programme. Misa reported that she enjoyed English as a subject but felt at a disadvantage compared to her kikokushijyo peers. Misa's questionnaire and interview responses indicated that she viewed study abroad as a means to develop her English competence and improve her chances with university entrance exams and later career. In effect, Misa's motivations reflect the conventional social imaginary of study abroad and the benefits it will inculcate in sojourners (Kubota, 2016). Despite this, she expressed reservations about the idea of spending a full year abroad and only decided to apply to AFS after a close friend also expressed a desire to apply. Misa reportedly opted for a placement in America due to it being the only English-speaking destination still available at that time. One detail that helps to contextualise Misa's experience is that several times during her interviews, she expressed regret that she had missed many opportunities to interact with others while abroad.

## Passivity and Learning through Osmosis

Misa received the contact details of her host family prior to departing and exchanged several messages with her host sister in this period. An excerpt of these conversations shown to me after our first interview focused on Misa's own imagined experience, including her desire to wear a gown at graduation and the subjects she would take at school. These interactions were perhaps foretelling of how their relationships would later play out, lacking reciprocity in the form of questions from the host sister and in Misa's curiosity about the host family itself. Importantly, they highlighted how Misa's imagination of American high school life was located in the performance of certain rituals rather than developing interpersonal connections.

Upon arriving at her host family's suburban residence in the US Midwest, these romanticised notions of life abroad collided with the practices of her host family.

| | |
|---|---|
| ミサ： | 朝、アメリカは、やっぱ海外は普通かもしれないんだけど、朝ご飯作ってくれなくて、自分でなんか、シリアル勝手にとって食べたりとか […] 日本ではその、お母さんが作ってくれるから、やっぱりそこは自分で用意しなくてはいけないのが大変だった。 |
| **Misa:** | In America, in the morning, this is probably normal overseas but, breakfast isn't made for you. You need to get your own |

cereal to eat [...] In Japan, your mother makes breakfast for you, and it was hard having to get it ready yourself. (Misa, Interview 1)

In moving into a new social context, Misa finds herself needing to orient towards different expectations; getting yourself breakfast is perceived as an American practice while having 'your mother' cook it for you is Japanese. Putting aside other critiques we could make of these notions, they demonstrate important orientations to scale that are taking place as Misa grapples with a new and unfamiliar order of cultural norms, reading them at national scales rather than the more localised scales of the family. This reflects an imagination of study abroad as occurring at national scales; Misa saw herself as a representative Japanese high school student travelling to live with a 'typical' American family.

Misa quickly found that she lacked the linguistic resources to operate on a day-to-day level, both to complete simple tasks such as understanding how to operate her locker at school and to interact with classmates. Misa struggled to understand and contribute to the conversations happening around her, impacting her ability to form meaningful relationships and contributing to a growing sense of isolation. As Misa revealed, this inability to participate was not purely a matter of linguistic repertoires.

ミサ: 普通の友達みたいな関係が全然できなくて。やっぱり留学生だからみたいな感じで接してくる人も多くて、なので、それは本当に、つらかったですね[...]アメリカ人同士は、やっぱすごいジョークとか言えるし[...]今までその幼稚園の話とか、[...]でも私は、そのつい2〜3ヶ月前に来た、ただの日本人という感じだったので、やっぱ話の内容もそんなに深くまでできないし。ただなんか、「さっきの授業大変だったね」とかその簡単な会話しかできなかった。

**Misa:** I couldn't make any connections that were like normal friends. There were lot of students there who were [not interested] because I was an exchange student and so that was really tough. [...] The Americans were able to joke with each other [...] and they would talk about what had happened back in pre-school [...] but for me, I had only arrived two or three months before, I was just the Japanese student, so I couldn't say much about those things. All I could say was 'That last class was difficult' or something, those kinds of simple conversations. (Misa, Interview 1)

Misa's sense of positioning as a *stranger* is emphasised by her peers' choice of topics that allowed them to demonstrate their insider status. By maintaining a topic on which localised knowledge was required,

Misa was excluded from participation, not only through her linguistic repertoire but also through the status conferred through her lack of shared history. This returns us again to the role of the host community in facilitating the participation of the sojourners and mediating their positionality from that of the *stranger*. Putting aside questions of intentionality, this episode again illustrates the power of locals, both through their linguistic competence and shared role as insiders, to determine who could and could not participate at an interactional level.

Misa's response to these difficulties is instructive, since it stands in contrast to those of Manabu and Megumi who also felt marginalised at different points during their time abroad by their inability to participate in local practices of interaction.

| | |
|---|---|
| リーバイ： | その時どうしたんですか？ |
| **Levi:** | What did you do at those times? |
| ミサ： | その時は、もう何もできなくて。えっと、日本人の一緒に留学している子に相談してるとか、でも実際向こうも同じような問題抱えてて。(うん、うん、うん)でもえっと、AFS通信という、AFSが2、3ヶ月に一回出してる新聞みたいな記事があって、で、そこに「やっぱり慣れるまではしょうがない」って書いてあって。その時英語も分かるようになるし、なんか、そういう、「コミュニケーション取れるようになる」って書いてあったの。それを本当に信じるしかなくて。ひたすら時が過ぎるの待ってました。 |
| **Misa:** | At those times, there was nothing I could do. I talked to another Japanese student who I was on exchange with, but they said they were actually dealing with the same problem. ((mm, mm, mm)) There was something called 'AFS *tsūshin*', every two or three months AFS would put out like a newspaper with articles in it and in there it said 'it can't really be avoided until you get used to it'. 'When you get used to [life in the host community] you'll become able to understand English'. It said in there, 'You'll become able to communicate with others'. So there was nothing but to believe in that. I just waited for that time to pass. (Misa, Interview 1) |

The first point to note is that Misa sought support from a fellow Japanese sojourner, which makes sense given her linguistic repertoire and will be discussed in more detail in the next section. The second point though, is how Misa found reassurance in AFS communications that promoted a discourse of language learning by osmosis – a generally held notion that the immersive contexts of study abroad can lead to gains in target language ability simply by being there (discussed further in Kubota [2016]). Misa's uncritical acceptance of this discourse and her resolution to wait until she acquired English competence in order to communicate more effectively contrast with Manabu's response to the same reported discourse. While they both encountered this discourse in relation to their time abroad, their diverging reactions to it underscore how complex interactions between individuals and their environments lead to the emergence of different approaches to language learning.

## Local (Im)Mobilities

In addition to the reported sense of exclusion at school, Misa also explained that as time went on, the relationship with her host sister also began to deteriorate.

| | |
|---|---|
| ミサ： | 私のホストシスターは、まあ優しかったんですけど、(はい)そんなにフレンドリーではなかったので、その、質問したりとか、向こうが、指摘しても、その反応が結構薄くて、(うん)、で、私がそれに、なんか嫌われてるんじゃないかって思っちゃったりとか。(うん)結構怖い印象、を、あの、得たので。それで結構、あの、喋ることに、抵抗感じてしまって。でどんどん、どんどん、向こうもそれ気がついて、どんどん喋れなくなってお互い、(うん)その距離ができて、壁ができてしまって。 |
| Misa: | My host sister was, well she was kind, but she wasn't that friendly. So if I asked her questions, her reaction was pretty half-hearted, ((mm)) So, because of that I thought that maybe she didn't like me. ((mm)) I got quite a negative impression from her. I felt that she was quite reluctant to speak to me. Then over time she noticed that I felt like that and we gradually stopped speaking to each other. ((mm)) The distance grew between us and there was like a wall between us. (Misa, Interview 1) |

As in the accounts of other informants, this relationship became more strained over time. However, the breakdown in this relationship had ramifications for Misa's opportunities for interaction and her mobility in the host community. The town where Misa lived required a car to travel almost anywhere. This included travel to and from school each day. The car used was not a neutral space but belonged to the host sister, who drove and therefore controlled not only the departure time and route, but also how that space was used. It would therefore have been implicitly understood as a space orientated to English language use. Under different circumstances the car could have become a place where regularly recurring interactions may have provided opportunities for language and cultural learning to take place. Instead, the only sound during these trips came from the car radio. Misa reported a lot of anxiety around communicating in the car, which again she attributed to more than her own linguistic repertoire.

| ミサ: | 結構、その子は文句言う子だったので、友達とかすごく仲良い友達の悪口とかを普通にお母さんとかに言ってたので、[...] 自分の意見を言ったらそれにすごい反抗してくるんじゃないかと思って。 |
|---|---|
| Misa: | [My host sister] was actually someone who complained quite a lot. About her friends for example, friends she was really close to, she would just say terrible things about them to [my host] mother. [...] I thought that if I ever said what I thought, she would go against me. (Misa, Interview 1) |

The localised space of the car became, at that time, associated with silence and anxiety for Misa through the daily routine of driving to and from school. By possessing more resources for initiating and encouraging interaction under localised norms, Misa's host sister would also be able to enforce practices which limited that interaction. The dynamic of non-interaction would have been difficult to resist, even if Misa's ability to renegotiate the nature of this space had been greater. However, Misa's local mobility was tied to her use of the car and her lack of any resources beyond those granted to her by the host family thus limited her ability to modify her circumstances.

The tension with her host sister also extended into the space of the home, complicating Misa's relationships with her host parents.

| リーバイ: | コミュニケーションしにくい場面、車以外ありましたか？ |
|---|---|
| Levi: | Were there places other than the car where it was difficult to communicate? |
| ミサ: | 車以外、二人っきりではなかったんですけれど、やっぱり一緒にご飯食べる時は [...] 4人、私とホストシスターとペアレンツ（うん）[...] やっぱり結構沈黙が続くとどうしようかなと思ったりとか、（うん）あとは、はい、結構、そのファミリーが、あの、内輪ネタが多かったりとかして、その全然、あの、昔のこととかは知らないので理解できなかったりとか。 |
| Misa: | Other than the car, it wasn't just the two of us but when we ate meals together [...] the four of us, me, my host sister and [host] parents ((yeah)) [...] I wondered what I should do if that silence was to continue a lot. ((yeah)) Also, yeah, the host family had a lot of inside jokes, and I had no idea about things that had happened long ago and couldn't understand [their conversations] at all. (Misa, Interview 1) |

Again, Misa felt marginalised by topic selection and the way it deprived her of opportunities to engage. This illustrates how the structures of power that exist within the localised space of host families can limit a sojourner's ability to contribute to family life. Effectively, orientation to (un)shared histories again highlighted Misa's role as *stranger* and excluded her participation, even in a passive role. Moreover, Misa again sees herself as relatively powerless to resist or renegotiate these situations.

However, Misa was not entirely powerless, as digital communication afforded her the ability to interact beyond her host family with a Japanese friend also on exchange in the United States. Prior to encountering difficulties in the host family, Misa had already been spending her evenings talking to this friend on Skype. Misa explained that earlier in the sojourn, her friend had encountered issues with her own host sister and these conversations had developed into nightly sessions of support and solidarity. I asked her about the content of these conversations.

ミサ: お互いどういう状況とか、悩みが本当に大きかったですね。それぞれやっぱり ホストファミリーとかにも結構不満を持ってたりとかも、それでどうしたいかとかもありましたし、あとホームシックお互いになって、[...]で今日本こういう事が起きてるんだよみたいな報告し合って、(うん)はい、相談とかもし合ってました。

Misa: [We talked about] each other's situations for example, we were both really troubled by them. We both had a lot of complaints about each of our host families and talked about what we wanted to do about the situation. We both became homesick [...] we would let each other know about things that were happening in Japan we heard about. ((mm)) Yeah. We would discuss what we should do. (Misa, Interview 1)

It is difficult to know to what extent hearing about her friend's difficulties served to reinforce Misa's interpretation of her own situation, however, it is clear she experienced feelings of homesickness and isolation.

Due to her limited ability to interact in English and a social context in which Misa felt excluded, she was unable to develop or draw on social networks in the host community in the same way that other informants such as Nikko and Nagisa did when faced with similar issues. In this way, digital technology served to mediate translocal connections outside the host community. In Misa's account, we therefore find an experience that aligns with notions of digital technology as facilitating sojourners' disengagement from the host community. What Misa's account shows is, at least in her case, the practice was not born of a desire to disengage, but rather a way to help cope with the interpersonal difficulties she was facing in a place where she was already feeling isolated.

Later, Misa suffered a broken leg, which meant she could not participate in extracurricular sporting activities at school, further limiting her already constrained mobility and interaction outside of the host family. Her host sister was active in a different sporting club and was out with her host parents at related events most evenings, leaving Misa at home by herself. Feeling estranged and confined to the house, Misa spent most her evenings alone at home watching Japanese language videos on YouTube.

| | |
|---|---|
| ミサ： | もう、その時やることがなくて、ずっとYouTube見てたりとか、で、それも結構日本のものを見てしまったので、それを本当に後悔ですよね。 |
| **Misa:** | There was nothing to do anymore, so I just watched YouTube and stuff like that the whole time. And what I watched was pretty much just Japanese stuff which I really regret now. |
| リーバイ： | 後悔ですか？なんで後悔って言いますか？ |
| **Levi:** | You regret it? Why do you say you regret it? |
| ミサ： | やっぱりその、アメリカに行って、アメリカにいるのに、その日本のものから離れないというのは、やっぱり来てる意味がないと思ったので、あと英語の勉強になりませんし。 |
| **Misa:** | So, despite going to America, being in America, I couldn't, how do you say, get away from Japanese stuff. I thought there was no point in me going there, and it didn't help me study English. (Misa, Interview 1) |

Although many of the other informants used YouTube as a resource for language learning, it became a way for Misa to pass the time, and perhaps more importantly, cope with the isolation she was experiencing as she waited for her sojourn to end. In retrospect, she admits regretting spending her time this way, yet it is apparent from her statements that there was an element of comfort to be found in media that connected her with Japan. Ecologically, Misa's engagement with Japanese language media online can be located in the intersecting conditions of isolation at school and home, exacerbated by the material conditions of her injury. It was also interdependent with a personal disposition towards passivity and a perceived lack of English language development. She had subscribed to the study abroad imaginary of language learning through osmosis but now found herself feeling disempowered and despondent. Disengagement from the host community and attendant language learning was therefore something arrived at through a confluence of overlapping elements of the social, material and psychological circumstances . In effect, they limited not only her motivation, but also her agency to engage in the appropriation of local communicative practices.

With around two months remaining in the United States, an AFS representative arrived to resolve a situation that had now deteriorated to a complete communication breakdown between Misa and her host family. Misa was granted a change of host family for the final months of her stay. The day after she graduated from her host high school, Misa collected her things and left her host family without speaking to any of them.

## Host Family Contexts and their Impact on Linguistic Development

Misa's host new family lived in a town about half an hour away from the previous host family. In contrast, they were an older couple whose children had already left home and had hosted exchange students several times in the past. This change stood as a point of demarcation in Misa's account as the new environment was instrumental in reshaping her orientation to language learning. The most significant difference that Misa described was the opportunities to communicate and engage with her host parents.

| | |
|---|---|
| リーバイ： | 前のホストファミリーと新しいホストファミリーで何が一番違ったんですか？ |
| **Levi:** | What was the biggest difference between your previous host family and your new host family? |
| ミサ： | やっぱり、その、質問ちゃんとしてくれたりとか、なんか、自分が喋るような機会を与えてくれたので、その自分が思ったより積極的になれるような、前のホストファミリーは、やっぱりシスターがいたので、やっぱりシスター中心に家族が回ってて、なので、あの、はい、会話に入るような機会があまりなかったですけど、2番目の家族は、そのちゃんと待って、私が言うまで待ってくれるみたい、その話す機会はちゃんと与えてくれたので、それは本当に自分の意見もしっかり言いましたし、すごく、はい、いい時間でしたね。 |
| **Misa:** | So, [the new host family] would actually ask me questions, like, they would give me chances to speak. I could be more active in conversations than I thought. With the previous host family, [my host] sister was there and so she was the centre of everything and the rest of the family revolved around her. So, yeah, there weren't really many chances for me to join conversations. But with the second [host] family, they would wait for me, like, wait until I spoke. They gave me proper chances to speak, so I was actually able express my opinions clearly. I had a great time with them. (Misa, Interview 1) |

Misa found her mobility markedly improved in her new environment. Her new host parents were both retired and so could provide transport to both see friends and visit places that Misa had been unable to go with her previous family. This episode demonstrates how, in Misa's case, the nature of her host family and the types of support they offered her were crucial to her experience. Furthermore, the contrast between the two host families underscores how dependent adolescents are on their host family and how this can structure their opportunities while abroad.

Misa also found that she was now living close to an exchange student from Thailand who she had been friendly with during AFS meetups. With school finished, Misa began spending a lot of time at this friend's host family's house, swimming in the family pool and watching English language movies together. In response to this, I asked whether these changes had also affected her social media use and she explained that she hadn't opened her computer once since making the move.

| | |
|---|---|
| ミサ: | まず2番目のホストファミリーが結構そのwi-fiがない状況でとりあえずそのケータイは使わないような使えない状況だったので、本当にあの全然見れなかったというのはひとつだし、あとはやっぱり一緒にいる時間が多かったのでやっぱ家にいないということもなかったのでその少しでも暇な時間があったらどこかに連れてってくれたので。 |
| **Misa:** | One reason is my second host family didn't have wifi and I couldn't use my mobile phone, so I couldn't really watch those things, and the other is I spent a lot of time with them, so I wasn't always at home. When we had free time my host parents would take me somewhere. (Misa, Interview 1) |

Again, Misa's account illustrates how affordances for, and the agency to engage in, language learning are entwined with issues of power, access and local material realities. Geographical proximity to another exchange student, a change in hosts and more free time provided Misa with the circumstances to transform her relationship to English language learning. Upon completion of these final months, Misa reported a marked difference in her ability to comprehend and participate in English language interactions to the point that she experienced a strangeness when she could again use Japanese to communicate upon returning.

It is important also to note that Misa saw the lack of connectivity as a positive contribution to her final months. It contrasts with Nagisa's experience where a lack of connectivity at school was detrimental to her participation in local peer communities. Perceptions of, and engagement with, affordances for language learning emerge at the intersection of the individual and the contextual, highlighting the particularity of sojourner experiences and the need to view elements such as digital communications and host families, not in absolute terms but as dynamic elements of context.

## Return to Normality

Arriving back in Japan during the summer vacation of her final year in high school, Misa was immediately immersed in jyuken. In some sense, this was reassuring since Misa described the situation as 「全然違和感がない」 'not feeling out of place at all' (Misa, Interview 2). She was able to share her experiences with the friend that she had been Skyping with while in the United States, and now found herself able to participate in the same classes as her kikokushijyo peers. The impact of the time spent with her first host family was still tangible and associated with strong feelings of regret.

ミサ： そういう[ホストファミリー]ことを考えると、ちょっと気が引けるし。結構後悔するような部分はたくさんあるんで、そういうこと考えると、落ち込む時もあるし、あと、たまに夢に出てきたりとか@、そういうこともしますね。

**Misa:** When I think about [that time with the host family], I feel a bit ashamed. There is quite a lot of parts I regret. When I think about it, there are times it makes me depressed. Also, occasionally I will have dreams about it @ That happens too. (Misa, Interview 2)

More than the positive experiences in the final months of her time abroad and the development of her English repertoire in those months, the time spent with her first host family had defined how she understood her time abroad. The one major difference she identified in herself was an improved ability to communicate both within her own family and among her friends at school that she tied to increased tolerance and empathy.

One area of Misa's account that particularly resonated with the other informants was the sense of restriction that she felt upon returning to high school in Japan.

ミサ： やっぱりもう勉強量が違うので、もう宿題の量も多いし、テストを、毎日テストがあったりとか、塾も行ってるので、アメリカに行った時はもう家に6時ぐらいに帰ってきたら、ずっと自由時間だったんですけど。もう最近は夜の9時ぐらいまで塾にいなきゃいけないので。もう、あの、自分の自由な時間をあまり持ってない、で大変。

**Misa:** Of course the amount we have to study [in Japan] is different, there's so much more homework, tests, every day we have a tests for example. I'm going to *jyuku*[1] too. When I went to America, I'd already be home by 6pm and then it would just be free time. But recently I have to be at *jyuku* until 9pm, so now I don't really have any free time and that's tough. (Misa, Interview 2)

Contrasting with other informants but aligning with her own ongoing sense of powerlessness to shape the circumstances she found herself in, she sees the surrounding environment as something immutable that she must simply bear,「日本の[...] 文化というか、[...] 受験生なので、しょうがないことかなと思います」 'You could say it's Japanese [...] culture [...] and since I'm a jyukensei, I don't think it can be helped' (Misa, Interview 2). Importantly though, it again demonstrates how local imaginaries of identity, in this case the jyukensei, serve to structure sojourners' orientations to identities aligned with their time abroad.

In the year after she returned, the only person she appeared to remain in contact with was her friend from Thailand, who came to Japan as part of a university exchange programme. During an opportunity they had to reconnect in person, Misa stated that they found it harder to communicate than they had while in the United States but were still able to enjoy the moment. Regarding Misa's plans for the future, she was focused on moving on to higher education in Japan. Misa stated that any future study abroad would be short term and probably in Europe, remaining ambivalent about further experiencing different ways of living or learning language abroad.

## Reflections: Disengagement and Localised Regimes of Power and Mobility

Earlier in this book, I pointed out how 'disengagement perspectives' of technology have been prominent in the study abroad language learning literature. On the surface, Misa's account would seem to support this perspective, as her interactions with a co-sojourner in Japanese on Skype and her retreat into Japanese language channels on YouTube co-occur with a general disengagement with her host family. The ecological details of Misa's account problematise the reductionism of this perspective, demonstrating the array of social, geographical and individual factors that contributed to her use of social media in Japanese and providing a ready counterexample in her second host family. Importantly, it shows how Misa's disengagement emerged through an array of different environmental and personal factors.

The study abroad literature has demonstrated the degree to which homestays can shape opportunities for language learning, being sojourners' primary form of social contact and providing (or preventing) access to new settings for language use (Dewey *et al.*, 2013; Grieve, 2015; Shiri, 2015). In Misa's case, a limited repertoire of English and her dependence on her host family constrained her ability to negotiate or exist beyond the confines of home and school. Localised regimes of power structured interactional dynamics and Misa's access to transportation, with effects on her ability to engage in language learning. The benefit of viewing sojourners' experiences ecologically is that we can identify the way that unequal relations of power manifest through a variety of practices that serve to shape their language learning.

In this way too, we can see how Misa's usage of social media is situated both within her own individual predispositions and the wider ecology in which she found herself. As she described it, Misa's use of social media, primarily in Japanese, was prompted by the circumstances she found herself thrust into, driven not by a desire to disengage but a sense of despair. The structuring effect of the host family on her social media habits is underscored by her account of transitioning to a second host family. The new familial arrangement was more accommodating and characterised by increased interaction and opportunities to engage with an exchange student from Thailand. This helped to redefine Misa's relationship with the English language and affirm her status as someone worthy of interaction; even as her desire to use social media was diminished.

Misa's account also serves to further illustrate how the tension that emerges between widespread imaginaries of study abroad and local realities shapes their experiences. As Manabu also reported, Misa subscribed to the belief that language learning would occur simply by being immersed in English. However, unlike Manabu, Misa perceived herself as without agency in the process, finding affirmation for this in the materials she received from AFS. What Misa's account reveals is that local homestay conditions were a key structuring condition on her opportunities for language learning.

In the context of the other informants' accounts, Misa's case highlights the particularity of individuals' experiences and the way that the translocal affordances of digital communications technology may be differently perceived. In spite of Misa's struggles, it is significant that the closest relationship developed outside of her host family was a fellow exchange student, with implications for her learning of English. That they met up again in Japan only further emphasises the need to view language learning abroad from perspectives that move past parochial notions of host communities.

### Note

(1) Privately run schools which offer supplementary classes after school hours and on weekends with a primary focus on entrance exams; sometimes called 'cram schools' in English.

# 8 Translocal Language Learning and Belonging during and beyond Study Abroad

## What Did This Book Set Out to Do?

When first designing the project which informed this book, I wanted it to address areas I saw as crucial yet underattended to in studies of language learning abroad. Primary among these were the experiences of adolescent sojourners who were travelling from non-Anglophone backgrounds to locations across the globe. When I encountered these people through my work in Japan, I was struck by the way they sought out and grappled with deep challenges to their identities at a period in their lives when status among their peers was pre-eminent, while also undertaking the often knotty and exhausting enterprise of language learning.

Although I incorporated methods designed to capture the sojourners' use of digital media into the design of the project, I hadn't anticipated the degree to which it would emerge in the narratives of their experiences. During the interviews and later analysis, it became apparent that social media was used differently across the cohort, both abroad and in the year after returning. Their accounts demonstrated the intrinsic importance that online communication had in adolescent social life across Japan, Brazil, Canada, the United States, Germany and Hungary.

Their accounts were also revealing of the way that other transnational populations were a significant influence on how they perceived themselves and approached language learning abroad. The presence and influence of other sojourners have been a reoccuring theme in the study abroad literature (e.g. Coleman, 2015; Hasegawa, 2019; Murphy-Lejeune, 2002; Twombly, 1995); however, the presence of extant communities connected to transnational migration has been less prominent and yet has played an important role in many of the participants' experiences covered in this book.

Therefore, what we see emerging are experiences of studying abroad and return that involve the translocal negotiation of interpersonal connections, identity and language learning. In many cases, these negotiations are mediated by digital communications technology and local instantiations of English. The informants' encounters with language at local scales conflicted with globalised imaginaries of study abroad as an immersive experience of parochialised linguistic and cultural absorption. They found themselves prioritising certain varieties as they orientated to the linguistic practices of their communities and confronted a revaluation of ensuing transnational identities upon returning to Japan. In the following sections, I discuss what I believe to be the key findings of this study and their implications for study abroad research and planning.

## Conceptualising Digital Communications in Study Abroad Language Learning

This book has grappled with the ways that digital communications, in particular social media, intersect with experiences of language learning abroad. Although there may be some nostalgic yearning for an era of study abroad when contact home was limited to postal services or long-distance calling cards, the interactive reality of host communities is now very much intertwined with the online. Affordances for language learning can emerge through interpersonal connections made, maintained or developed online, while the asynchronicity and visually centred multimodality of social media offer alternative ways to appropriate and exercise the communicative practices of the host community. Although an ongoing focus on experiences abroad has generally meant that the research has primarily dealt with the affordances of digital communications in host countries, this book has also highlighted how ongoing connections can serve to support participants' linguistic development in the months and years that follow. Digital communications technology and the current iteration of social media platforms allow both local and international vectors of interaction and therefore must be accounted for across the totality of participants' experiences, including the pre- and post-sojourn phases.

The informants' journeys included in this book identified affordances they perceived digital media offering them and how these affordances emerged ecologically. The case studies demonstrate that the ways informants used digital technology were co-constitutive of the communities they inhabited. They also show how the affordances they percived this technology offering them were transformed between communities and across borders. Below, I outline three main ideas that must inform our thinking moving forward.

### The affordances of digital communications technology are interrelated to local realities

Digital communications cannot be regarded as something external to, or additive of, the contexts of study abroad. As the case studies have illustrated, the affordances that the informants perceived digital connectivity offering them were intimately tied to the social, material and symbolic contexts they inhabited. During their time abroad, this manifested as an ability to connect with locals as a normative part of peer sociality and facilitated deepening connections and intimacy. Language learning abroad research has continuously affirmed the centrality of interpersonal connections to sojourners' linguistic development (Isabelli-García, 2006; Kurata, 2004), particularly the positive influence of network size (Dewey *et al.*, 2014) and relationships across diverse contexts (Zappa-Hollman & Duff, 2015). Social media in particular represents not only an additional context for these connections, but also one that allows them to be extended beyond immediate spatial and temporal circumstances.

The desire to be seen as a legitimate member of local communities also means appropriating the linguistic means to claim associated identities. Social media and other attendant online resources can mediate both appropriation of and engagement with locally relevant varieties. This was seen in informants' attempts to develop their communicative repertoires through their observations of, and participation in, platforms such as YouTube. The use of language associated with host communities online also demonstrated how social media served as a platform for deploying language appropriated through other means. It also mediated the performance of identities tied to their sojourn, particularly for audiences situated at home, as local resources were identified and curated for their ability to be read exotically by Japanese language audiences elsewhere. Posting habits for several of the informants then evolved as their familiarity with their local environments, social networks and online audiences changed, again demonstrating how their online interactions were intertwined with their ongoing experiences.

Social media has also been identified as a source of social support when issues of adjustment to unfamiliar circumstances arise (Mikal & Grace, 2012; Rapley, 2019). This is also seen in the informants' accounts, particularly in Misa's case with her nightly Skype sessions to a fellow Japanese sojourners and the use of Japanese language video on YouTube. However, Nagisa's account shows that this functionality is not limited to being abroad as she sought social support from her host community when facing issues back in Japan. This again demonstrates that social media use is tied to and shaped by both local and translocal processes of being and belonging.

This brings us to the overriding issue of access. Using any of the affordances of digital communications technology was shown in the informants' accounts to be contingent on local material realities. Connectivity (or lack thereof), particularly at school where they spent a significant amount of time, shaped their interactions with peers who were also consistently online. This had implications for their sense of belonging and the degree to which they could actively participate in ongoing interaction. Nagisa's case, in particular, highlights the consequences of limited connectivity, leading to feelings of exclusion and reliance on classmates' devices for resources such as translation software. On the other hand, Misa, in a change of homestay circumstances found the lack of connectivity in her second host family to be productive in her engagement with the learning of English. Yet, even this was contingent on the host family's attitude towards her participation and it is difficult to imagine that a lack of connectivity in her first host family would have improved her situation, particularly given it would have denied her access to the social support she sought online.

When crossing borders, sojourners can arrive without geographical frames of reference or knowledge of the socially constructed places that exist within their new environment. From a materialist perspective, the geography and physical affordances of a space impact the opportunities for interaction that sojourners can perceive and access. Links between the social and the physical environment are inevitable since 'the organisation and meaning of space is a product of social translation, transformation, and experience' (Soja, 1989: 80). It is through language and interaction that space is transformed into place (Tuan, 1991) and that place becomes interwoven with emotion (White & Bown, 2017). In her book, Murphy-Lejeune (2002) argues that the social fabric of a place is sustained by its spatial fabric and so the first step in the process of belonging is adapting to the physical surroundings in a new location. The different ways that people experience space mean that certain geographical settings may suit different sojourners, impacting their ability to interact and develop interpersonal connections. Misa's case demonstrates how those residing with host families in remote locations or reliant on private transportation are highly dependent on their hosts for access to opportunities beyond home and school. Consequently, this local immobility can also limit opportunities to form or develop in-person connections that subsequently lead to online connections. The nature of the physical surroundings and the sojourner's ability to navigate it therefore has implications for their ability to build social connections. Although participants in study abroad are often viewed as being 'mobile', emphasising their ability to move across transnational spaces, the material realities of more localised spaces can also result in immobilities (De Fina & Mazzaferro, 2022). While there is some evidence to suggest that sojourners' digital communications technology use across linguistic varieties is tied to how they perceive their surrounds (Durbidge, 2019), this is an area that would benefit from further research.

Broadly, the emerging picture that can be gleaned from these studies supports the notion that the online activities of sojourners are interrelated with their offline realities. In a study that emerged from the same project as this book, an examination of self-reported use of digital technology compared against challenges faced while abroad suggested 'that technology is being used as part of a strategy to deal with difficulties faced abroad' (Durbidge, 2019: 229). Yet, as the cases in this book demonstrate, this is only part of the story, as a desire to enact and occupy new identity positions tied to the host community affect what is posted on social media. For this reason, online spaces also need to be understood as places offering sojourners opportunities for creation, curation and experimentation with the ways they are seen and interact. What goes on in social networks online is in a dialogical relationship with the contexts in which participation is situated; therefore, study abroad research must account for those intersections.

The emerging interest in *new materialism* (Canagarajah, 2018; Pennycook, 2018; Toohey, 2019) offers a number of vital insights for language learning abroad research as it highlights the significance of materiality, embodiment and agency in the learning process. Importantly, new materialism challenges the notion that language learning is solely a human-centred activity. It acknowledges the role of non-human actors, such as technologies, objects and environmental factors, in shaping learners' experiences and agency and sees them in dynamic interrelationships (or entanglements) with each other. These perspectives can therefore provide new and vital insights into the role of technology as it is used during study abroad, particularly as new affordances become available such as those of generative artificial intelligence (GenAI).

Semiotic assemblages and spatial repertoires offer one method for conceptualising language learning through the perspectives of new materialism. The concept of assemblages offers a framework to comprehend how different trajectories of people, semiotic resources and objects converge at specific moments and places (Pennycook & Otsuji, 2017). Understanding language learning as situated within semiotic assemblages may further allow us to explore the complex interplay of various elements and their influence on the meanings and outcomes of language use.

## Use of digital communications is co-constitutive of participation in translocal communities

Directly connected to the observations outlined above is the realisation that the ways in which sojourners use social media abroad and upon return are both facilitative of, and determined by, their participation in local and transnational communities. For the adolescents who shared their stories for this project, social media use was intimately tied to interactions with peers at school, both at home and abroad. This reflects boyd's (2019) observations that relationships formed at school are fundamental to adolescents' conceptions of identity and friendships, and underscore social media's role in mediating those conceptions as adolescents' online practices are driven by a desire for interpersonal connection. Looking at the totality of the content posted on the informants' Instagram accounts, many of them had recently begun their accounts or had only posted a few times before departing. Therefore, their sojourns provided impetus to use Instagram more frequently and also to invest in the normative communicative practices of the platform. Consequently, social media use is not adjacent, augmentative or undermining of the in-person social lives of sojourners; rather, it is co-constitutive of them, being part of their total interaction space and reflecting the nature of the in-person connections they are (or are not) forming. That is to say, the way that sojourners use social media cannot be separated from the way they experience questions of identity, power and interaction locally and translocally.

We can observe this in the way that the informants' online activities were intertwined with their localised relationships. No better was this illustrated than in the account of Megumi and her encounters with racism and marginalisation in her first school. This meant that her main source of interaction during her first few months was her host mother and her online interactions remained limited until she changed schools. The acceptance and belonging she found there were then translated into commensurate multilingual interaction on Instagram and Snapchat.

The informants' accounts revealed how the modalities of online communication allowed them to observe and engage in translanguaging practices that were fundamental to interaction in local adolescent communities. Therefore, social media was an important site for observing and interacting in local teenage vernaculars. Given the tightly knit connections between language and identity, the appropriation of these forms of communication was viewed as essential to occupying legitimate positions within these communities. More broadly, the translingual nature of the informants' interactions also became more prominent as they developed social connections in their respective host communities. The connections between linguistic diversity online and social connections in host contexts have been observed elsewhere (Back, 2013; Martínez-Arbelaiz et al., 2017) and also speak to the ways that sojourners deploy linguistic strategies of audience design as their online connections diversify.

To varying degrees too, curatorial practices observed in the informants' online posts also pointed to their participation in transnational communities of their peers. Many of the events they memorialised on Instagram represented specific dimensions of their experiences, mainly highlighting those that held combinations of the exotic, the social and the affirming. For many of the informants, their posts represented a type of 'digital postcard' that communicated these notions through multimodal and multilingual practices to online audiences, located both within and beyond host contexts. Importantly, the visual affordances of Instagram appear to have better facilitated their ability to communicate through developing multilingual competences. As Lee and Barton (2011) found, the multimodal affordances of social media mean that users with even limited competence in a given variety can use this with visual modes to maximise their audiences. However, this did not always appear to be the case with the informants, as early during their stays, they often posted in the host language even while all comments on their posts were in Japanese. This suggests that their use of the host language varieties, at least during the initial weeks and months, was largely performative – indexing affiliation with their host community through the adoption of the local communicative practices. In effect, this allowed the informants to perform 'study abroad identities' for their audiences at home, particularly when done in conjunction with images of local cultural practices or food.

Over time though, both the nature of the images and the linguistic content and complexity of what they posted changed. The reasons for this are multifarious. Firstly, as Umino and Benson (2016) demonstrated in their study of photo records of international students, the subject of images often switches from the touristic to the social as their social networks in the host community develop. This was certainly the case for the informants and was particularly visible in the Instagram content of Nikko and Manabu who, by the end of their sojourns, rarely appeared in images alone. Increases in the comments on posts in the host language varieties and the increasing sophistication with which the informants engaged with these comments also demonstrated concomitant developments in host social networks and linguistic repetoires. This relationship has been strongly supported through other methods in the language learning abroad literature (e.g. Dewey *et al.*, 2013; Isabelli-García, 2006; Shiri, 2015). As the linguistic and geographical diversity of their online audience increased, it allowed the informants to author themselves as transnational, multilingual young people for an audience at home. Simultaneously, these linguistic identities could also be recognised and responded to by members of the host community, thereby affirming their affiliation with host speech communities. An increasing sophistication of the informants' posts over time in this study also point to their developing competence in the types of self-presentation legitimised by their peers and the norms and structures of the platforms they used.

The ways that linguistic resources are deployed on social media among a given community are also subject to *media ideologies* (Gershon, 2010) that determine what is appropriate to do with language online. Moving forward, we must also examine the ways that discourses of language learning which circulate in the communities that sojourners frequent, including those online, shape the ways they approach language learning and use while abroad. While it is certainly important that we provide students with cutting-edge understandings of language learning, we must also recognise the value they can place on ideas that emanate from other communities they inhabit.

### The affordances of digital communications are multifaceted and transform through mobility

Taking these findings a step further, we can see how, in the year after returning from their sojourns, the affordances of online interaction continued to play a role in the informants' lives and the interpersonal connections they had forged abroad. What's more, their accounts demonstrate how the affordances of social media were transformed as they returned to Japan.

As discussed above, social media served to facilitate increased connection and intimacy between sojourners and other young people they encountered abroad. However, upon returning the emphasis shifted towards maintaining, reconnecting and extending these relationships. Campbell (2015), in particular, has demonstrated how interpersonal connections formed abroad can be maintained through digital interaction many years after a sojourn and continue to offer both a connection with host language practices and opportunities to interact using these practices. This can be seen in the multitude of ways that the informants used digital communications to continue to interact with friends and members of host families, to follow the lives of members of their host communities as they were posted to social media and to continue to perform the multilingual identities they had formed while abroad. Moreover, there is a general sense from the participants that maintaining connections with host families contributed to their well-being, bridging the geographical gap and fostering an ongoing sense of connection to their host communities.

The way the informants understood digital communications in relation to the development of their linguistic repertoires also shifted from the appropriation of new linguistic forms towards maintaining those developed abroad. As several of the informants explained, after returning to Japan they sought out resources and interaction online tied to their multilingual repertoires as a means of remaining in contact with varieties they had appropriated. These affordances appeared to be particularly urgent given the widespread apathy towards their multilingualism they encountered upon returning to schools in Japan.

Finally, the informants' accounts revealed a shift in the performance of identities connected with their sojourns. While abroad, social media platforms were used to curate and showcase their experiences, presenting themselves as study abroad participants in new cultural and linguistic contexts. However, upon returning to Japan, the focus shifted to maintaining multilingual identities that were often denied to them in return contexts. The accounts of the informants demonstrate how social media can serve as a means to reinvoke the identities and connections in contexts far from the contexts in which they were originally formed. Social media thus served as a means for sustaining and articulating 'study abroad' identities, transcending the geographical boundaries that separated them from their initial formation.

Together, this demonstrates that digital communications afforded the informants vectors of interaction where their multilingual identities were recognised and validated. Although their multilingual abilities were often marginalised in local contexts, the removal of proximal constraints on interaction through social media allowed them to transcend the normative control of local linguistic attitudes. Effectively, social media reflects, maintains and extends the social worlds of sojourners across time and space. It allows them, post-return, to relive the experiences of their year abroad even as they are immersed in the vicissitudes of returned life. Scholars such as Murphy-Lejeune (2002) and Doerr (2016) have pointed to the way that a sojourn is often experienced as compressed and intensive. An individual sojourner may then spend months and years after their return, processing what has occurred and the changes it has fostered in them. Although study abroad has often been constructed as a demarcated experience, bounded by the arrival and departure of the individual from host contexts, the reality is much more porous and processual. As the accounts of the informants show, the availability of digital communications technology makes this process more apprehensible and perhaps more potent. Although ongoing interactions with members of host communities are now situated in the contexts of home, the sense of ongoing continuity has become decidedly less abstract and more immediately interactive. The fact that many of the informants returned to or received visits from their host communities demonstrates how, through global flows of people, they may continue to also be proximally entwined with those contexts even after returning.

From a theoretical standpoint, it is crucial to recognise that perceptions of what the affordances of social media offer sojourners undergo transformations as borders are crossed. What may be feasible and desirable in one context may no longer hold true in another. Likewise, what may have been readily accessible in one context may prove more challenging to obtain in another. The manner in which sojourners engage with digital communications is contingent upon the social, material and symbolic contexts in which they are situated. Consequently, changes in these contexts inevitably alter the considerations involved in using it over time and space.

## Language Learning Abroad is Social, Multilingual and Translocal

All this brings us to what we can say about language learning as it occurs in the contexts of study abroad. Although the social imaginary of study abroad constructs language learning as an outcome of immersive contexts, what we observe in the informants' accounts is an agentic orientation to language learning as a means of obtaining belonging and a reimagination of the self. This means an orientation to varieties and practices deemed valuable at local scales (and translocally with online audiences). It also meant, for these informants coming from non-Anglophone backgrounds, weighing the translocal and neoliberal value afforded to English in globalising imaginaries against its indexical value at local scales. Significantly, the need to negotiate these tensions was not limited to their time abroad, but also the return contexts of their high schools. In investigations of language learning during study abroad, it is important that we now move beyond parochial conceptualisations and recognise the dynamic, multilingual and, indeed, translocal nature of host communities. The communities that sojourners travel to are not static entities, but rather subject to flows of people and information that characterise the contemporary social landscape.

What emerges from this study is the important role of local communities with transnational connections in shaping localised discourses of identity, language and belonging. Nagisa's encounters with essentialising discourses of Japaneseness in Brazil were tempered by her knowledge of and interactions with local Japanese immigrant communities. Manabu initially found belonging at school among a local immigrant population while Megumi's positive experiences at her second school were also fostered by the population of immigrant students she encountered there. Both Manabu and Megumi also showed an awareness of local attitudes towards these populations and their link to the use of English at school. The presence of these communities complexifies what it means to be part of a place and, as seen through the experiences of the informants, provides them with alternative ways of negotiating identities abroad. Returning to Spenader's (2011) study of American students in a Swedish high school, we see a similar pattern in the experience of Max who also found belonging among an English-speaking immigrant community. In an era when human mobility is continuing to reshape the cultural and linguistic milieux of communities around the world, language learning abroad research needs to engage with the ways this can shape the reception and learning of sojourners abroad. Thus, the recognition of so-called 'superdiversity' (Vertovec, 2007) in study abroad contexts calls for us to move beyond ideas of language learning that remain tied to territorialised notions of language and culture.

This speaks to the ongoing need to investigate study abroad from a holistic perspective and see the presence of sojourners in these communities as part of eco-dialogic processes. As Cook (2006) noted, encounters with Americans at the table of Japanese host families created moments of learning, not only for the participant, but also for the family. So too, did the presence of the informants appear to contribute to engagement with Japanese cultural and linguistic practices. Therefore, we need to be cautious not to understand study abroad contexts as rarefied opportunities for immersion, but as dynamic social contexts that are shaped and reshaped by those acting within and through flows of people and information.

We can see the complexity of these processes in the role that multilingual host siblings played during the initial months of the informants' stays. Those who possessed some competence in Japanese or English communicative practices mediated initial interactions between the informants and other members of the host family. That these relationships then often became sources of tension underscores their dynamism as patterns of interaction and accommodation negotiated around and through the abilities of the host sibling needed to be renegotiated. Host siblings may find themselves in complex positions as their linguistic repertoires are instrumentalised to mediate interaction between sojourners and the rest of the host family, while they simultaneously possess the power to determine when and on what terms interactions take place. What is evident though is that their multilingual contributions to the communicative practices of the host family served to broker an interactional space for the informants to find their place in the host family. Importantly, in each of these cases, the informants described the linguistic ecology in their host families in terms that indicated its fluidity and development over time, signifying how the role of host siblings may also have changed across the period of the sojourn.

Returning again to the ways that the informants experienced host contexts, they often found themselves in situations where diverse linguistic repertoires in the host community created complex communicative and ideological environments that the informants were required to negotiate in order to participate and belong. The fact that the informants in this study actively used the linguistic resources they were appropriating early in their stay emphasises the need for a conceptual move away from perfunctory views of sojourners as 'language learners'. As Cook (2016) has argued, the notion of learner is necessarily reductive and fails to account for what it is that sojourners are actually doing with language abroad. It dismisses the competencies they already possess and assumes a unidirectional process whereby the sojourner is entailed to learn the language of the hosts, when in reality sojourners themselves may also be involved in developing and reconfiguring the linguistic repertoires of host community members. Moreover, sojourners arrive in host contexts bearing the vestiges of socialisation processes they have already undergone and, to varying degrees, bring with them multilingual repertoires that can alter both the ways they engage with those they encounter and the opportunities they have to learn local language varieties.

What is also apparent from the informants' accounts is the way they strategically approached the processes of language learning, drawing on their own agency and the affordances they perceived to appropriate and negotiate the use of particular varieties of language tied to specific communities. This brings us to the important question of the status of English in multilingual study abroad contexts, particularly where other varieties are used by members of the host community in day-to-day interactions. As studies such as Brown (2021), Mitchell *et al.* (2017) and Trentman (2013a) show, Anglophone speakers may encounter difficulty when attempting to interact in multilingual settings, particularly when interlocuters insist in interacting in English. What is instructive about the experiences described in this study is that sometimes there was resistance to speaking varieties other than English, despite the informants not being, or racialised as, from Anglophone backgrounds themselves.

Although the particularities of the informants' cases mean that English served different communicative and symbolic purposes throughout each informant's stay, overall, it is apparent that English use was not necessarily indexical of whiteness, but of alterity as it maintained informants' positioning to that of the earlier discussed *stranger* (Murphy-Lejeune, 2002). The informants inferred that legitimate positionality of inclusion and belonging in local communities could not be obtained through English and therefore struggled to be heard and accepted through local varieties. That is not to say that English language competence was not actively pursued by these informants, since many of them expressed a recognition of its value, both within the Japanese education system and as a globalising resource. Indeed, Nagisa's decision to travel to Brazil was predicated on a conscious rejection of the instrumental benefits she perceived in learning English over the desire to forge stronger transnational ties with family. Rather, the decision of which varieties to pursue, appropriate and use were dictated by the communities of which they sought membership.

This demonstrates how ideologies of language function across different communities of study abroad, creating environments where the overall multilingual competence of its community is deployed in different ways and requiring sojourners to approach practices of linguistic appropriation strategically and reflectlocal political realities. Although the way a participant negotiates these environments is crucial to their own linguistic development, language learning opportunities can be limited or denied through ideological regimes which partition the use of linguistic resources on the basis of insider/outsider identities. Moreover, attitudes regarding the learning and use of particular varieties and the availability of the resources for doing so can differentiate across communities and individuals, as well as across time, throughout host contexts. This means that what a sojourner can learn and do with language is situated in, and determined by, the shifting interactional and social contexts in which they find themselves, emphasising the need to understand processes of language learning ecologically and across scales.

In negotiating linguistic practices and attitudes re-encountered abroad and upon return and in seeking to identify the constellations of communicative resources essential for participation and belonging across the communities they inhabit, sojourners are also learning underlying ideologies of language and their relativity to different social milieux. These observations can be extended to online spaces, which as Nikko's account reveals, facilitate and mediate interaction that occurs translocally, presenting an additional dimension through which sojourners encounter and use language. Yet, as Nikko's accounts of Skyping friends together with Kristel reveal, the communicative practices of a given community can also be invoked independent of surrounding material and social circumstances through a physical and online co-presence. These findings emphasise how our understandings of language learning abroad must simultaneously account for and transcend the geographical and material realities of host community contexts and take in the possibilities offered through digital communications.

A multilingual perspective on study abroad must therefore also recognise the translocal nature of language learning, where interpersonal connections and larger global processes influence what a sojourner chooses to learn. We should therefore ask what varieties are legitimately spoken by whom and under what circumstances. As Iino's (1996) study of homestay interactions in Japan pointed out, ideological attitudes towards the use of Kansai dialectical patterns meant that while hosts used these forms with each other, they switched to 標準語 hyōjyungo[1] when addressing the sojourners. Moreover, when sojourners attempted to deploy local 関西弁 kansaiben,[2] they were met with laughter or discouraged from doing so. Similar attitudes were also found by Iwasaki (2011), where some male American sojourners observed the use of vernacular masculine forms of language among Japanese peers but were discouraged from this use themselves. On the other hand, one participant found that access to extracurricular activities such as club activities or a church choir provided them with opportunities to learn 'honorific' formal styles that infrequently appear in quotidian interactions. Although it is important to consider the interactions of so-called 'named languages' in host contexts, it is also important to recognise how attitudes towards different varieties also shape language learning abroad.

Acknowledging the heteroglossia (Bakhtin, 1981) that sojourners will encounter abroad allows us to see how specific varieties of language and the orders of indexicality associated with them are intertwined with the positionalities that sojourners are able to legitimately occupy. Importantly, a heteroglossic view conceives of language use as situated within particular social, cultural and historical milieu, and given the role of both youth culture and online discourse in shaping contemporary forms of communication, this allows us to better understand why sojourners chose to invest in, and appropriate, specific practices and the extent those practices were available to them. It also provides us with a perspective on the longer-term linguistic development of participants after they have returned from study abroad. This means considering the extent that investment in the practices of certain communities continues to hold relevance once participants are no longer in proximal contact with members of the host community. The ability of digital communications technology to transcend geographical space only serves to underscore the need to understand language learning abroad not as an isolated or demarcated phenomenon, but as emergent of the social contexts in which an individual is engaged.

By considering the fluidity and translocalism of host communities, the influence of global flows of people and information and the dynamics of language development, researchers can develop a more nuanced understanding of language learning during study abroad. This broader perspective allows for a comprehensive exploration of the sociocultural, material and contextual factors that shape and inform language learning experiences in diverse study abroad settings.

## Rethinking Some Assumptions of Study Abroad

The interdisciplinary nature of study abroad and the research that it engenders are both its biggest strength and its greatest challenge. Embracing the complexity of language learning in study abroad requires engaging with diverse perspectives, not only from linguistics but also from other fields including sociology, geography, cultural studies, psychology and technology studies. Therefore, it is essential to continuously reassess the foundational assumptions that underpin our understanding of study abroad, ensuring that we do so in light of the many changes taking place beyond the immediate concerns of language learning in study abroad. The findings presented in this book underscore the importance of examining commonly accepted concepts in the field of study abroad, particularly from a sociological and critical perspective. Based on the results, I describe three concepts that warrant consideration in both study abroad research and planning.

### Immersion

As I detailed in Chapter 1 of this book, the notion of immersion has been fundamental to conceptions of study abroad and requires urgent reassessment in light of a world of overlapping and flowing cultural and linguistic diversity that has been intensified by the global reach of digital communications technology. While there is little doubt that the contexts of study abroad can offer participants experiences and opportunities for language learning that may not be available to them at home, we also need to consider what we mean when we talk about immersion and whether it maintains conceptual validity when dealing with the on-the-ground realities of sojourners' experiences of language and language learning.

Perhaps most concerning is that reified notions of immersion serve to perpetuate ideas of a homogeneous and monolithic host linguaculture, disregarding the diversity and heterogeneity within any given context. It overlooks the fact that study abroad contexts are subject to the same global flows of people that brought the sojourners to them, and can contain many individuals and social groups who diverge from presumed norms. Assuming an all-encompassing experience of immersion fails to acknowledge the linguistic and cultural complexities that cut across the locations to which sojourners travel. As the experiences of the informants demonstrate, the presence of other transnational communities, access to language resources both in home and host varieties, as well as host community members' multilingualism and own mobility experiences all contributed to complex, linguistically diverse environments that sojourners needed to navigate strategically. Questions of language learning abroad shouldn't be understood in degrees of immersion, but rather in terms of linguistic varieties seen as (un)desirable, (ir)relevant and (un)obtainable and the ways that sojourners seek to appropriate them.

Parochial views of host communities as ideal, immersive sites for target language learning should therefore be discarded for understandings that reflect wider cross-border flows of people and information. Translocal perspectives of language learning abroad are vital here. We are then better positioned to understand the complexity of sojourners' experiences and provide them with the critical tools they need to understand the ideological implications of the environments they will encounter. This also means interrogating the ongoing focus of language learning research on Anglophone communities and recognising it as a product of, and a contributor to, the hegemonic status of English as a medium of international interaction.

## Life stage as structuring feature

A strong and developing literature now recognises the complex ways that different aspects of social identity, including race and ethnicity, nationality and gender may intersect to shape the way that study abroad and attendant language learning are experienced. What continues to be overlooked is the way that life stage may also contribute to these experiences, particularly given the social, cultural, legal and physiological forces that can shape how study abroad is understood and experienced. As discussed previously, notions of maturity, independence and responsibility can vary as a sojourner moves between home and host communities and this needs to be accounted for in our understandings of language learning abroad. Although there are undoubtedly many features of university-level sojourners' experiences of study abroad that are applicable across all populations, failure to critically engage with the sociological differences in language learning across different life stages leaves epistemological blind spots in our understandings.

Reflecting on the experiences of the informants detailed in this book, their adolescence appears as a structuring feature of their experiences. Socially and legally, it determined the institutions in which they were required to inhabit – school and family. Developmentally, approval of their peers was paramount to their sense of belonging, determining the varieties of language they sought to appropriate.

Turning to the homestay first, Kinginger (2015) has already highlighted how adolescents are often received differently in homestay settings and are more readily accepted as members of the family than university-aged sojourners. The informants' accounts in this project again further contribute to this perspective, as they readily show the central role that the host family plays in the lives of adolescent sojourners, both in terms of the support they can offer and the degree to which the sojourner is subject to their control. The most salient relationship that most of the informants identified in their host families was the one they shared with their host mother. Reflecting gendered divisions of labour in host families, host mothers were a significant source of support for the adolescents in this study, contributing to a number of vitally important aspects of their lives. Their availability and willingness to engage with the informants not only offered opportunities for interaction, but also provided embedded support that came with the trust and stability of the relationship they adopted. While it is certainly true that those observing sojourners departing from tertiary institutions have also reported on the important role that host mothers play (Knight & Schmidt-Rinehart, 2002; Shiri, 2015), the role of host families in the lives of these adolescent sojourners appears to be particularly pronounced.

On the other hand, Misa's account in particular demonstrates how reliant adolescents can be on their host family and how they are subject to dynamics of power in adult-controlled spaces. It demonstrates how the local geography and infrastructure can intersect with and amplify the power that host parents possess, particularly when the sojourner's local mobility is dependent upon the host family's willingness to provide transportation. The contrast here is visible in accounts such as Manabu and Nikko, who, residing in cities with substantial public transportation systems, were able to independently travel to meet peers and attend activities. More broadly though, all of the informants lacked independent financial means while abroad and were dependent upon their host parents to support them throughout their stay. Although we often think about sojourners in terms of mobility, we must also recognise that mobility occurs across scales and that local relations of power, geography and material resources can intersect to determine the availability of, and access to, local contexts of interaction.

Alongside the host family, high school attendance stood as an important structuring context on the informants' experiences abroad. It was their main context for sociality outside of the host family and, given adolescents' orientation towards their perception and status among their peers (Milner, 2004), had deep ramifications for their sense of belonging and language learning. Embedded in the social milieux of the local schools they attended, the informants negotiated their positionality and status in circumstances where they needed to learn not only the local social practices of their peers, but also the cultural and linguistic practices of the community more broadly. As the informants' accounts show, the right to participate in those communities and the ability to legitimately use local linguistic practices often needed to be negotiated and was, at times, resisted through the use of English. Unaccommodating and marginalising cultural and linguistic contexts constrained or removed their ability to negotiate a viable position for themselves. This signifies the type of dissociation that sojourners can experience as strangers in host contexts, as their 'past, both personal and collective, ceases to exist in the eyes of those around [them]... strangers are in no position to participate in the taken-for-granted pattern of the new group, nor in their heritage' (Murphy-Lejeune, 2002: 17). However, the requirement to attend school meant that daily, they needed to return to communities that were not prepared to accept them, extracting a psychological toll on their wellbeing. This again highlights how the adolescent sojourners had very little agency to alter the environments in which they spent much of their time and were limited to lobbying adults who held the power to make those changes, including the local branch of AFS.

The focus on status also demonstrates how the life stage of a sojourner can influence the types of relationships they prioritise abroad and the nature and circumstances in which they are developed. Peers played a vital role in determining the types of linguistic practices the sojourners sought to appropriate and often emerged in their narratives as important sources of learning about wider community attitudes. In many of the informants' accounts, there appeared key individuals who significantly contributed to informants' peer network development and socialisation as well as providing various forms of support. While I have discussed these phenomena in detail elsewhere (Durbidge, 2021), the importance of certain individuals in providing newcomers with access to their social networks was noted by Tomiya (1997) in her study of non-Japanese women who married Japanese men. The findings of her study highlighted how the social networks of her participants expanded through knowing someone who already had developed networks that were shared with her participants. In much the same way, it appears that developing close contact with certain individuals provided access to friendships groups and wider peer networks.

The accounts and Instagram streams of the informants indicated that time spent with their peers was not limited to the contexts of school, but also included activities such as sleepovers, sports, eating out, sightseeing and watching Netflix, in addition to the online interactions they reported. The multiplex nature of these contexts of interaction, a significant contributor to linguistic development (Kurata, 2004), combined with their frequent and recurring nature would have provided the conditions of 'progressively more complex reciprocal interaction'

(Bronfenbrenner, 1995: 620) that characterise developmentally effective processes. However, an important distinction here is that the possibility and development of sexual relationships have been shown to be an important aspect of many university-age sojourners' experiences abroad (Anya, 2016; Mitchell *et al.*, 2017; Murphy-Lejeune, 2002). The intimacy experienced by the adolescent sojourners in this study (at least as it was reported to me) remained limited in its physicality and opportunities to meet in person were undoubtedly subject to the strictures of adult control and supervision.

This study also shows that, broadly speaking, the motivations for studying abroad and language learning of those who completed these year-long programmes were founded on notions of cosmopolitanism and transnational interaction. International student numbers from many areas of the world can be driven by instrumental motivations for studying internationally, including professional and citizenship considerations (Tran & Nguyen, 2016). Apart from Misa, all the informants expressed a desire to pursue some part of their higher education abroad, while Nikko selected her university based on the opportunities it offered to study with international students. Although among the informants there was an awareness of neoliberalist discourses that related English competence to career opportunities (see Kubota and Takeda [2021] for a detailed discussion of this phenomenon in a Japanese context), they were largely interested in pursuing ongoing opportunities that prioritised friendship and adventure. This, in part, probably reflects the economic stability of their middle-class lives, but it also demonstrates the heterogeneity in the motivation of those seeking to study beyond their country of origin.

Although this study only examined the lives of the informants in the year after their return, I have continued to follow many of them on Instagram and can anecdotally report that they have continued to pursue international connections and relationships, travelling overseas and posting pictures that reveal friendships and love interests which cross cultural and linguistic borders. Greater recognition of the role that life stage plays in unfolding perceptions of what takes place abroad naturally highlights the way that a sojourn can fit into the transition between these stages. Study abroad may therefore become a liminal space between one life stage and the next, with significant impacts on the way that the successive life stage is pursued and understood. Indeed, we can see this in research by Mitchell *et al.* (2020: 339–340) that showed that for students of a UK university, participation in a two-semester study abroad programme during the third year of tertiary education had an 'enduring impact […] on their developing personal and intercultural competence, reflected in their current personal self-confidence and independence, international orientation, and intercultural openness' that they carried into their professional careers.

## Reverse culture shock

The accounts detailed in this book also provide evidence for re-evaluating the notion of *return culture shock*. As it currently stands in the study abroad literature, it is conceived of primarily as a widely experienced, yet ultimately individual psychological process. The difficulties the informants faced upon their return to Japan and their struggles to reconcile the people they had become abroad with the expectations they returned to, would seem to fit the description for this phenomenon offered by Ting-Toomey and Dorjee (2019: 95) as 'the realignment of one's new identity with a once-familiar home environment', and who identify the 'home culture's demand for conformity and expectations for performing old roles' as contributing to this. Many other studies though have focused on individuals' reactions to the experience of return and have located these phenomena within that individual, implicitly construing the social milieu they return to as the baseline to which they must now 'reacculturate' or 'reassimilate' (e.g. Gaw, 2000; Presbitero, 2016).

The informants' accounts described in this book demonstrate how an ecological perspective provides a means of critically evaluating these assumptions. The informants reported similar difficulties, struggling to have identities developed abroad valued and dealing with a universal sense of curtailment and restriction. They had come to be defined by their linguistic mobility abroad, finding belonging abroad through their ability to translanguage identities among their peers and host families. Yet, these same impulses became a liability as they needed to renegotiate their positionality within a social milieu that constructed the diverse multilingual and intercultural practices with which they returned as in conflict with a legitimate Japanese identity. In enacting cultural and social behaviours that deviated from accepted norms, they were viewed as demonstrating a freshly developed alterity.

Throughout their accounts, we observe that their sense of alienation arose not only from shifts in their own perceptions – seeing old worlds through new eyes if you will – but also through systemic processes of 'othering' based on rigid cultural notions of Japaneseness that lacked space for hybrid, transnational identities. Looking at the informants' return experiences both contextually and longitudinally, we can see how the phenomena commonly associated with reverse cultural shock emerged from the penumbra where the individual encounters their social surrounds. That is to say, the dissonance the informants experienced that would normally be attributed to individual psychological phenomena emerged in a social context that was unaccepting of the changes they had undergone abroad.

We can observe too how the institutional contexts which they returned to were also facilitative of these attitudes. There was little support for those who had spent time abroad, even in schools where it was encouraged and viewed as a personal choice, with limited bearing on educational priorities. Those who had been abroad were not seen as a resource or benefit to the school – rather the time spent abroad represented a potential liability as the individual bore the responsibility for catching up on work they had missed, or in some cases, forced to remain in the grade from which they had departed. Despite the funding, support and encouragement offered by government agencies for study abroad, at the classroom level the informants' experiences really only served to mark them as different from their peers.

This illustrates the importance of not only return interventions such as guided critical reflection (Jackson, 2015) and academic mentoring (Giovanangeli *et al.*, 2017), but also of examining attitudes towards international experience more widely in return contexts. Although the way that various aspects of identity intersect with language learning has been explored extensively in the study abroad literature, this project demonstrates the need to extend these explorations to return contexts, noting the ramifications for the ongoing development of linguistic repertoires tied to communities elsewhere. If the wider cultures of the institutions' sojourners remain ambivalent towards, or inhospitable to, the identities that sojourners return with, then experiences of 'reverse cultural shock' will no doubt emerge among those who come back changed by experiences of studying abroad.

## Final Thoughts

Following the discussions included in the book, the value of bringing ecological and scalar perspectives to investigations of study abroad should be apparent. The experiences of individuals studying abroad are emergent of and stratified across the complex and dynamic social, cultural and material contexts they encounter. The development of participants' communicative repertoires is not linear, but dynamic and agentic, shaped by changes in external contexts and within the participants themselves. Moreover, these processes are taking place at a particular societal moment, shaped by rapid developments in digital technology and movements of people across the globe. Apprehending all this complexity requires metaphors that not only make sense but also allow us to keep sight of the humanity embedded in the interactions that unfold between all those a sojourn can touch. At a moment when the Earth's bioecological systems are increasingly threatened and transformed by human activity, the notion of study abroad as intersecting with wider ecologies seems appropriate and, perhaps, points towards a need for the field to also begin to grapple with the environmental and biological dimensions of language learning abroad.

## Notes

(1) 'Standard' Japanese originating in Tokyo-based linguistic varieties.
(2) A group of linguistic features found in Kansai area varieties of Japanese.

# References

Adami, E. (2014) Retwitting, reposting, repinning; reshaping identities online: Towards a social semiotic multimodal analysis of digital remediation. *LEA-Lingue e Letterature d'Oriente e d'Occidente* 3, 223–243.
AFS Intercultural Programs (2022) AFS timeline. https://afs.org/archives/timeline/
Agha, A. (2003) The social life of cultural value. *Language & Communication* 23 (3), 231–273. https://doi.org/10.1016/S0271-5309(03)00012-0
Alfurayh, L. (2022) From ideal to real: The impact of study abroad on the identity of Saudi women in Australia. Doctoral dissertation, Monash University. https://doi.org/10.26180/19195313.v1
Allen, H.W. and Dupuy, B. (2012) Study abroad, foreign language use, and the communities standard. *Foreign Language Annals* 45 (4), 468–493. https://doi.org/10.1111/j.1944-9720.2013.01209.x
Anderson, B. (2006) *Imagined Communities: Reflections on the Origin and Spread of Nationalism*. Verso Books.
Anderson, T. (2019) Reproductions of Chinese transnationalism: Ambivalent identities in study abroad. *Applied Linguistics* 40 (2), 228–247. https://doi.org/10.1093/applin/amx018
Androutsopoulos, J. (2006) Introduction: Sociolinguistics and computer-mediated communication. *Journal of Sociolinguistics* 10 (4), 419–438. https://doi.org/10.1111/j.1467-9841.2006.00286.x
Androutsopoulos, J. (2014) Languaging when contexts collapse: Audience design in social networking. *Discourse, Context & Media* 4, 62–73. https://doi.org/10.1016/j.dcm.2014.08.006
Anya, U. (2016) *Racialized Identities in Second Language Learning: Speaking Blackness in Brazil*. Routledge.
Anya, U. (2021) When the foreign is familiar: An Afro-Dominican-American woman's experience translanguaging race, ethnicity and cultural heritage learning Portuguese in Brazil. In W. Diao and E. Trentman (eds) *Language Learning in Study Abroad: The Multilingual Turn* (pp. 43–71). Multilingual Matters.
Appadurai, A. (1990) Disjuncture and difference in the global cultural economy. *Theory, Culture & Society* 7 (2), 295–310.
Appadurai, A. (1996) *Modernity at Large: Cultural Dimensions of Globalization*. University of Minnesota Press.
Ayano, M. (2006) Japanese students in Britain. In M. Byram and A. Feng (eds) *Living and Studying Abroad: Research and Practice* (pp. 11–37). Multilingual Matters.
Back, M. (2013) Using Facebook data to analyze learner interaction during study abroad. *Foreign Language Annals* 46 (3), 377–401. https://doi.org/10.1111/flan.12036

Badwan, K. and Simpson, J. (2022) Ecological orientations to sociolinguistic scale: Insights from study abroad experiences. *Applied Linguistics Review* 13 (2), 267–286. https://doi.org/10.1515/applirev-2018-0113

Bakhtin, M.M. (1981) *The Dialogic Imagination: Four Essays*. University of Texas Press.

Barkhuizen, G., Benson, P. and Chik, A. (2013) *Narrative Inquiry in Language Teaching and Learning Research*. Routledge. https://doi.org/10.4324/9780203124994

Baron, N.S. (2008) *Always On: Language in an Online and Mobile World*. Oxford University Press.

Barton, D. and Lee, C. (2013) *Language Online: Investigating Digital Texts and Practices*. Routledge.

Barton, D. and Potts, D. (2013) Language learning online as a social practice. *TESOL Quarterly* 47 (4), 815–820. https://doi.org/10.1002/tesq.130

Bauman, Z. (2000) *Liquid Modernity*. Polity Press.

Bauman, Z. (2004) *Identity*. Polity Press.

Bell, A. (1984) Language style as audience design. *Language in Society* 13 (2), 145–204. https://doi.org/10.1017/S004740450001037X

Benson, P., Barkhuizen, G., Bodycott, P. and Brown, J. (2013) *Second Language Identity in Narratives of Study Abroad*. Palgrave Macmillan. https://doi.org/10.1057/9781137029423

Bernstein, B. (2000) *Pedagogy, Symbolic Control, and Identity: Theory, Research, Critique*. Rowman & Littlefield.

Block, D. (2000) Interview research in TESOL – Problematizing interview data: Voices in the mind's machine? *TESOL Quarterly* 34 (4), 757–763.

Block, D. (2003) *The Social Turn in Second Language Acquisition*. Edinburgh University Press.

Block, D. (2007) *Second Language Identities*. Continuum.

Blommaert, J. (2007) Sociolinguistic scales. *Intercultural Pragmatics* 4 (1), 1–19. https://doi.org/10.1515/IP.2007.001

Blommaert, J. (2010) *The Sociolinguistics of Globalization*. Cambridge University Press. https://doi.org/10.1017/CBO9780511845307

Blommaert, J. (2018a) *Dialogues with Ethnography: Notes on Classics, and How I Read Them*. Multilingual Matters.

Blommaert, J. (2018b) *Durkheim and the Internet: On Sociolinguistics and the Sociological Imagination*. Bloomsbury Publishing.

Blommaert, J. (2021) Sociolinguistic scales in retrospect. *Applied Linguistics Review* 12 (3), 375–380. https://doi.org/10.1515/applirev-2019-0132

Blommaert, J. and Rampton, B. (2011) Language and superdiversity. *Diversities* 13 (2), 1–21.

Blommaert, J., Leppänen, S., Pahta, P. and Räisänen, T. (2012) *Dangerous Multilingualism: Northern Perspectives on Order, Purity and Normality*. Palgrave Macmillan.

boyd, d. (2008) *Taken Out of Context: American Teen Sociality in Networked Publics*. University of California.

boyd, d. (2019) Friendship. In M. Ito, S. Baumer, M. Bittanti, d. boyd, R. Cody, B. Herr Stephenson, H.A. Horst, P.G. Lange, D. Mahendran, K.Z. Martínez, C.J. Pascoe, D. Perkel, L. Robinson, C. Sims and L. Tripp (eds) *Hanging Out, Messing Around, and Geeking Out* (pp. 79–115). The MIT Press. https://doi.org/10.7551/mitpress/8402.003.0007

Bronfenbrenner, U. (1995) Developmental ecology through space and time: A future perspective. In P. Moen, G.H.J. Elder and K. Luscher (eds) *Examining Lives in Context: Perspectives on the Ecology of Human Development* (pp. 619–647). American Psychological Association. https://doi.org/10.1037/10176-000

Bronfenbrenner, U. (1999) Environments in developmental perspective: Theoretical and operational models. In S.L. Friedman and T.D. Wachs (eds) *Measuring Environment*

*Across the Life Span: Emerging Methods and Concepts* (pp. 3–28). American Psychological Association. https://doi.org/10.1037/10317-001

Bronfenbrenner, U. and Morris, P.A. (2006) The bioecological model of human development. In W. Damon and R.M. Lerner (eds) *Handbook of Child Psychology* (6th edn, Vol. 1, pp. 793–828). Wiley.

Brown, L. (2021) 'Sorry, I don't speak any English': An activity-theoretic account of language choice in study abroad in South Korea. In W. Diao and E. Trentman (eds) *Language Learning in Study Abroad: The Multilingual Turn* (pp. 145–169). Multilingual Matters.

Cabinet Office (2021) *Reiwa 3 nendo seishōnen no intānetto riyō kankyō jitai chōsa hōkokusho [Report on the 2021 Survey of Adolescent Internet Usage]*. Government of Japan. https://www8.cao.go.jp/youth/kankyou/internet_torikumi/tyousa/r03/net-jittai/pdf/2-1-1.pdf

Campbell, R. (2011) The impact of study abroad on Japanese language learners social networks. *New Voices* 5, 25–63. https://doi.org/10.21159/nv.05.02

Campbell, R. (2015) Life post-study abroad for the Japanese language learner: Social networks, interaction and language usage. In R. Mitchell, N. Tracy-Ventura and K. McManus (eds) *Social Interaction, Identity and Language Learning during Residence Abroad* (pp. 241–262). The European Second Language Association.

Canagarajah, S. (2018) Materializing 'competence': Perspectives from international STEM scholars. *The Modern Language Journal* 102 (2), 268–291. https://doi.org/10.1111/modl.12464

Chudacoff, H.P. (1989) *How Old Are You?: Age Consciousness in American Culture*. Princeton University Press. https://doi.org/10.2307/j.ctv173f2tp

Coleman, J.A. (2013) Researching whole people and whole lives. In C. Kinginger (ed.) *Social and Cultural Aspects of Language Learning in Study Abroad* (pp. 17–44). John Benjamins. https://doi.org/10.1075/lllt.37

Coleman, J.A. (2015) Social circles during residence abroad: What students do, and who with. In R. Mitchell, N. Tracy-Ventura and K. McManus (eds) *Social Interaction, Identity and Language Learning During Residence Abroad* (Vol. 4, pp. 33–52). The European Second Language Association.

Coleman, J.A. and Chafer, T. (2010) Study abroad and the internet: Physical and virtual context in an era of expanding telecommunications. *Frontiers: The Interdisciplinary Journal of Study Abroad* 19, 151–167.

Cook, H.M. (2006) Joint construction of folk beliefs by JFL learners and Japanese host families. In M.A. DuFon and E. Churchill (eds) *Language Learners in Study Abroad Contexts* (pp. 120–150). Multilingual Matters.

Cook, H.M. (2008) *Socializing Identities Through Speech Style: Learners of Japanese as a Foreign Language*. Multilingual Matters. https://doi.org/10.21832/9781847691026

Cook, V. (2016) Premises of multi-competence. In V. Cook and Li Wei (eds) *The Cambridge Handbook of Linguistic Multi-Competence* (pp. 1–25). Cambridge University Press. https://doi.org/10.1017/CBO9781107425965.001

Darvin, R. (2023) Sociotechnical structures, materialist semiotics, and online language learning. *Language Learning* 27 (2), 28–45.

Davies, B. and Harré, R. (1990) Positioning: The discursive production of selves. *Journal for the Theory of Social Behaviour* 20 (1), 43–63. https://doi.org/10.1111/j.1468-5914.1990.tb00174.x

Dawson, S. (2019a) 'Bitch I'm back, by popular demand': Agency and structure in a study abroad setting. *Gender and Language* 13 (4), 449–468. https://doi.org/10.1558/genl.39399

Dawson, S. (2019b) Identities and ideologies in study abroad contexts: Negotiating nationality, gender, and sexuality. Doctoral dissertation, Victoria University of Wellington. http://researcharchive.vuw.ac.nz/handle/10063/8538

De Costa, P., Park, J. and Wee, L. (2016) Language learning as linguistic entrepreneurship: Implications for language education. *The Asia-Pacific Education Researcher* 25 (5–6), 695–702. https://doi.org/10.1007/s40299-016-0302-5

De Fina, A. and Mazzaferro, G. (2022) *Exploring (im)Mobilities: Language Practices, Discourses and Imaginaries*. Multilingual Matters.

Dewey, D.P., Belnap, R.K. and Hillstrom, R. (2013) Social network development, language use, and language acquisition during study abroad: Arabic language learners' perspectives. *Frontiers: The Interdisciplinary Journal of Study Abroad* 22, 84–110.

Dewey, D.P., Bown, J., Baker, W., Martinsen, R.A., Gold, C. and Eggett, D. (2014) Language use in six study abroad programs: An exploratory analysis of possible predictors. *Language Learning* 64 (1), 36–71. https://doi.org/10.1111/lang.12031

Diao, W. (2021) Language use, class and study abroad in China. In W. Diao and E. Trentman (eds) *Language Learning in Study Abroad: The Multilingual Turn* (pp. 121–144). Multilingual Matters.

Diao, W. and Trentman, E. (2021) *Language Learning in Study Abroad: The Multilingual Turn*. Multilingual Matters.

Doerr, N.M. (2013) Do 'global citizens' need the parochial cultural other? Discourse of immersion in study abroad and learning-by-doing. *Compare: A Journal of Comparative and International Education* 43 (2), 224–243. https://doi.org/10.1080/03057925.2012.701852

Doerr, N.M. (2016) Chronotopes of study abroad: The cultural other, immersion, and compartmentalized space–time. *Journal of Cultural Geography* 33 (1), 80–99. https://doi.org/10.1080/08873631.2015.1065030

Doerr, N.M. and Suarez, R. (2018) Immersion, immigration, immutability: Regimes of learning and politics of labeling in study abroad. *Educational Studies* 54 (2), 183–197. https://doi.org/10.1080/00131946.2017.1356309

Dovchin, S. and Lee, J.W. (2019) Introduction to special issue: 'The ordinariness of translinguistics'. *International Journal of Multilingualism* 16 (2), 105–111. https://doi.org/10.1080/14790718.2019.1575831

Dovchin, S., Pennycook, A. and Sultana, S. (2017) *Popular Culture, Voice and Linguistic Diversity: Young Adults On-And Offline*. Springer.

Dressler, R., Crossman, K. and Kawalilak, C. (2021) Pre-service teachers' learning about language learning and teaching: A nexus analysis of study abroad blogging. *Journal of Language, Identity & Education*, 1–13. https://doi.org/10.1080/15348458.2021.1938573

Duff, P.A. (2008) *Case Study Research in Applied Linguistics*. Routledge.

Duff, P.A. (2019) Social dimensions and processes in second language acquisition: Multilingual socialization in transnational contexts. *The Modern Language Journal* 103, 6–22. https://doi.org/10.1111/modl.12534

Dufva, H. (2012) Bakhtin and second language acquisition. In C.A. Chapelle (ed.) *The Encyclopedia of Applied Linguistics*. Blackwell Publishing Ltd. https://doi.org/10.1002/9781405198431.wbeal0072

Durbidge, L. (2017) Duty, desire and Japaneseness: A case study of Japanese high school study abroad. *Study Abroad Research in Second Language Acquisition and International Education* 2 (2), 206–239. https://doi.org/10.1075/sar.15016.dur

Durbidge, L. (2019) Technology and L2 engagement in study abroad: Enabler or immersion breaker? *System* 80, 224–234. https://doi.org/10.1016/j.system.2018.12.004

Durbidge, L. (2020) Study abroad in multilingual contexts: The linguistic investment and development of Japanese adolescents in and beyond year-long exchange programs. Doctoral dissertation, Monash University. https://doi.org/10.26180/5ecb8e158ded3

Durbidge, L. (2021) Social network development and language learning in multilingual study abroad contexts. In A. Carhill-Poza and N. Kurata (eds) *Social Networks in Language Learning and Language Teaching* (pp. 209–233). Bloomsbury.

Durbidge, L. (2022) Sojourners online: Social media and online communication as a data source in study abroad research. In J. McGregor and J.L. Plews (eds) *Designing Second Language Study Abroad Research* (pp. 229–248). Springer International Publishing. https://doi.org/10.1007/978-3-031-05053-4_12

Endō, S. (1965) *Ryūgaku*. Shinchōsha.

Engle, J. and Engle, L. (2002) Neither international nor educative: Study abroad in the time of globalization. In W. Grünzweig and N. Rinehart (eds) *Rockin'in Red Square: Critical Approaches to International Education in the Age of Cyberculture* (pp. 25–39). Transaction.

Engle, L. and Engle, J. (2003) Study abroad levels: Toward a classification of program types. *Frontiers: The Interdisciplinary Journal of Study Abroad* 9 (1), 1–20. https://doi.org/10.36366/frontiers.v9i1.113

Erikson, E.H. and Erikson, J.M. (1998) *The Life Cycle Completed (Extended Version)*. W.W. Norton & Company.

Fisseha, R. (2021) Say something in your language. In L. Carranza, E. Fantetti and A. Tsabari (eds) *Tongues: On Longing and Belonging through Language* (1st edn, pp. 85–91). Book*hug Press.

Freed, B.F. (1995) Language learning and study abroad. In B.F. Freed (ed.) *Second Language Acquisition in a Study Abroad Context* (pp. 3–33). John Benjamins.

Gaw, K.F. (2000) Reverse culture shock in students returning from overseas. *International Journal of Intercultural Relations* 24 (1), 83–104. https://doi.org/10.1016/S0147-1767(99)00024-3

Georgalou, M. (2016) 'I make the rules on my wall': Privacy and identity management practices on Facebook. *Discourse & Communication* 10 (1), 40–64. https://doi.org/10.1177/1750481315600304

Gershon, I. (2010) *The Breakup 2.0: Disconnecting Over New Media*. Cornell University Press.

Gibson, J.J. (1979) *The Ecological Approach to Visual Perception*. Houghton Mifflin Harcourt.

Giddens, A. (1990) *The Consequences of Modernity*. Polity Press.

Giovanangeli, A., Oguro, S. and Harbon, L. (2017) Mentoring students' intercultural learning during study abroad. In J. Jackson and S. Oguro (eds) *Intercultural Interventions in Study Abroad* (pp. 88–102). Routledge.

Goldoni, F. (2013) Students' immersion experiences in study abroad. *Foreign Language Annals* 46 (3), 359–376. https://doi.org/10.1111/flan.12047

Goldoni, F. (2017) Race, ethnicity, class and identity: Implications for study abroad. *Journal of Language, Identity, and Education* 16 (5), 328–341. https://doi.org/10.1080/15348458.2017.1350922

Grant, N. and Fabrigar, L. (2007) Exploratory factor analysis. In N. Salkind (ed.) *Encyclopedia of Measurement and Statistics* (pp. 333–335). Sage Publications.

Greiner, C. and Sakdapolrak, P. (2013) Translocality: Concepts, applications and emerging research perspectives. *Geography Compass* 7 (5), 373–384. https://doi.org/10.1111/gec3.12048

Grieve, A.M. (2015) The impact of host family relations and length of stay on adolescent identity expression during study abroad. *Multilingua* 34 (5), 623–657. https://doi.org/10.1515/multi-2014-0089

Hail, H.C. (2015) Patriotism abroad: Overseas Chinese students' encounters with criticisms of China. *Journal of Studies in International Education* 19 (4), 311–326. https://doi.org/10.1177/1028315314567175

Hall, S. (1992) The question of cultural identity. In S. Hall, D. Held and A.G. McGrew (eds) *Modernity and its Futures* (pp. 273–375). Polity Press. https://philpapers.org/rec/HALMAI

Hall, S. (1997) The spectacle of the other. In S. Hall (ed.) *Representation: Cultural Representations and Signifying Practices* (Vol. 7, pp. 223–290). Sage London.

Han, Y. (2019) Exploring multimedia, mobile learning, and place-based learning in linguacultural education. *Language Learning and Technology* 23 (3), 29–38.

Hasegawa, A. (2019) *The Social Lives of Study Abroad: Understanding Second Language Learners' Experiences through Social Network Analysis and Conversation Analysis*. Taylor & Francis.

Hasnain, A. and Hajek, J. (2022) Understanding international student connectedness. *International Journal of Intercultural Relations* 86, 26–35. https://doi.org/10.1016/j.ijintrel.2021.10.008

Hassall, T. (2013) Pragmatic development during short-term study abroad: The case of address terms in Indonesian. *Journal of Pragmatics* 55, 1–17. https://doi.org/10.1016/j.pragma.2013.05.003

Hjorth, L. (2003) Cute@keitai.com. In N. Gottlieb and M.J. McLelland (eds) *Japanese Cybercultures* (pp. 68–77). Routledge.

Hofer, B.K., Thebodo, S.W., Meredith, K., Kaslow, Z. and Saunders, A. (2016) The long arm of the digital tether: Communication with home during study abroad. *Frontiers: The Interdisciplinary Journal of Study Abroad* 28, 24–41.

Holliday, A. (2016) *Doing & Writing Qualitative Research* (3rd edn). Sage Publications.

Hymes, D. (1967) Models of the interaction of language and social setting. *Journal of Social Issues* 23 (2), 8–28. https://doi.org/10/b57br4

Hymes, D. (1970) Linguistic aspects of comparative political research. In R.T. Holt and J.E. Turner (eds) *The Methodology of Comparative Research: A Symposium from the Center for Comparative Studies in Technological Development and Social Change and the Department of Political Science, University of Minnesota* (pp. 295–341). Free Press.

Hymes, D. (1972) On communicative competence. In J. B. Pride and J. Holmes (eds) *Sociolinguistics* (pp. 269–293). Harmondsworth.

IBGE (2008) *Resistência & integração: 100 anos de imigração japonesa no Brasil / IBGE, Centro de Documentação e Disseminação de Informações*. https://biblioteca.ibge.gov.br/biblioteca-catalogo.html?id=238935&view=detalhes

Ichimoto, T. (2007) *Recrafting 'Self/s': Identity Transformation among Japanese Women Students in Australian Universities*. Fukurō.

Iino, M. (1996) 'Excellent foreigner!' Gaijinization of Japanese language and culture in contact situations. An ethnographic study of dinner table conversations between Japanese host families and American students. Doctoral dissertation, University of Pennsylvania.

Iino, M. (2006) Norms of interaction in a Japanese homestay setting: Toward a two-way flow of linguistic and cultural resources. In M.A. DuFon and E. Churchill (eds) *Language Learners in Study Abroad Contexts* (pp. 151–173). Multilingual Matters.

Isabelli-García, C. (2006) Study abroad social networks, motivation and attitudes: Implications for second language acquisition. In M.A. DuFon and E. Churchill (eds) *Language Learners in Study Abroad Contexts* (pp. 231–258). Multilingual Matters.

Isabelli-García, C., Bown, J., Plews, J.L. and Dewey, D.P. (2018) Language learning and study abroad. *Language Teaching* 51 (4), 439–484. https://doi.org/10.1017/S026144481800023X

Ito, M. and Okabe, D. (2005) Intimate connections: Contextualizing Japanese youth and mobile messaging. In R. Harper, L. Palen and A. Taylor (eds) *Inside the Text: Social, Cultural and Design Perspectives on SMS* (pp. 127–145). Springer.

Itō, M., Baumer, S. and Bittanti, M. (2019) *Hanging Out, Messing Around, and Geeking Out: Kids Living and Learning with New Media* (10th Anniversary edn). The MIT Press.

Iwasaki, N. (2011) Learning L2 Japanese 'politeness' and 'impoliteness': Young American men's dilemmas during study abroad. *Japanese Language and Literature* 45 (1), 67–106.

Iwasaki, N. (2018) 'Hāfu' no gakusei no nihon ryūgaku: Gengo pōtorēto ga shimesu aidentiti henyō to raifusotōrī [A "half" student's study abroad in Japan: Identity change and life story as revealed through a language portrait]. In I. Kawakami, K. Miyake and N. Iwasaki (eds) *Idō to kotoba [Mobility and Language]* (pp. 16–38). Kuroshio.

Jackson, J. (2008) *Language, Identity and Study Abroad: Sociocultural Perspectives*. Equinox Publishing.

Jackson, J. (2015) "Unpacking" international experience through blended intercultural praxis. In R.D. Williams and A. Lee (eds) *Internationalizing Higher Education* (pp. 231–251). Sense.

Jackson, J. (2017) Intervening in the intercultural learning of L2 study abroad students: From research to practice. *Language Teaching* 51 (3), 1–18.

Jacquemet, M. (2005) Transidiomatic practices: Language and power in the age of globalization. *Language & Communication* 25 (3), 257–277. https://doi.org/10.1016/j.langcom.2005.05.001

James, A. and Prout, A. (eds) (2015) *Constructing and Reconstructing Childhood: Contemporary Issues in the Sociological Study of Childhood* (Classic edition). Routledge.

Jewitt, C. (2016) Multimodal analysis. In A. Georgakopoulou and T. Spitoli (eds) *The Routledge Handbook of Language and Digital Communication* (pp. 69–84). Routledge.

Jin, L. (2018) Digital affordances on WeChat: Learning Chinese as a second language. *Computer Assisted Language Learning* 31 (1–2), 27–52. https://doi.org/10.1080/09588221.2017.1376687

Jovanovic, D. and Van Leeuwen, T. (2018) Multimodal dialogue on social media. *Social Semiotics* 28 (5), 683–699. https://doi.org/10.1080/10350330.2018.1504732

Juveland, S.R. (2011) Foreign language students' beliefs about homestays. Doctoral dissertation, Portland State University. https://doi.org/10.15760/etd.289

Kalocsai, K. (2013) *Communities of Practice and English as a Lingua Franca: A Study of Students in a Central European Context*. Walter de Gruyter.

Kamada, L.D. (2010) *Hybrid Identities and Adolescent Girls: Being 'Half' in Japan*. Multilingual Matters.

Kanno, Y. (2003) *Negotiating Bilingual and Bicultural Identities: Japanese Returnees Betwixt Two Worlds*. Routledge.

Kaplan, A.Y. (2018) *French Lessons: A Memoir: Enlarged*. The University of Chicago Press.

Kawai, Y. (2015) Deracialised race, obscured racism: Japaneseness, Western and Japanese concepts of race, and modalities of racism. *Japanese Studies* 35 (1), 23–47. https://doi.org/10.1080/10371397.2015.1006598

Kell, C. (2015) 'Making people happen': Materiality and movement in meaning-making trajectories. *Social Semiotics* 25 (4), 423–445. https://doi.org/10.1080/10350330.2015.1060666

Kinginger, C. (2008) Language learning in study abroad: Case studies of Americans in France. *The Modern Language Journal* 92 (s1), 1–124. https://doi.org/10.1111/j.1540-4781.2008.00821.x

Kinginger, C. (2013) Identity and language learning in study abroad. *Foreign Language Annals* 46 (3), 339–358. https://doi.org/10.1111/flan.12037

Kinginger, C. (2015) Language socialization in the homestay: American high school students in China. In R. Mitchell, N. Tracy-Ventura and K. McManus (eds) *Social Interaction, Identity and Language Learning During Residence Abroad* (pp. 53–74). The European Second Language Association.

Kinginger, C. (2017) Second language learning in a study abroad context. In N. Van Deusen Scholl and S. May (eds) *Second and Foreign Language Education* (pp. 125–136). Springer International Publishing.

Kinginger, C. and Carnine, J. (2019) Language learning at the dinner table: Two case studies of French homestays. *Foreign Language Annals* 52 (4), 850–872. https://doi.org/10.1111/flan.12431

Kinginger, C. and Lee, S.-H. (2019) The dialects of control and connection in the study abroad homestay. *Study Abroad Research in Second Language Acquisition and International Education* 4 (1), 19–44. https://doi.org/10.1075/sar.17014.kin

Kinginger, C., Gourvès-Hayward, A. and Simpson, V. (1999) A tele-collaborative course on French-American intercultural communication. *The French Review* 72 (5), 853–866.

Kinginger, C., Wu, Q., Lee, S.-H. and Tan, D. (2016) The short-term homestay as a context for language learning: Three case studies of high school students and host families. *Study Abroad Research in Second Language Acquisition and International Education* 1 (1), 34–60. https://doi.org/10.1075/sar.1.1.02kin

Knight, S.M. and Schmidt-Rinehart, B.C. (2002) Enhancing the homestay: Study abroad from the host family's perspective. *Foreign Language Annals* 35 (2), 190–201. https://doi.org/10.1111/j.1944-9720.2002.tb03154.x

Kobayashi, Y. (2007) Japanese working women and English study abroad. *World Englishes* 26 (1), 62–71.

Kobayashi, Y. (2018) *The Evolution of English Language Learners in Japan: Crossing Japan, The West, and South East Asia*. Routledge.

Kobayashi, Y. (2022) *Attitudes to English Study Among Japanese, Chinese and Korean Women: Motivations, Expectations and Identity*. Routledge.

Kramsch, C. (2002) Introduction: 'How can we tell the dancer from the dance?' In C. Kramsch (ed.) *Language Acquisition and Language Socialization: Ecological Perspectives* (pp. 1–30). Continuum.

Kramsch, C. (2008) Ecological perspectives on foreign language education. *Language Teaching* 41 (3), 389–408. https://doi.org/10.1017/S0261444808005065

Kramsch, C. (2009) *The Multilingual Subject*. Oxford University Press.

Kubota, R. (2016) The social imaginary of study abroad: Complexities and contradictions. *The Language Learning Journal* 44 (3), 347–357. https://doi.org/10.1080/09571736.2016.1198098

Kubota, R. and Takeda, Y. (2021) Language-in-education policies in Japan versus transnational workers' voices: Two faces of neoliberal communication competence. *TESOL Quarterly* 55 (2), 458–485. https://doi.org/10.1002/tesq.613

Kurata, N. (2004) Communication networks of Japanese language learners in their home country. *Journal of Asian Pacific Communication* 14 (1), 153–178.

Kytölä, S. (2016) Translocality. In A. Georgakopoulou and T. Spitoli (eds) *Routledge Handbook of Language and Digital Communication* (pp. 620–644). Routledge.

Leander, K.M. and Mckim, K.K. (2003) Tracing the everyday 'sitings' of adolescents on the internet: A strategic adaptation of ethnography across online and offline spaces. *Education, Communication & Information* 3 (2), 211–240. https://doi.org/10.1080/14636310303140

Lee, C.K.M. and Barton, D. (2011) Constructing glocal identities through multilingual writing practices on Flickr.com®. *International Multilingual Research Journal* 5 (1), 39–59. https://doi.org/10.1080/19313152.2011.541331

Leung, C. (2005) Convivial communication: Recontextualizing communicative competence. *International Journal of Applied Linguistics* 15 (2), 119–144. https://doi.org/10.1111/j.1473-4192.2005.00084.x

Ling, R. and Yttri, B. (2006) Control, emancipation, and status: The mobile telephone in teens' parental and peer relationships. In R. Kraut, M. Brynin and S. Kiesler (eds) *Computers, Phones, and the Internet: Domesticating Information Technology* (pp. 219–234). Oxford University Press.

Llanes, À., Arnó, E. and Mancho-Barés, G. (2016) Erasmus students using English as a lingua franca: Does study abroad in a non-English-speaking country improve L2 English? *The Language Learning Journal* 44 (3), 292–303. https://doi.org/10.1080/09571736.2016.1198099

Lomicka, L. and Lord, G. (2019) Reframing technology's role in language teaching: A retrospective report. *Annual Review of Applied Linguistics* 39, 8–23. https://doi.org/10.1017/S0267190519000011

Lomicka, L. and Ducate, L. (2021) Using technology, reflection, and noticing to promote intercultural learning during short-term study abroad. *Computer Assisted Language Learning* 34 (1–2), 35–65. https://doi.org/10.1080/09588221.2019.1640746

Luke, C. and Gore, J. (1993) *Feminisms and Critical Pedagogy*. Routledge. https://doi.org/10.4324/9781315021287

Magnan, S.S. and Lafford, B. (2012) Learning through immersion during study abroad. In S. Gass and A. Mackey (eds) *The Routledge Handbook of Second Language Acquisition* (pp. 525–540). Routledge.

Malinowski, B. (1923) The problem of meaning in primitive languages. In C.K. Ogden and I.A. Richards (eds) *The Meaning of Meaning* (pp. 296–336). Kegan Paul.

Malkki, L. (1992) National geographic: The rooting of peoples and the territorialization of national identity among scholars and refugees. *Cultural Anthropology* 7 (1), 24–44. https://doi.org/10.1525/can.1992.7.1.02a00030

Marijuan, S. and Sanz, C. (2018) Expanding boundaries: Current and new directions in study abroad research and practice. *Foreign Language Annals* 51 (1), 185–204. https://doi.org/10.1111/flan.12323

Martin, F. and Rizvi, F. (2014) Making Melbourne: Digital connectivity and international students' experience of locality. *Media, Culture & Society* 36 (7), 1016–1031. https://doi.org/10.1177/0163443714541223

Martínez-Arbelaiz, A., Areizaga, E. and Camps, C. (2017) An update on the study abroad experience: Language choices and social media abroad. *International Journal of Multilingualism* 14 (4), 350–365. https://doi.org/10.1080/14790718.2016.1197929

Marwick, A.E. and boyd, d. (2011) I tweet honestly, I tweet passionately: Twitter users, context collapse, and the imagined audience. *New Media & Society* 13 (1), 114–133.

Matsuda, M. (2006) Mobile communication and selective sociality. In M. Ito, D. Okabe and M. Matsuda (eds) *Personal, Portable, Pedestrian: Mobile Phones in Japanese Life* (pp. 123–142). MIT Press.

Matsui, M. (1995) Gender role perceptions of Japanese and Chinese female students in American universities. *Comparative Education Review* 39 (3), 356–378.

McQuillan, D. (2022) *Resisting AI: An Anti-Fascist Approach to Artificial Intelligence*. Bristol University Press.

Mercer, K. (1990) Black hair/style politics. In R. Fergerson, M. Gever, T.T. Minh-ha and C. West (eds) *Out There: Marginalization and Contemporary Cultures* (pp. 247–264). MIT Press.

Mikal, J.P. and Grace, K. (2012) Against abstinence-only education abroad: Viewing Internet use during study abroad as a possible experience enhancement. *Journal of Studies in International Education* 16 (3), 287–306.

Miller, D., Costa, E., Haynes, N., McDonald, T., Nicolescu, R., Sinanan, J., Spyer, J., Venkatraman, S. and Wang, X. (2016) *How the World Changed Social Media* (Vol. 1). UCL Press.

Milner, M. (2004) *Freaks, Geeks, and Cool Kids: American Teenagers, Schools, and the Culture of Consumption*. Routledge.

Ministry of Foreign Affairs of Japan (2022) *Burajiru kiso deeta* [*Basic Data on Brazil*]. Ministry of Foreign Affairs of Japan. https://www.mofa.go.jp/mofaj/area/brazil/data.html

Mitchell, R., Tracy-Ventura, N. and McManus, K. (2017) *Anglophone Students Abroad: Identity, Social Relationships and Language Learning*. Routledge.

Mitchell, R., Tracy-Ventura, N. and Huensch, A. (2020) After study abroad: The maintenance of multilingual identity among Anglophone languages graduates. *The Modern Language Journal* 104 (2), 327–344. https://doi.org/10.1111/modl.12636

Morales, A. and Hanson, W.E. (2005) Language brokering: An integrative review of the literature. *Hispanic Journal of Behavioral Sciences* 27 (4), 471–503. https://doi.org/10.1177/0739986305281333

Morinaga Williams, E. (2018) Motehen: A case study of shifting perceptions of Japanese masculinity and desirability through study abroad. *Journal of International Students* 8 (4). https://doi.org/10.32674/jis.v8i4.219

Morinaga Williams, E. (2019) Perceptions of desirability and enactment of agency among Japanese male university students abroad. *GALE Journal* 11, 49–70.

Morita, M. and Nagasawa, K. (1999) Developing intercultural communication abilities through telecollaborative projects in Japanese English classes. *The Bulletin of the Faculty of Education, Ibaraki University* 48, 185–232.

Morris-Suzuki, T. (1998) *Re-inventing Japan: Time, Space, Nation*. M.E. Sharpe.

Murphy-Lejeune, E. (2002) *Student Mobility and Narrative in Europe: The New Strangers*. Routledge.

National Centre for University Entrance Examinations (2022) Summary of results from the 2022 national center test for university admissions [Reiwa 4 nendo daigaku nyūshi sentāshiken jisshi kekka no gaiyō]. https://www.dnc.ac.jp/albums/abm.php?d=58&f=abm00000702.pdf

Nogami, Y. (2013) Negotiation of second language identities in shifting power relations: Voices of Japanese L2 English users. *Hiroshima Journal of International Studies* 19, 81–100.

Norton, B. (2000) *Identity and Language Learning*. Pearson Education Ltd.

Norton Peirce, B. (1995) Social identity, investment, and language learning. *TESOL Quarterly* 29 (1), 9–31.

Norušis, M.J. (2009) *PASW Statistics 18 Statistical Procedures Companion*. Prentice Hall.

Ogden, A. (2008) The view from the veranda: Understanding today's colonial student. *Frontiers: The Interdisciplinary Journal of Study Abroad* 15, 35–55.

Ong, A. (1999) *Flexible Citizenship: The Cultural Logics of Transnationality*. Duke University Press.

Ortega, L. (2021) Research on language learning during study abroad: What next? In W. Diao and E. Trentman (eds) *Language Learning in Study Abroad: The Multilingual Turn* (pp. 213–224). Multilingual Matters.

Pangrazio, L. (2019) Technologically situated: The tacit rules of platform participation. *Journal of Youth Studies* 22 (10), 1308–1326. https://doi.org/10.1080/13676261.2019.1575345

Papastergiadis, N. (2000) *The Turbulence of Migration: Globalization, Deterritorialization, and Hybridity*. Polity Press.

Pascoe, C.J. (2019) Intimacy. In M. Ito, S. Baumer, M. Bittanti, d. boyd, R. Cody, B. Herr Stephenson, H.A. Horst, P.G. Lange, D. Mahendran, K.Z. Martínez, C.J. Pascoe, D. Perkel, L. Robinson, C. Sims and L. Tripp (eds) *Hanging Out, Messing Around, and Geeking Out* (pp. 117–148). The MIT Press. https://doi.org/10.7551/mitpress/8402.003.0007

Pavlenko, A. (2007) Autobiographic narratives as data in Applied Linguistics. *Applied Linguistics* 28 (2), 163–188.

Pavlenko, A. and Blackledge, A. (2004) *Negotiation of Identities in Multilingual Contexts*. Multilingual Matters.

Pennycook, A. (2018) *Posthumanist Applied Linguistics*. Routledge.

Pennycook, A. and Otsuji, E. (2017) Fish, phone cards and semiotic assemblages in two Bangladeshi shops in Sydney and Tokyo. *Social Semiotics* 27 (4), 434–450. https://doi.org/10.1080/10350330.2017.1334391

Piller, I. (2016) *Linguistic Diversity and Social Justice: An Introduction to Applied Sociolinguistics*. Oxford University Press.

Plews, J.L. (2015) Intercultural identity-alignment in second language study abroad, or the more-or-less Canadians. In R. Mitchell, N. Tracy-Ventura and K. McManus (eds) *Social Interaction, Identity and Language Learning during Residence Abroad* (pp. 281–304). The European Second Language Association.

Polanyi, L. (1995) Language learning and living abroad. In B.F. Freed (ed.) *Second Language Acquisition in a Study Abroad Context* (pp. 271–237). John Benjamins.

Potter, J. (2012) *Digital Media and Learner Identity: The New Curatorship*. Palgrave Macmillan.

Pozzi, R., Quan, T. and Escalante, C. (2021) *Heritage Speakers of Spanish and Study Abroad*. Routledge. https://doi.org/10.4324/9780429289163

Presbitero, A. (2016) Culture shock and reverse culture shock: The moderating role of cultural intelligence in international students' adaptation. *International Journal of Intercultural Relations* 53, 28–38. https://doi.org/10.1016/j.ijintrel.2016.05.004

Rapley, D. (2019) Online support for Japanese students studying abroad: A virtual umbilical cord. *New Zealand Studies in Applied Linguistics* 25 (1), 64–78.

Rymes, B. (2012) Recontextualizing YouTube: From macro–micro to mass-mediated communicative repertoires. *Anthropology & Education Quarterly* 43 (2), 214–227. https://doi.org/10.1111/j.1548-1492.2012.01170.x

Salaberry, M.R., White, K. and Burch, A.R. (2019) Language learning and interactional experiences in study abroad settings: An introduction to the special issue. *Study Abroad Research in Second Language Acquisition and International Education* 4 (1), 1–18. https://doi.org/10.1075/sar.18015.sal

Sanz, C. and Morales-Front, A. (eds) (2018) *The Routledge Handbook of Study Abroad Research and Practice*. Routledge.

Sauro, S. and Zourou, K. (2019) What are the digital wilds? *Language Learning & Technology* 23 (1), 1–7. https://doi.org/10125/44666

Schumann, F.M. (1980) Diary of a language learner: A further analysis. In R. Scarcella and S. Krashen (eds) *Research in Second Language Acquisition: Selected Papers of the Los Angeles Second Language Acquisition Research Forum* (pp. 51–57). Newbury Housen.

Seibert Hanson, A.E. and Dracos, M. (2019) The digital dilemma: L1 and L2 technology use, language learning, and motivation among US university students studying abroad. *Study Abroad Research in Second Language Acquisition and International Education* 4 (2), 224–251. https://doi.org/10.1075/sar.18003.sei

Sekiguchi, K. and Kanazawa, H. (2022) Toritsukō no 'burakku kōsoku' 5 kōmoku zenpai e kami no kurozome, shitagi no iro shitei... [Five 'black school rules' at metropolitan high schools to be abolished: Dyeing hair black, specifying underwear color]... *Asahi Shinbun Dejitaru*, 11 March. https://www.asahi.com/articles/ASQ3C6FTJQ3CU-TIL01J.html?iref=ogimage_rek

Shiri, S. (2015) The homestay in intensive language study abroad: Social networks, language socialization, and developing intercultural competence. *Foreign Language Annals* 48 (1), 5–25. https://doi.org/10.1111/flan.12127

Siegal, M. (1995) Individual differences and study abroad. In B.F. Freed (ed.) *Second Language Acquisition in a Study Abroad Context* (pp. 225–244). John Benjamins.

Simmel, G. (1921) The sociological significance of the stranger. In E.W. Burgess and R.E. Park (eds) *Introduction to the Science of Sociology* (pp. 322–327). University of Chicago Press.

Soja, E.W. (1989) *Postmodern Geographies: The Reassertion of Space in Critical Social Theory*. Verso.
Spenader, A.J. (2011) Language learning and acculturation: Lessons from high school and gap-year exchange students. *Foreign Language Annals* 44 (2), 381–398. https://doi.org /10.1111/j.1944-9720.2011.01134.x
Spence-Brown, R. (1993) Japanese exchange students overseas: The effect of communicative inadequacies on presentation of self. *Journal of Asian Pacific Communication* 4 (4), 193–207.
Steffensen, S.V. and Fill, A. (2014) Ecolinguistics: The state of the art and future horizons. *Language Sciences* 41, 6–25. https://doi.org/10.1016/j.langsci.2013.08.003
Steffensen, S.V. and Kramsch, C. (2017) The ecology of second language acquisition and socialization. *Language Socialization*, 17–32. https://doi.org/10.1007/978-3-319-02255-0_2
Tajima, C. and Cookson, S. (2011) English language anxiety in learners during study abroad: Language use in homestay context. *Obirin Gengo Kyōiku Ronsō* 7, 79–97.
Takahashi, K. (2013) *Language Learning, Gender and Desire: Japanese Women on the Move*. Multilingual Matters.
Talburt, S. and Stewart, M.A. (1999) What's the subject of study abroad? Race, gender, and 'living culture'. *The Modern Language Journal* 83 (2), 163–175.
Tanaka, K. (2007) Japanese students' contact with English outside the classroom during study abroad. *New Zealand Studies in Applied Linguistics* 13 (1), 36.
Taylor, C. (2004) *Modern Social Imaginaries*. Duke University Press.
The Douglas Fir Group (2016) A transdisciplinary framework for SLA in a multilingual world. *The Modern Language Journal* 100 (S1), 19–47. https://doi.org/10.1111/modl.12301
Ting-Toomey, S. and Dorjee, T. (2019) *Communicating Across Cultures* (2nd edn). The Guilford Press.
Tomiya, R. (1997). Nihonjin to kekkonshita gaikokujin jyosei no nettowāku to nihonngo gakushū no katei [The networks of foreign women who married a Japanese and Japanese language learning processes]. In Nihongo Kyōiku Gakkai Nettowāku Chōsa Kenkyū Iinkai [Japanese Language Teaching Society Network Research and Survey Committee] (ed.) *Kokunai no nihongo kyōiku nettowākuzukuri nikansuru chōsa kenkyū [Research and study on the creation of Japanese language education networks in Japan]* (pp. 74–93). Nihongo Kyouiku Gakkai.
Toohey, K. (2019) The onto-epistemologies of new materialism: Implications for applied linguistics pedagogies and research. *Applied Linguistics* 40 (6), 937–956. https://doi .org/10.1093/applin/amy046
Tsuda, T. (2003) *Strangers in the Ethnic Homeland: Japanese Brazilian Return Migration in Transnational Perspective*. Columbia University Press.
Tran, L.T. and Nguyen, N.T. (2016) The cosmopolitan sojourners: Understanding international Korean, Vietnamese and Chinese students' motivations to study overseas. In D.K. Sharpes (ed.) *Handbook on Comparative and International Studies in Education* (pp. 561–584). Information Age Publishers.
Trentman, E. (2013a) Arabic and English during study abroad in Cairo, Egypt: Issues of access and use. *The Modern Language Journal* 97 (2), 457–473.
Trentman, E. (2013b) Imagined communities and language learning during study abroad: Arabic learners in Egypt. *Foreign Language Annals* 46 (4), 545–564. https://doi.org/10 .1111/flan.12054
Tuan, Y.-F. (1991) Language and the making of place: A narrative-descriptive approach. *Annals of the Association of American Geographers* 81 (4), 684–696.
Tullock, B. (2018) Identity and study abroad. In C. Sanz and A. Morales-Front (eds) *The Routledge Handbook of Study Abroad Research and Practice* (pp. 261–274). Routledge. https://www.taylorfrancis.com/chapters/edit/10.4324/9781315639970-17/ identity-study-abroad-brandon-tullock

Tullock, B. (2021) Encountering multilingualism in study abroad: Sojourners' orientations to linguistic diversity and language hierarchies in Barcelona. In W. Diao and E. Trentman (eds) *Language Learning in Study Abroad: The Multilingual Turn* (pp. 190–212). Multilingual Matters.

Tupas, R. (ed.) (2015) *Unequal Englishes: The Politics of Englishes Today*. Palgrave Macmillan UK. https://doi.org/10.1057/9781137461223

Twombly, S.B. (1995) Piropos and friendships: Gender and culture clash in study abroad. *Frontiers: The Interdisciplinary Journal of Study Abroad* 1 (1), 27.

Umino, T. and Benson, P. (2016) Communities of practice in study abroad: A four-year study of an Indonesian student's experience in Japan. *The Modern Language Journal* 100 (4), 757–774. https://doi.org/10.1111/modl.12351

van Dijk, J.A. (2017) Digital divide: Impact of access. *The International Encyclopedia of Media Effects*, 1–11. https://doi.org/10.1002/9781118783764.wbieme0043

van Lier, L. (2000) From input to affordance: Social-interactive learning from an ecological perspective. In J.P. Lantolf (ed.) *Sociocultural Theory and Second Language Learning* (pp. 245–259). Oxford University Press.

van Lier, L. (2004) *The Ecology and Semiotics of Language Learning: A Sociocultural Perspective*. Springer Science & Business Media.

van Lier, L. (2008) Ecological-semiotic perspectives on educational linguistics. In F.M. Hult and B. Spolsky (eds) *The Handbook of Educational Linguistics* (pp. 596–605). Blackwell Publishing.

Vertovec, S. (2007) Super-diversity and its implications. *Ethnic and Racial Studies* 30 (6), 1024–1054. https://doi.org/10.1080/01419870701599465

Wakana, T. (2018) Study abroad as transformative learning opportunity: Willingness to communicate, social interactions, and identity development among Japanese students. Doctoral dissertation, University of Wisconsin-Madison. https://search.library.wisc.edu/digital/A2DOEBJRGSBPPQ8F

Warschauer, M. (1999) *Electronic Literacies: Language, Culture, and Power in Online Education*. L. Erlbaum Associates.

Weedon, C. (1996) *Feminist Practice and Poststructuralist Theory*. Basil Blackwell.

Wertsch, J.V. (1991) *Voices of the Mind: Sociocultural Approach to Mediated Action*. Harvard University Press.

White, C. and Bown, J. (2017) Emotion in the construction of space, place and autonomous learning opportunities. In G. Murray and T. Lamb (eds) *Space, Place and Autonomy in Language Learning* (pp. 29–43). Routledge.

Wilkinson, S. (1998a) On the nature of immersion during study abroad: Some participant perspectives. *Frontiers: The Interdisciplinary Journal of Study Abroad* 4 (2), 121–138.

Wilkinson, S. (1998b) Study abroad from the participants' perspective: A challenge to common beliefs. *Foreign Language Annals* 31 (1), 23–39.

Willis, T.Y. (2015) "And still we rise…": Microaggressions and intersectionality in the study abroad experiences of Black women. *Frontiers: The Interdisciplinary Journal of Study Abroad* 26 (1), 209–230. https://doi.org/10.36366/frontiers.v26i1.367

Wolcott, T. (2013) An American in Paris: Myth, desire, and subjectivity in one student's account of study abroad in France. In C. Kinginger (ed.) *Social and Cultural Aspects of Language Learning in Study Abroad* (pp. 127–154). John Benjamins.

Wolcott, T. (2016) Introduction to the special issue: Study abroad in the twenty-first century. *L2 Journal* 8 (2), 3–11.

Yashima, T., Zenuk-Nishide, L. and Shimizu, K. (2004) The influence of attitudes and affect on willingness to communicate and second language communication. *Language Learning* 54 (1), 119–152.

Yoneyama, S. (1999) *The Japanese High School: Silence and Resistance*. Routledge.

Zappa-Hollman, S. and Duff, P.A. (2015) Academic English socialization through individual networks of practice. *TESOL Quarterly* 49 (2), 333–368. https://doi.org/10.1002/tesq.188

Zheng, D. (2012) Caring in the dynamics of design and languaging: Exploring second language learning in 3D virtual spaces. *Language Sciences* 34 (5), 543–558. https://doi.org/10.1016/j.langsci.2012.03.010

# Index

Adolescence 44, 46, 165-167
Affordance 37
AFS intercultural programs 3, 53, 62, 120-121, 141, 146
Appadurai, Arjun 1-3, 79

Bauman 116
Blommaert, Jan 7-8, 40, 111, 116, 118

case selection 49-52
cluster analysis 57-59
connectivity 94-95, 153-154

digital communication
    adolescent use of 22-23, 30-32, 155-156
    digital sociality 18-25, 30-31, 65-66, 70-73, 153
    disengagement perspective of 23-24, 103, 144-145, 149-150
    facilitating connections 65-66, 76, 99-101, 113-114, 128-129, 144, 155-157
    instrumentalist perspective of 24
    and intimacy 72-73
    and language learning 68-69, 125-126,
    platform architechture 19-21, 156-157
    situatedness of 3, 17, 20, 34-35, 65-66, 93-95, 130, 150, 154-155
    and Study Abroad 2-3, 23-25, 33-35, 68-73, 93-95, 113-114, 128-129, 145, 152-159
Doerr, Neriko Musha 28, 159

ecological approach 37-40
Endo, Shushaku 26

English(es) 4-5, 8-9, 47-49, 159-162
    as international Language 77-80, 165, 168
    and Japan 47-49
    as language of the stranger 71, 75, 109-111, 127-128, 162
    as lingua franca 62-63, 67, 69, 78, 84-85, 109-113, 124-125

factor analysis 55-56
flows 1-3, 5, 7, 28-29, 79, 116-118, 159-165

host family
    host mother's role 63-64, 86, 106, 123, 166
    host sibling's role 63, 65, 85-86, 122
    and language learning 86, 106, 126, 146-147, 161
    power 44-45, 64, 143-145, 150, 166

identity 33, 40-43
    online 99-101
    negotiation of 79-80, 102-103, 116-117, 121-122, 128, 135-136
    Japanese 48-49, 56, 87-93, 131
    Stranger 42-43
Imaginaries 9-10, 78-80, 102-103, 117-118, 125-126, 150
Immersion 24, 25-29, 34-35, 63, 69, 164-165
    learning through 'osmosis' 125, 139-142

Kaplan, Alice 2
key individual 65, 167

Kinginger, Celeste 6, 24, 44, 102, 135, 166
Kramsch, Claire 37, 49-42
Kubota, Ryuko 9-10, 25, 141, 168

life stage 44-46, 165-168

migrant communities 106, 124, 160
mobility 69-70, 77-78, 149-150, 154
Murphy-Lejeune, Elizabeth 42-43, 64, 73, 154, 159, 167

narrative analysis 49
Norton, Bonny 14, 111

orders of Indexicality 8-9, 80, 102,

positioning theory 42

racialization 106-111, 117
reverse cultural shock 169-170

scales 7-9, 77-79, 97-99, 118, 136, 159-160
second language learning and use
   English 68-69, 145, 147,
   French 121, 123-124, 128, 136
   German 109-110, 112, 114
   Hungarian 67, 70-71, 77-78
   Japanese 63, 89, 122, 129
   Mandarin 70, 107
   Portuguese 70, 83, 88-89, 94
social network
   formation 65, 70, 86-87, 112, 128, 157, 167
   maintainance 18, 20, 76, 83, 101, 115-116, 158

territorialisation 25, 27-29
translanguaging 70-71, 84, 93-94, 97, 129, 133
translocality 5-6, 28-29, 76, 117, 136-137
transnationality 6-7, 80, 102-103 136

van Lier, Leo 37-38

For Product Safety Concerns and Information please contact our EU Authorised Representative:

Easy Access System Europe

Mustamäe tee 50

10621 Tallinn

Estonia

gpsr.requests@easproject.com